INSIDE

LANGUAGE • LITERACY • CONTENT

NATIONAL GEOGRAPHIC LEARNING | CENGAGE Learning

NATIONAL GEOGRAPHIC LEARNING | CENGAGE Learning

Acknowledgments

Grateful acknowledgment is given to the authors, artists, photographers, museums, publishers, and agents for permission to reprint copyrighted material. Every effort has been made to secure the appropriate permission. If any omissions have been made or if corrections are required, please contact the Publisher. **Amelia Fusion:** Excerpt from *The Log of Christopher Columbus*, translated by Robert H. Fusion. Copyright © 1987 by Robert H. Fusion. Reprinted by permission of Amelia Fusion. **Houghton Mifflin Harcourt Publishing Company:** Excerpts from *The Hobbit* by J.R.R. Tolkein. Copyright © 1937 by George Allen & Unwin Ltd., © 1966 by J.R.R. Tolkein, © renewed 1994 by Christopher R. Tolkein, John F.R. Tolkein. Copyright © restored 1996 by the Estate of J.R.R. Tolkein, assigned 1997 to the J.R.R. Tolkein Copyright Trust. Reprinted by permission of Houghton Mifflin Harcourt Publishing Company and HarperCollins, Ltd. All rights reserved. **LifeTime Media, Inc.:** Excerpt from *Pressure is a Privilege* by Billie Jean King, foreword by Christine Brennan. Copyright © 2008 by Billie Jean King. Reprinted by permission by LifeTime Media, Inc. All rights reserved. **National Geographic Society:** "Bionics" by John Fishman from *National Geographic*, January 2010. Copyright © 2010 by the National Geographic Society. Reprinted by permission of the National Geographic Society. All rights reserved. Excerpt from "A Conflict Close to Home" from *A Blog for Peace in Israel-Palestine* by Aziz Abu Sarah, from NationalGeographic.com. Reprinted by permission of the National Geographic Society. All rights reserved. **Simon & Schuster, Inc.:** Excerpt from Abundance: *The Future is Better than You Think* by Peter H. Diamandis and Steven Kotler. Copyright © 2012 by Peter H. Diamandis and Steven Kotler. Reprinted with the permission of Free Press of Simon & Schuster. All rights reserved.

Photography

Cover, Back cover ©Andrew Masur/Flickr/Getty Images. **7** ©Caro/Alamy. **8** ©Matthew Wakem/Aurora Photos. **14** ©Horst Petzold. **23** ©Stephanie Maze/National Geographic. **29, 30, 31** Courtesy of NASA. **43** ©DLILLC/Corbis. **57** ©Charles Gupton/Corbis. **58** ©Mary Evans Picture Library/Alamy Images. **59** ©Harald Sund. **60** ©Brent Stirton/Staff/Getty Images News/Getty Images. **65** ©Ted Nasmith. **67** ©AP Photo/Warner Bros. **79** ©Raymond Gehman/National Geographic Image Collection. **85** ©Margo Silver/Photonica World/Getty Images. **86** ©HMS Group Inc./Getty Images. **92** ©Mario Tama/Getty Images News/ Getty Images. **93** © Dennis MacDonald/Alamy. **94** ©The Granger Collection, New York. **100** ©Look and Learn/The Bridgeman Art Library. **101** ©Ilina S/ Getty Images. **112** Superstudio/Getty Images. **119** ©Patrik Giardino/Corbis. **126** ©Ullstein - CARO/Riedmiller/Peter Arnold. **127** ©Nik Wheeler/Corbis. **129** ©Wayne Eastep/Photographer's Choice/Getty Images. **132** ©Mark Thiessen/National Geographic Stock. **133** ©Mark Thiessen/National Geographic Stock. **134–135** ©Bryan Christie Design/National Geographic Stock. **147** ©De Agostini/Getty Images. **148** ©Robert Harding Picture Library Ltd/ Alamy Images. **149** ©M. Timothy O'Keefe/Alamy. **154** ©Albert Lorenz. **156** ©Bridgeman Art Library. **163** ©Institute for Exploration/University of Rhode Island & Mystic Aquarium. **168** ©rescomovie/Shutterstock. **169** (b) ©Cobalt88/ Shutterstock. **180** ©Toby Talbot/AP Images. **182** ©Hulton Archive/Getty Images. **187** ©Michael Newman/PhotoEdit. **188** ©Robert W. Ginn/PhotoEdit. **189** ©AFP/Getty Images. **195** © Eric Meola/Getty images. **196** ©GERARD MALIE/AFP/Getty Images. **200** ©Aziz Abu Sarah/National Geographic Explorer. **212** ©Associated Press/Ted S. Warren. **215** ©Digital Vision/Getty Images. **219** ©AFP/Getty Images. **221** ©Trip/Art Directors & TRIP/Alamy. **225** ©Ernst Haas/Getty Images. **226** ©moodboard/Corbis. **229** ©Owaki/Kulla/Terra/ Corbis. **232** ©PhotoDisc/Getty Images. **233** ©Bettmann/Corbis. **244** ©Dominic Burke/Alamy Images. **245** ©David Young-Wolff/PhotoEdit. **214** Compliments of NASA Orbital Debris Program Office. **245** ©David Young-Wolff/PhotoEdit. **264** Library of Congress. **265** ©Don Grall/Visuals Unlimited/Getty Images.

Illustration

258 Stefano Vitale.

Fine Art

169 ©*The Landing of Christopher Columbus in the New World* (oil on canvas), Kemmelmeyer, Frederick (d.1821) (attr. to)/Private Collection/Peter Newark Pictures/The Bridgeman Art Library.

For product information and technology asistance, contact us at
Cengage Learning Customer & Sales Support, 1-800-354-9706

For permission to use material from this text or product, submit all requests online at **www.cengage.com/permissions**
Further permissions questions can be emailed to
permissionrequest@cengage.com

National Geographic Learning | Cengage Learning
1 Lower Ragsdale Drive
Building 1, Suite 200
Monterey, CA 93940

Cengage Learning is a leading provider of customized learning solutions with office locations around the globe, including Singapore, the United Kingdom, Australia, Mexico, Brazil, and Japan. Locate your local office at **www.cengage.com/global**.

Visit National Geographic Learning online at **ngl.cengage.com**
Visit our corporate website at **www.cengage.com**

Printer: RR Donnelley, Harrisonburg, VA

ISBN: 978-12854-38955 (Practice Book)
ISBN: 978-12854-39006 (Practice Book Teacher's Annotated Edition)

ISBN: 978-12857-62395 (Practice Masters)

Printed in the United States of America

13 14 15 16 17 18 19 20 21 22

10 9 8 7 6 5 4 3 2 1

INSIDE

LANGUAGE • LITERACY • CONTENT

Contents: Reading

Unit 3

Unit 4

Contents: Grammar

Unit 1

Unit 2

Unit 3

Unit 4

Unit 5

Unit 6

Unit 7

Unit 8

Proofreader's Marks

Mark	Meaning	Example
≡	Capitalize.	I love new york city.
/	Do not capitalize.	I'm going shopping at my favorite Store.
⊙	Add a period.	Mr Lopez is our neighbor.
?	Add a question mark.	Where is my black pen
!	Add an exclamation point.	Look out
" "	Add quotation marks.	You are late, said the teacher.
^,	Add a comma.	Amy how are you feeling today?
^;	Add a semicolon.	This shirt is nice however, that one brings out the color of your eyes.
:	Add a colon.	He wakes up at 6 30 a.m.
—	Add a dash.	Barney he's my pet dog has run away.
( )	Add parentheses.	I want to work for the Federal Bureau of Investigation FBI .
=	Add a hyphen.	You were born in mid September, right?
'	Add an apostrophe.	I m the oldest of five children.
#	Add a space.	She likes him alot.
⁐	Close up a space.	How much home work do you have?
^	Add text.	My keys are ^ on the table.
[delete mark]	Delete.	I am going too my friend's house.
[change mark]	Change text.	We have ~~to~~ too much garbage.
[transpose mark]	Transpose words, letters.	Did you see thier new car?
(sp)	Spell out.	Today he is turning 16. (sp)
¶	Begin a new paragraph.	"I win!" I shouted. "No you don't," he said.
(ital)___	Add italics.	The Spanish word for table is mesa. (ital)
(u/s)___	Add underlining.	(u/s) Little Women is one of my favorite books.

Name ________________________________

Mind Map

Use the Mind Map to show your ideas about solving problems. As you read the selections in this unit, add new ideas to the Mind Map.

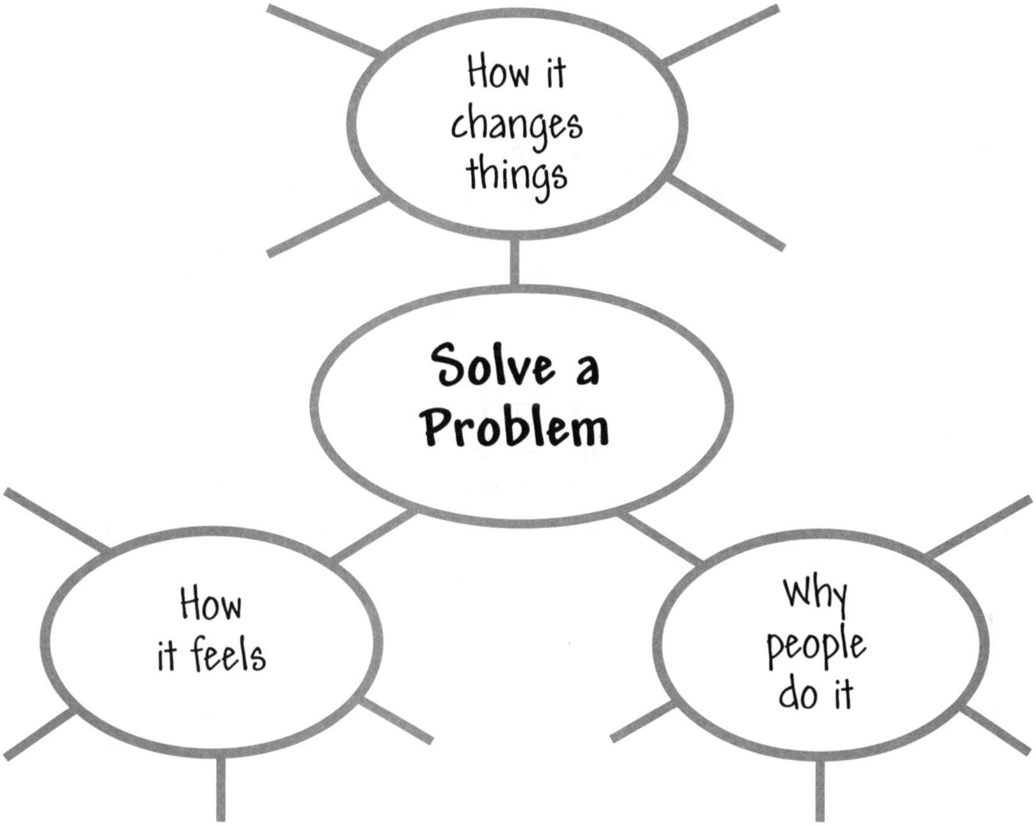

Academic Vocabulary

Think about a time you had to solve a problem. What **possibilities** did you think about to help solve the problem? Use the word **possibility** in your answer.

____

____

____

____

Name ______________________________

Reading Strategies: Plan, Monitor, Visualize, and Determine Importance

A. Read the headings and first two sentences to preview the passage. What do you predict the text is about? What will be your purpose for reading?

____

____

B. Read the passage. Monitor your understanding as you read.

A Ride Like No Other

Organizers of the 1893 World's Fair wanted a new and unique attraction to draw visitors' attention. George Ferris had an idea. The young engineer designed a huge rotating wheel that would serve as both a ride and a way for people to view the event from above. At first, most people thought his idea was crazy. His ambitious design called for a structure that looked like a giant bicycle wheel with seats. The wheel turned on a 46-ton axle set between two pyramid-shaped steel structures.

Persistence Pays Off

His critics did not discourage George. After finding support from fellow engineers and investors, Ferris had his plan approved. A few months later, crowds of amazed fair-goers were treated to a ride like no other. The Ferris Wheel allowed for 2,160 passengers at a time to ride in 36 deluxe cars. The 20-minute ride amazed over 1.5 million attendees during the fair.

C. Answer the questions.

1. What is meant by *draw visitors' attention*? Which words in the text support this?

____

____

2. What words help you visualize how people would ride Ferris's invention?

____

3. Summarize the main idea of the passage.

____

Academic Vocabulary

Describe how you think fair-goers reacted to George Ferris's new ride. What words in the text support your ideas?

____

____

Focus on Reading

Name ______________________________

Reading Strategies: Ask Questions, Make Connections, and Make Inferences

A. Read the passage. Think about any questions you have as you read.

Frank Henry Fleer created the first bubble gum in 1906. He called it Blipper-Blubber. Unfortunately, it was not a successful invention and never went on sale. It was too sticky and came apart when people chewed it. However, Fleer's early work was not the end of the Fleer Company's interest in bubble gum.

In 1928, Walter E. Diemer, an employee of the Fleer company, accidentally solved the bubble gum problem. Diemer was an accountant, not a scientist or an inventor. He stumbled upon the right combination of ingredients while experimenting in his spare time. This new gum was strong enough and elastic enough to stretch when filled with air. It also did not stick to your face if the bubble popped. The new product was a great success. Diemer named his gum Dubble Bubble. The pink concoction is still sold today.

B. Answer the questions.

1. Ask yourself what the word *concoction* means. In your own words, write a definition of *concoction*. Explain how you found the answer.

____

____

2. What connections can make with this story? Choose one and tell about it.

____

____

3. Reread the second paragraph of the passage. What can you infer about the kind of person Walter Diemer was? Support your answer with details from the text.

I read ______________________________

I know ______________________________

And so ______________________________

Name ______________________________

Reading Strategies: Synthesize

A. Read the passage.

I decided to start babysitting on the weekends. I talked to my friend Sara because she already has a successful babysitting business. We both like children, and we are both willing to work hard. Sara encouraged me to babysit. She said, "Marciano, you'll do a great job."

I had some doubts about whether I would be successful. Sara is very organized, but I am not. Sara also has younger brothers and sisters. Unlike Sara, I am an only child. I have no experience taking care of children. I asked Sara how she was able to get so many families to hire her. She said that once she started, people recommended her. Sara said she would recommend me!

B. Answer the following questions.

1. What is a conclusion you can draw about Marciano as a babysitter? Include details from the text to support your conclusion.

____

____

2. What is a conclusion you can draw about why Sara is a successful babysitter?

____

____

3. What are two generalizations you could make about babysitters from the text?

____

____

Academic Vocabulary

How might Marciano **solve** the problem of his lack of experience?

____

____

____

Name ______________________________

Some Word Parts

Some Word Parts
Suffix: *-ful* means "having traits of"
Suffix: *-ous* means "full of"
Suffix: *-ion* means "act of"

Use Word Parts

Read the passage. Follow these steps.

1. Look closely at the word to see if you know any of the parts. If you see two base words, think about the meaning of each one.
2. Do you see a prefix or a suffix? If yes, cover it.
3. Think about the meaning of the base word. Then uncover the prefix or suffix, and think about its meaning.
4. Put the meanings of the word parts together to understand the whole word. Be sure the meaning make sense in the text.

Follow the directions above. Write the meaning of each underlined word.

> The first bubble gum was made in 1906. Nobody was happy with the gum at the time. It was too sticky and came apart when people chewed it. In 1928, Walter E. Diemer invented the first successful bubble gum. This gum did not come apart when people chewed it. Walter became famous for his invention. He called his gum "Double Bubble." Today gum lovers everywhere are thankful for his creation!

1. **nobody** ______________________________
2. **successful** ______________________________
3. **famous** ______________________________
4. **invention** ______________________________
5. **everywhere** ______________________________
6. **thankful** ______________________________
7. **creation** ______________________________

Academic Vocabulary

Newspaper is a **compound** word because ______________________________

____

____

______________________________.

Name ______________________________

Critical Viewing Guide

Take Notes

A. View the video. Take notes on at least three things that you learned.

____

____

____

____

____

____

____

____

Analyze the Video

B. Review your notes to help answer these questions.

1. Write two sentences to explain what was in the video.

____

____

____

2. What was the most interesting thing you learned?

____

____

____

3. Explain why scientists have to ask questions in order to **solve** problems.

____

____

____

____

____

Name ______________________________

Hitching a Ride: Key Vocabulary

A. Study each word. Circle a number to rate how well you know it. Then complete the chart.

Rating Scale	1	2	3
	I have never seen this word before.	I am not sure of the word's meaning.	I know this word and can teach the word's meaning to someone else.

▲ The Wright Brothers **test** their **invention**.

Key Words	Check Understanding	Deepen Understanding
❶ **attach** (u-**tach**) *verb* Rating: 1 2 3	You can **attach** pictures of your friends to a wall. **Yes** **No**	Do you attach anything to the walls of your bedroom? What? How? ______
❷ **captive** (**kap**-tiv) *adjective* Rating: 1 2 3	People at a zoo are **captive** visitors. **Yes** **No**	Where do captive animals live? ______
❸ **challenge** (**chal**-unj) *noun* Rating: 1 2 3	Winning a race is a **challenge**. **Yes** **No**	What is a challenge you have had? ______
❹ **experiment** (ik-**sper**-i-ment) *verb* Rating: 1 2 3	When you **experiment**, you want to understand something better. **Yes** **No**	What are some tools that scientists experiment with? ______

Name ______________________________

When **scientists experiment**, they **record** data. They use this data to **test** their results. ▶

Key Words	Check Understanding	Deepen Understanding
❺ **invention** (in-**ven**-chun) *noun* **Rating:** 1 2 3	A good **invention** solves a problem. **Yes** **No**	What inventions make your life easier? ____________
❻ **record** (ri-**kord**) *verb* **Rating:** 1 2 3	We usually **record** songs and poems we don't like. **Yes** **No**	What would you want to record in a diary? Why? ____
❼ **scientist** (**sī**-un-tist) *noun* **Rating:** 1 2 3	Some **scientists** study objects in space. **Yes** **No**	What makes someone a great scientist? ____________
❽ **test** (test) *verb* **Rating:** 1 2 3	If someone **tests** something, they already know how it works. **Yes** **No**	Tell about a time that you tested something. ________

B. Imagine you work at a zoo. Use at least two Key Vocabulary words to describe your job.

____

____

____

Name ______________________________

Hitching a Ride: Reading Strategies Log

Complete at least one row of the Reading Strategies Log for each section of "Hitching a Ride."

Text I read	Strategy I used	How I used the strategy
Page: 17 Text: Brightly colored fish swirled around Greg Marshall as he glided over the reef.	☐ Plan ☐ Monitor ☐ Ask Questions ☐ ______	To plan my reading, I predicted that the story will be about swimming with fishes.
Page: ______ Text: ______	☐ Plan ☐ Monitor ☐ Ask Questions ☐ ______	
Page: ______ Text: ______	☐ Plan ☐ Monitor ☐ Ask Questions ☐ ______	

Selection Review

Name ______________________________

Key Vocabulary	
attached	invention
captive	record
challenge	scientists
experiments	test

Hitching a Ride

A. Read the paragraph.
Write a Key Vocabulary word in each blank.
Reread the paragraph to make sure the words make sense.

It is true that ____________ learn a lot by studying zoo animals. But ____________ animals may not act as they would in the wild. Studying wild animals in nature is a bigger ____________. What would it be like to see things from an animal's point of view? These are some of the reasons that Greg Marshall created an ____________ called the Crittercam. The device can be ____________ to animals in the wild. Greg had to ____________ the Crittercam many times to make sure it would work correctly. When it was finally ready, field workers could ____________ what the animals were doing. They could track movements and conduct ____________. Studying wildlife can be a wild life!

B. Write complete sentences to answer these questions about "Hitching a Ride."

1. What **invention** might help you get a better view of a bird?

____

____

____

____

____

____

2. Why is it important to **record** wildlife?

____

____

____

____

____

____

Vocabulary Study

Name ______________________________

Use Compound Words

Follow the steps below to figure out the meaning of each compound word.

1. Find the base words.
2. Figure out the meaning of the base words.
3. Put the meanings of the base words together to figure out what the word means.
4. Write the definition.
5. Read the sentence to make sure the word makes sense.

1. **moonlight** ______________________________

   The bright moonlight came through my bedroom window.

2. **sunflower** ______________________________

   The sunflower grew so tall that it reached the roof of our house.

3. **sailboat** ______________________________

   The sailboat moved quickly across the water.

4. **eyesight** ______________________________

   My eyesight is so good that I can see the flowers at the end of our street.

5. **daydream** ______________________________

   Michael had a daydream during class about flying to the moon in a rocket.

6. **ballpark** ______________________________

   We went to the ballpark early to watch the teams practice.

7. **raindrop** ______________________________

   As soon as I felt the first raindrop, I opened my umbrella.

8. **bookmark** ______________________________

   Jocelyn frowned when her bookmark fell from her book.

9. **underground** ______________________________

   The train travels underground to all parts of the city.

Name ________________________________

Academic Vocabulary	
compound	research
describe	solve
possibility	

Hitching a Ride: Academic Vocabulary Review

A. Write the Academic Vocabulary words next to their definitions.

Meaning	Word
1. to find the answer to a problem	
2. made of two or more parts	
3. one way to do, have, or make something	
4. to tell what something is like	
5. to collect information about a subject	

B. Use each Academic Vocabulary word in a sentence.

1. **compound** ________________________________

____

2. **describe** ________________________________

____

3. **research** ________________________________

____

4. **solve** ________________________________

____

5. **possibility** ________________________________

____

Name ________________________________

Critical Viewing Guide

Take Notes

A. View the video. Take notes on at least three things that you learned.

____
____
____
____
____
____
____
____

Analyze the Video

B. Review your notes to help answer these questions.

1. Write two sentences to explain what was in the video.

____
____
____

2. What was the most interesting thing you learned?

____
____
____

3. Could time travel **solve** problems? How?

____
____
____
____
____

Learn Key Vocabulary

Name ______________________________

LAFFF: Key Vocabulary

A. Study each word. Circle a number to rate how well you know it. Then complete the chart.

Rating Scale	1	2	3
	I have never seen this word before.	I am not sure of the word's meaning.	I know this word and can teach the word's meaning to someone else.

▲ Seagulls fly **forward** to their **destination.**

Key Words	Check Understanding	Deepen Understanding
1 backward (bak-**wurd**) *adverb* Rating: 1 2 3	☐ to move toward the back ☐ to move side to side	A driver might need to move a car backward ________ .
2 concentrate (**kon**-sun-trāt) *verb* Rating: 1 2 3	☐ to think about what to do ☐ to speak loudly to a group of people	It is hard to concentrate when ________ .
3 convince (kun-**vints**) *verb* Rating: 1 2 3	☐ to argue with someone ☐ to make someone think the same thing you do	Sometimes I try to convince my friends to ________ .
4 destination (des-tu-**nā**-shun) *noun* Rating: 1 2 3	☐ the place where you want to go ☐ the place where you are now	One way I can figure out how to get to a destination is ________ .

Name ______________________________

Did You Know?

Michael Kevin Kearney is a child **genius** who started college at age 6. He has a very bright **future**.

Key Words	Check Understanding	Deepen Understanding
❺ **forward** (for-wurd) *adverb* **Rating:** 1 2 3	☐ to the front ☐ in a circle	It is difficult to move forward when ________________________.
❻ **future** (fyū-chur) *noun* **Rating:** 1 2 3	☐ some time yesterday ☐ some time tomorrow	One thing I hope to do in the future is ________________________.
❼ **genius** (jen-yus) *noun* **Rating:** 1 2 3	☐ someone who is very smart ☐ someone who is very strong	A genius is special because ________________________.
❽ **machine** (mu-shēn) *noun* **Rating:** 1 2 3	☐ source of information ☐ a tool that helps us make or do something	Some machines that I use often are ________________________.

B. What if you could travel forward through time? Use at least two Key Vocabulary words to describe what your life would be like.

____

____

____

Name ____________________

LAFFF: Reading Strategies Log

Complete at least one row of the Reading Strategies Log for each section of "LAFFF."

Text I read	Strategy I used	How I used the strategy
Page: 40 Text: frizzy white hair, thick glasses	☐ Make Connections ☐ Make Inferences ☐ Visualize ☐ ________	I pictured a genius as an older person whose hair would be white and frizzy. It helps me see how Peter isn't the typical genius.
Page: ________ Text: ________	☐ Make Connections ☐ Make Inferences ☐ Visualize ☐ ________	
Page: ________ Text: ________	☐ Make Connections ☐ Make Inferences ☐ Visualize ☐ ________	

Selection Review

Name ______________________________

LAFFF

Key Vocabulary

backward	forward
concentrated	future
convinced	genius
destination	machine

A. Read the paragraph.
Write a Key Vocabulary word in each blank.
Reread the paragraph to make sure the words make sense.

Angela's neighbor Peter was so smart that she was ____________ that he was a ____________. Peter ____________ very hard on his schoolwork and had very few friends. One day, Angela peeked into Peter's garage and saw an odd-looking booth. Peter told her it was a time ____________. At first, Angela was not completely sure he was telling the truth. Peter showed her how he could travel ____________ into the future by bringing back a flower. He had one problem, though. He could not travel ____________ into the past.

Angela decided to use the device to help her win a writing contest. She set the ____________ for three weeks into the ____________ and copied the winning story. After she won the contest, she felt bad about taking the story. However, she soon realized that she actually took the story from herself!

B. Write complete sentences to answer these questions about "LAFFF."

1. At the end of the story, do you think Angela's opinion of herself has changed?

____

____

____

____

____

2. How did Peter help Angela? Why do you think he wanted to help her?

____

____

____

____

____

Name ______________________________

Use Prefixes

Prefix	Meaning
dis-	the opposite of
en-	to give
im-	into, inside, not
un-	not

Follow the steps below to figure out the meaning of each word.

1. Analyze the meaning of each word part.
2. Combine the meaning of each part to figure out the word meaning.
3. Write the definition.
4. Read the sentence in which the word appears. Make sure it makes sense.

1. **unwelcome** ______________________________

   The guest is unwelcome because he broke two plates the last time he came to our house.

2. **impossible** ______________________________

   I thought long division was impossible at first because there are so many steps.

3. **entrusted** ______________________________

   My mother entrusted me to babysit my baby brother.

4. **unhappy** ______________________________

   The basketball player is unhappy because his shot did not go into the basket.

5. **enclose** ______________________________

   The rancher must enclose the animals in a pen so they don't escape.

6. **impatient** ______________________________

   Wong's friend is so impatient that he taps his foot while he is waiting.

7. **improper** ______________________________

   My grandmother says that I am improper when I do not say hello to her friends.

8. **untied** ______________________________

   The boy's shoelace came untied as he ran down the stairs.

9. **dishonest** ______________________________

   The criminal has a very dishonest face.

Name ______________________

Academic Vocabulary	
analyze	possibility
compound	solve
describe	structure

LAFFF: Academic Vocabulary Review

A. Use your own words to tell what each Academic Vocabulary word means.

Word	My Definition
1. **analyze**	
2. **compound**	
3. **describe**	
4. **possibility**	
5. **solve**	
6. **structure**	

B. Circle the word that best fits into each sentence.

1. Chemists mix two ingredients to make a (**compound** / **structure**) substance.
2. When a scientist (**describes** / **analyzes**) an experiment to others, she tells about it.
3. When a scientist (**solves** / **analyzes**) a material, he studies it closely.
4. When you (**solve** / **compound**) a riddle, you figure out the answer.
5. The way something is built or put together is called its (**structure** / **research**).
6. Going to lunch earlier is a (**possibility** / **structure**) for solving our scheduling problem.

C. Read each sentence. Circle **Yes** or **No** to answer.

1. The best way to **analyze** something is to ignore it. **Yes** **No**
2. A skyscraper is an example of a **structure**. **Yes** **No**
3. If taking the bus is a **possibility**, it might happen. **Yes** **No**
4. *Toothpaste* is a **compound** word. **Yes** **No**
5. When the police **solve** a crime, it remains a mystery. **Yes** **No**
6. Travel writers often **describe** faraway places. **Yes** **No**

Build Background

Name ______________________________

Critical Viewing Guide

Take Notes

A. View the video. Take notes on at least three things that you learned.

____
____
____
____
____
____
____
____

Analyze the Video

B. Review your notes to help answer these questions.

1. Write two sentences to explain what was in the video.

____
____
____

2. What was the most interesting thing you learned?

____
____
____

3. Describe a problem you think should be **solved** with a new invention.

____
____
____
____
____

Learn Key Vocabulary

Name ______________________________

Kids Are Inventors, Too: Key Vocabulary

▲ A clock is a **device designed** to keep track of time.

A. Study each word. Circle a number to rate how well you know it. Then complete the chart.

Rating Scale	1	2	3
	I have never seen this word before.	I am not sure of the word's meaning.	I know this word and can teach the word's meaning to someone else.

Key Words	Check Understanding	Deepen Understanding
❶ **ability** (u-**bil**-ut-ē) *noun* Rating: 1 2 3	Everyone has the **ability** to be a gymnast. **Yes** **No**	List three abilities you have. ______
❷ **design** (di-**zīn**) *verb* Rating: 1 2 3	It helps to make a drawing when you **design** something. **Yes** **No**	List three projects for school that you've had to design. ______
❸ **device** (di-**vīs**) *noun* Rating: 1 2 3	All **devices** are helpful. **Yes** **No**	List three devices that are helpful to you. ______
❹ **exist** (ig-**zist**) *verb* Rating: 1 2 3	Scientists can prove that water does not **exist**. **Yes** **No**	List three things that exist in your town or city. ______

Name ______________________________

Kids Are Inventors, Too

Key Vocabulary	
ability	model
design	problem
device	solve
exist	suggestion

A. Read the paragraph.
Write a Key Vocabulary word in each blank.
Reread the paragraph to make sure the words make sense.

Kids have the ____________ to invent all kinds of useful items. Chester Greenwood invented earmuffs when he was fifteen to ____________ the ____________ of cold ears in winter. He invented earmuffs over a century ago, and many different kinds ____________ to this day!

Some inventors like Josh Parsons start with a paper ____________ of the special ____________ they want to make. Parsons' plan was to ____________ a baseball glove for a friend with no hands. Reeba Daniel used a ____________ from her mother to invent something that saves time. As a result, she won prizes for her diagram of a machine that would wash and dry clothes in one step. Kids have some amazing ideas!

B. Write complete sentences to answer these questions about "Kids Are Inventors, Too."

1. Which invention from "Kids Are Inventors, Too" seems most helpful? Explain your ideas.

____

____

____

____

____

____

2. Choose one inventor from the article. How would you describe this inventor to a friend?

____

____

____

____

____

Vocabulary Study

Name ______________________________

Use Suffixes

Suffix	Meaning
-al	relates to
-er/-or	person or thing that does the action
-ity	the quality of
-ize	to make
-less	without
-tion/-ion	the act or state of

Follow the steps below to figure out the meaning of each word.

1. Analyze the meaning of each word part.
2. Combine the meaning of each part to figure out the word meaning.
3. Write the definition.
4. Read the sentence in which the word appears. Make sure it makes sense.

1. **emotional** ______________________________

   The man became emotional when his first grandchild was born.

2. **purity** ______________________________

   Scientists tested the purity of the water after a company dumped chemicals into the lake.

3. **pollution** ______________________________

   The pollution in some cities is so bad that it is unhealthy to exercise outside.

4. **finalize** ______________________________

   She wanted to finalize her homework so she could go outside with her friends.

5. **shopper** ______________________________

   The shopper went to the store before it opened so he could be first in line to buy the new game.

6. **effortless** ______________________________

   Math class became effortless for Jackie because she studied every night.

7. **editor** ______________________________

   An editor needs to make sure every word is correct.

8. **subtraction** ______________________________

   I enjoy subtraction because we play games in class while learning how to do it.

Name ______________________________

Academic Vocabulary

analyze, research, compound, solve, possibility

Kids Are Inventors, Too: Academic Vocabulary Review

A. Read the paragraph.
Write an Academic Vocabulary word in each blank.
Reread the paragraph to make sure the words make sense.

There are many kinds of scientists. Food scientists carefully ____________ food to learn what it is made from. These scientists study the structure of a food's tiny parts, or molecules. Food scientists can also be inventors. They ____________ the way foods can be combined to create new foods. Some new foods can help ____________ problems such as hunger. Perhaps you can learn more about food scientists and some of their new ____________ creations.

B. Write a complete sentence for each Academic Vocabulary word.

1. **analyze**

____

____

2. **compound**

____

____

3. **possibility**

____

____

4. **solve**

____

____

5. **research**

____

____

The Evolution of a Great Idea

BY PETER DIAMANDIS AND STEVEN KOTLER

1 Sir Arthur C. Clarke, inventor of the **geostationary communication satellite** and author of dozens of best-selling science fiction books, knew something about the evolution of great ideas. He described three stages to their development. "In the beginning," says Clarke, "people tell you that's a crazy idea, and it'll never work. Next, people say your idea might work, but it's not worth doing. Finally, eventually, people say, I told you that it was a great idea all along!"

2 When Tony Spear was given the job of landing an unmanned rover on the Martian surface, he **had no inkling** that Clarke's three stages would be precisely his experience. A jovial, white-haired cross between Albert Einstein and Archie Bunker, Spear started his career at NASA's Jet Propulsion Laboratory in 1962. Over the next four decades, he worked on missions from Mariner to Viking, but it was his final assignment, project manager on the Mars Pathfinder, that he describes as his "greatest mission **challenge** ever."

3 The year was 1997, and the United States had not landed a probe on Mars since July 1976. That was Viking, a complex and expensive mission, costing some $3.5 billion (in 1997 dollars). Spear's assignment was to find a way to do everything that the previous mission had done, just "faster, better, cheaper." And when I say cheaper, I mean a *whole lot* cheaper: fifteen times cheaper, to be exact, for a fixed and total development cost of only $150 million. Out the window went the expensive stuff, the traditional stuff, and the proven stuff, including the types of retro-rockets for landing that got the job done on Viking.

4 "To pull this off under these impossible constraints, we had to do everything differently," reflects Spear, "from how I managed, to how we landed. That really scared people. At NASA headquarters, I was assigned six different managers in rapid sequence—each of the first five found a different excuse to get off the project. Finally I was assigned someone about to retire who didn't mind sticking with me

Key Vocabulary

- **challenge** *n.*, a task that is difficult

In Other Words

geostationary communication satellite satellite at a fixed point over Earth

had no inkling could not have imagined

An artist's depiction of the spacecraft descending toward the airbag landing pad on Mars.

at the end of his career. Even the NASA administrator, Daniel Golden, nearly flipped out when he received his initial mission briefing—he couldn't get past how many new things we were trying out."

Among the many things Spear tried out, nothing struck people as **zanier** than using airbags to cushion the initial impact, helping the craft bounce around like a beach ball on the Martian surface, before settling down into a safe landing spot. But airbags were cheap, they wouldn't **contaminate** their landing site with foreign chemicals, and Spear was pretty certain that they would work. The early tests, however, were a disaster, so the experts were summoned.

In Other Words
zanier more unusual
contaminate dirtyw

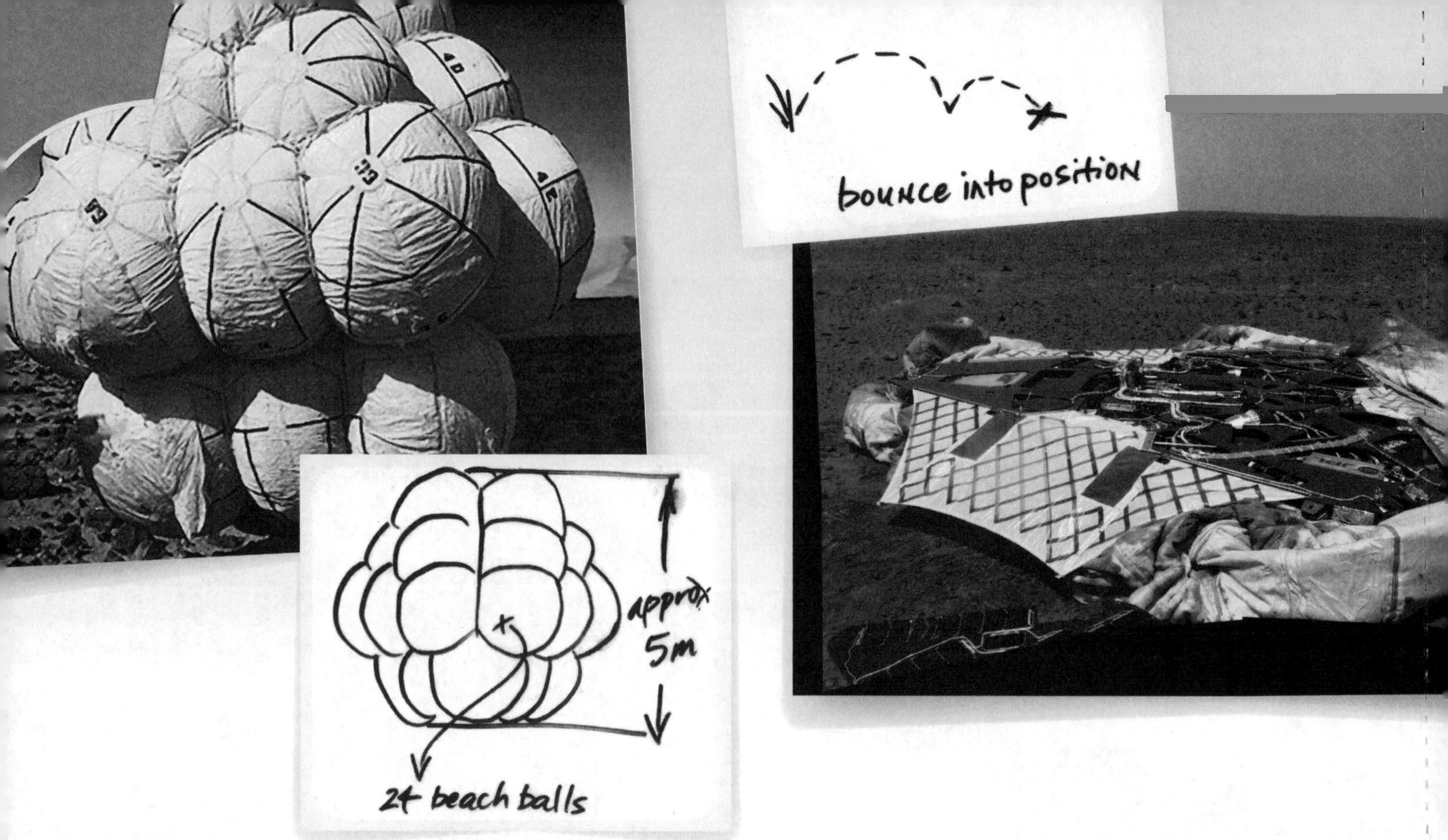

6 The experts had a pair of opinions. The first was: Don't use airbags. The second was: No, we're totally serious, don't even *consider* using airbags. "Two of them," recounts Spear, "told me flat out that I was wasting government money and should cancel the project. Finally, when they realized I wasn't going to give up, they decided to dig in and help me."

7 Together they tested more than a dozen designs, skidding them along a **faux** rocky Martian surface to see which would survive without shredding to pieces. Finally, just eight months prior to launch, Spear and his team completed qualification testing of a design composed of twenty-four interconnected spheres, loaded it aboard Pathfinder, and launched it into space. But the anxiety didn't end there. The trip to Mars took eight months, during which there was plenty of time to worry about the fate of the mission. "In the weeks just prior to landing," Spear recalls, "everyone was very nervous, **speculating** whether we'd have a big splat when we arrived. Golden himself was wondering what to do: should he come to the JPL control room for the landing or not? Just a few days before our July 4 descent to the surface, the administrator took a **bold tack**, holding a press conference and proclaiming, 'The Pathfinder mission demonstrates a new way of doing business at NASA, and is a success whether or not we survive the landing.' "

In Other Words
faux fake
speculating wondering
bold tack risk

← beach balls deflate/Pathfinder opens

8 The landing, though, went exactly as planned. They had spent one-fifteenth the cost of Viking, and everything worked perfectly—especially the airbags. Spear was a hero. Golden was so impressed, he insisted that airbags be used to land the next few Mars missions and was quoted as saying, "Tony Spear was a legendary project manager at JPL and helped make Mars Pathfinder the riveting success that it was."

"Demonstrating great ideas involves a considerable amount of risk."

9 The point here, of course, is that Clarke was right. Demonstrating great ideas involves a considerable amount of risk. There will always be **naysayers**. People will resist breakthrough ideas until the moment they're accepted as the new norm. Since the road to **abundance** requires significant **innovation**, it also requires significant **tolerance** for risk, for failure, and for ideas that strike most as absolute nonsense. As Burt Rutan puts it, "**Revolutionary** ideas come from nonsense. If an idea is truly a breakthrough, then the day before it was discovered, it must have been considered crazy or nonsense or both—otherwise it wouldn't be a breakthrough."

In Other Words

naysayers people who disagree
abundance many new ideas
innovation trying of new things
tolerance acceptance
Revolutionary Completely new

Name ______________________

Read for Understanding

A. From what kind of text is this passage taken? How do you know?

B. Write a sentence that tells the topic of the selection.

Reread and Summarize

C. On **Practice Book** pages 28–31, circle the 3–5 most important words in each section. Make notes about why you chose each word. Why is the word important in the section?

1. Section 1: (paragraphs 1–2)

2. Section 2: (paragraphs 3–4)

3. Section 3: (paragraphs 5–7)

4. Section 4: (paragraphs 8–9)

D. Use your topic sentence from above and your notes to write a summary of the selection.

Name ______________________________

Reread and Analyze

E. Analyze how the authors include clarifying details to help readers answer questions they have about the topic.

1. Reread paragraph 1 and the first sentence of paragraph 2 on **Practice Book** page 28. Who is Sir Arthur C. Clarke, and why do the authors choose to begin the selection with him? Underline words and phrases to support your answers. Use text evidence to support your answer.

____

____

____

2. Underline other words and phrases on **Practice Book** pages 28–31 that help you answer questions that you have about the topic as you read. Explain how each detail tells you more about the topic and answers a specific question you had.

____

____

F. Analyze how the authors include facts to help readers answer questions they have about the topic.

1. Read paragraph 3 on **Practice Book** page 28. How do the dates and information about the Viking mission help answer questions you have about Tony Spear's new assignment? Underline the words and phrases that support your answer. Use text evidence to support your answer.

____

____

____

2. Underline other words on **Practice Book** pages 28–31 to analyze how the authors include facts that develop the ideas in the text. Explain how each fact supports information the authors include.

____

____

Name ______________________________

Reread and Analyze

G. Analyze how the authors use text structure to develop the important ideas in the text.

1. Reread paragraphs 5 and 6 on **Practice Book** pages 29–30. What is the main idea of these paragraphs? How does the structure of these paragraphs help you figure out what is important? Underline words and phrases to support your answers. Use text evidence to support your answer.

____

____

____

2. Circle another important idea in a paragraph on **Practice Book** pages 28–31. Underline the details the authors include to support this idea. Explain how the structure of the paragraph helps you understand the main idea.

____

____

H. Analyze how the authors include supporting details to develop the ideas in the text.

1. Read paragraph 8 on **Practice Book** page 31. What is the important idea in this paragraph? How do the supporting details help readers understand what is important? Underline the words and phrases that support your answer. Use text evidence to support your answer.

____

____

____

2. On **Practice Book** pages 28–31, circle another important idea. Explain the details that help you figure out that this is an important idea.

____

____

Name ______________________________

Discuss and Write

I. Synthesize your ideas about how the authors present details that answer questions about their topic and show what is important.

1. With the class, discuss the various ways the authors support the idea that thinking of things in new ways can solve problems. List the examples you discuss.

____

____

____

2. Choose one of the examples that you listed. Write a paragraph to explain how the authors support this example through main ideas and details. Use the questions below to organize your thoughts.

- What do you think the authors want you to learn from the text?
- What parts of the text helped you answer questions you had? Give 2 examples.
- What parts of the text help you determine important ideas? Give 2 examples.

____

____

____

____

Connect with GUIDING QUESTION

J. Discuss the Guiding Question: What makes an idea powerful?

1. What did the naysayers say about this project?

____

____

2. Why did Tony Spear choose to ignore the naysayers?

____

____

3. How do you know that Spear's idea was a powerful one?

____

Unit 1 Review

Name ______________________________

Academic Vocabulary

analyze	possibility
compound	research
contrast	solve
describe	structure

Academic Vocabulary Review

A. Circle the word that best fits into each sentence.

1. To find information, you can go to a library and do (**solve** / **research**).
2. When you (**solve** / **structure**) a puzzle, you find the answer to it.
3. When you (**solve** / **contrast**) two things, you tell how they are different.
4. A (**compound** / **structure**) is how parts are arranged or organized.

B. Read each statement. Circle **Yes** or **No** to answer.

1. When you **describe** something, you use words to tell about it. **Yes** **No**
2. Something **compound** is made of only one part. **Yes** **No**
3. A scientist can **analyze** material closely with a microscope. **Yes** **No**
4. One way to get information is to **research** a topic. **Yes** **No**

C. Answer the questions in complete sentences.

1. **Describe** your favorite game or sport. **Contrast** it with your least favorite game or sport.

____

____

2. If you could **interview** any person in the world, who would it be? Explain why.

____

____

3. What would you do to **analyze** the steps you need to complete a task? Explain.

____

____

4. What subject would you like to **research**? Explain why.

____

____

Name ______________________________

Key Vocabulary Review

A. Read each sentence. Circle the word that best fits into each sentence.

1. A person who studies science is a (**device** / **scientist**).
2. Tomorrow is in the (**future** / **machine**).
3. If you want to know how to get to your (**experiment** / **destination**), use a map.
4. You can (**attach** / **solve**) pictures to a wall to decorate it.
5. A (**backward** / **captive**) animal might live in a cage.
6. It is hard to (**concentrate** / **convince**) when the TV is on.
7. You can use a notebook to (**experiment** / **record**) important ideas.
8. Reading is an important (**ability** / **design**).

B. Use your own words to write what each Key Vocabulary word means. Then write an example for each word.

Word	My Definition	Example
1. **backward**		
2. **convince**		
3. **experiment**		
4. **forward**		
5. **genius**		
6. **solve**		
7. **suggestion**		
8. **test**		

Name ______________________________

Unit 1 Key Vocabulary

ability	challenge	destination	forward	machine	scientist
attach	concentrate	device	future	model	solve
backward	convince	exist	genius	problem	suggestion
captive	design	experiment	invention	record	test

C. Answer the questions in complete sentences.

1. What is an example of an **invention**?

____

____

2. Think about a **machine**. How does this machine help you?

____

____

3. What is a **challenge** for you?

____

____

4. Tell about something you would like to **design**.

____

____

5. Describe a **device** in your home and tell how it helps you.

____

____

6. Tell about a **model** you have seen.

____

____

7. What is one **problem** that you can help **solve**?

____

____

8. Give an example of an animal that doesn't **exist**.

____

____

Unit 2 Launch

Name ______________________________

Mind Map

Use the Mind Map to show your ideas about how you could work on your talents. As you read the selections in this unit, add new ideas.

Talent	Knowledge	Skills	Outcome
1. Music	1. Read music	1. Take lessons	1. Play in public
2.	2.	2.	2.
3.	3.	3.	3.

Academic Vocabulary

Think about a **challenge** you have faced. Why might people try to **challenge** themselves? Use the word **challenge** in your answer.

____

____

____

____

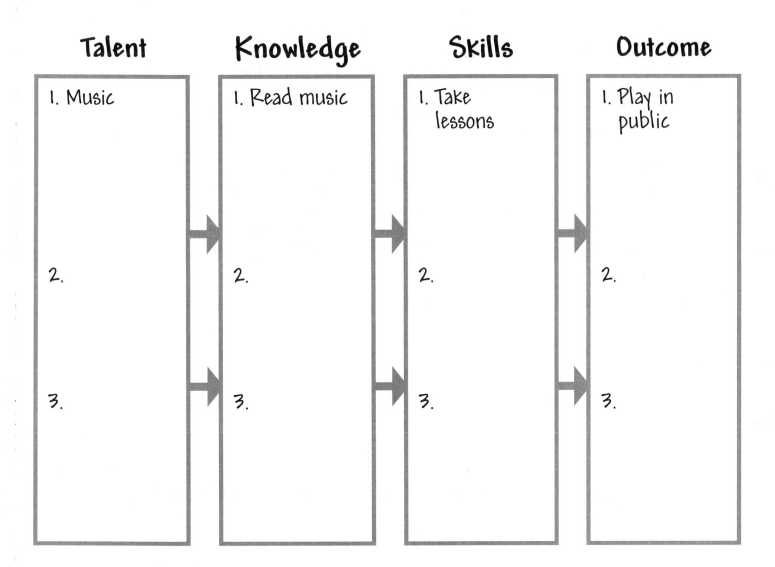

Name ______________________________

Analyze Elements of Fiction: Plot, Characters, and Setting

Read the passage. Underline the setting and the characters.
Look for clues that tell about the plot. Then answer the questions.

> One day out in the grassland, a jackal heard a lion moaning. The lion was trapped with thorns in his paws. The lion asked the jackal for help. The jackal refused. He was afraid the lion would eat him. The lion promised that he would not eat the jackal. So the jackal set the lion free.
>
> Then the lion pounced on the jackal and roared, "Now I will eat you!"
>
> The jackal quickly said, "Before you decide, you must ask some other animals."
>
> The lion asked a tiger and an elephant. Both animals said the lion should eat the jackal. Then the lion asked a wise old rabbit. The rabbit said he couldn't decide until he saw where it happened. So the three animals went back to the trap. The rabbit and the jackal pushed the thorns back into the lion's paws, set the trap again, and ran away. The jackal was sure to be careful after that!

1. What is the setting? How does this affect the story?

____

____

2. Who are the characters and what are they like?

____

____

3. What is the conflict? How do the animals' traits help them to resolve the conflict?

____

____

Academic Vocabulary

What **element** of friendship do you most enjoy? What **trait** do you look for in a friend? Explain.

____

____

____

____

Focus on Vocabulary

Name ______________________________

Relate Words: Synonyms

Read the passages. Follow these steps.

1. When you read, you can put words into groups, or categories, to help you understand their exact meanings.
2. Use a Synonym Scale to rank synonyms in order of their strength.

A. Read the passage. Make a Synonym Scale for the underlined words.

> My brother is a brilliant painter. We noticed he was talented at a young age. His ideas were clever. Now he is an adult. People buy his paintings. He is very skilled at what he does.

Synonym Scale

→

________ ________ ________ ________

B. Read the passage. Make a Synonym Scale for the underlined words.

> Everyone knew that the old house was haunted. One day, Michelle's friends dared her to explore the creepy house. She slowly opened the door of the frightening house. Inside it was dark and gloomy. She yelled a terrifying scream when she got tangled in a cobweb! She ran out the door and never returned to that old house!

Synonym Scale

→

________ ________ ________ ________

Academic Vocabulary

How would you make an **exact** copy of a painting?

____

____

____

____

Build Background

Name ______________________________

Critical Viewing Guide

Take Notes

A. View the video. Take notes on at least three things that you learned.

____

____

____

____

____

____

____

____

Analyze the Video

B. Review your notes to help answer these questions.

1. Write two sentences to explain what was in the video.

____

____

____

2. What was the most interesting thing you learned?

____

____

____

3. What **challenges** do you think an author faces when writing a story? Explain.

____

____

____

____

____

Learn Key Vocabulary

Name ____________________

The Challenge: Key Vocabulary

A. Study each word. Circle a number to rate how well you know it. Then complete the chart.

Rating Scale	1	2	3
	I have never seen this word before.	I am not sure of the word's meaning.	I know this word and can teach the word's meaning to someone else.

▲ You may **notice** that many people are afraid to **approach** spiders.

Key Words	Check Understanding	Deepen Understanding
❶ **approach** (u-**prōch**) *verb* **Rating: 1 2 3**	When you **approach** something, you move away from it. **Yes** **No**	What are you afraid to approach? ____________
❷ **assume** (u-**süm**) *verb* **Rating: 1 2 3**	When we **assume** something, we know it is true. **Yes** **No**	What would you assume if you saw someone smile? ____________
❸ **attention** (u-**ten**-chun) *noun* **Rating: 1 2 3**	It is important to pay **attention** to traffic signals. **Yes** **No**	Why would you give a teacher your attention? ____________
❹ **awkward** (**aw**-kwurd) *adjective* **Rating: 1 2 3**	It sometimes feels **awkward** to do something new. **Yes** **No**	What makes you feel awkward? ____________

Name ______________________________

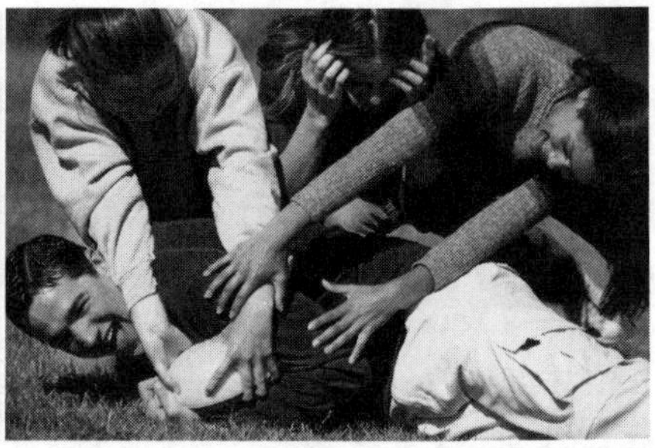

It is correct to **assume** that it takes a lot of **practice** to be good at football. ▶

Key Words	Check Understanding	Deepen Understanding
5 encourage (in-**kur**-ij) *verb* Rating: 1 2 3	You **encourage** someone when you want them to be successful. Yes No	Who encourages you? Explain. ______
6 notice (**nō**-tis) *verb* Rating: 1 2 3	When we **notice** something, we see it. Yes No	When do people notice you? Explain. ______
7 practice (**prak**-tis) *verb* Rating: 1 2 3	You do not need to **practice** to be good at something. Yes No	What do you practice? Why? ______
8 weight (**wāt**) *noun* Rating: 1 2 3	**Weights** are usually heavy. Yes No	What can lifting weights do for you? ______

B. Use at least two of the Key Vocabulary words. Write about a skill you improved and how you did it.

____

____

____

Name ______________________________

Analyze Plot

A. As you read "The Challenge," look for the parts of the plot. Complete the Plot Diagram.

B. Reread the passage and complete the Plot Diagram.

Climax: ______________________________

____

Complication: ______________________________

____

Complication: ______________________________

____

Complication: ______________________________

____

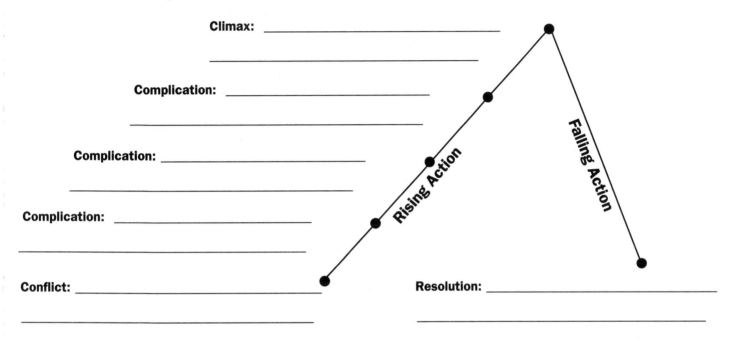

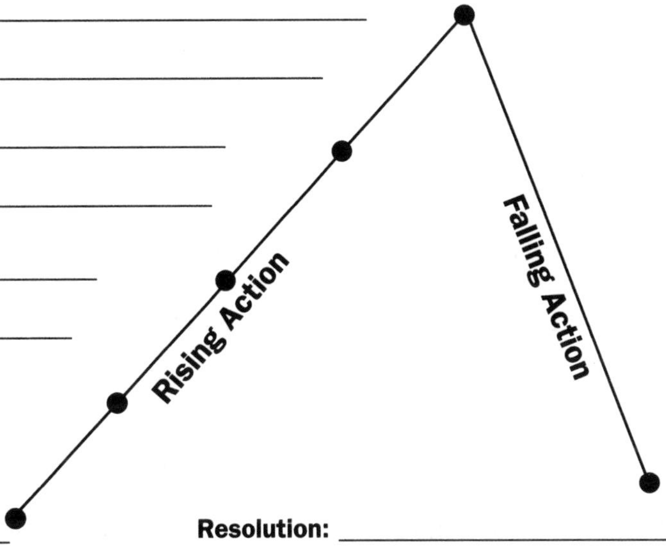

Conflict: ______________________________

____

Resolution: ______________________________

____

C. Give an example of how a setting influenced José's efforts to get Estela notice him.

____

____

D. Give an example of how a character's actions affect the events in the story.

____

____

____

Selection Review

Name ______________________________

The Challenge

Key Vocabulary	
approached	**encourage**
assumed	**notice**
attention	**practice**
awkward	**weights**

A. Read the paragraph.
Write a Key Vocabulary word in each blank.
Reread the paragraph to make sure the words make sense.

"The Challenge" is about a boy named José Camacho who wanted a girl called Estela to _______________ him. José _______________ Estela played racquetball because he saw a racket in her backpack. When he finally had enough courage, José _______________ her and began to talk. He thought challenging her to a racquetball game would be a great way to get her to pay _______________ to him. José did not know how to play and needed time to _______________, but he only had one day to learn! No one in his family could _______________ him to win the match.

The next day, José and Estela met at the court to play racquetball. José was very _______________ and did not hit the ball very well. He lost the match. José decided to lift _______________ so he could be stronger if Estela wanted another match. He hoped she wouldn't!

B. Write complete sentences to answer these questions about "The Challenge."

1. What made José think he could impress Estela by playing racquetball?

____

____

____

____

____

2. What do you think might happen the next time José and Estela meet?

____

____

____

____

____

____

Name ______________________________

Use Word Categories

Follow the steps to build a Word Web of related words for each category.

1. Look at the category words in the box.
2. Think about words that belong in that category.
3. Write these words in the ovals.

1. Types of weather

2. Types of music

3. Things to read

4. Furniture

5. Large cities

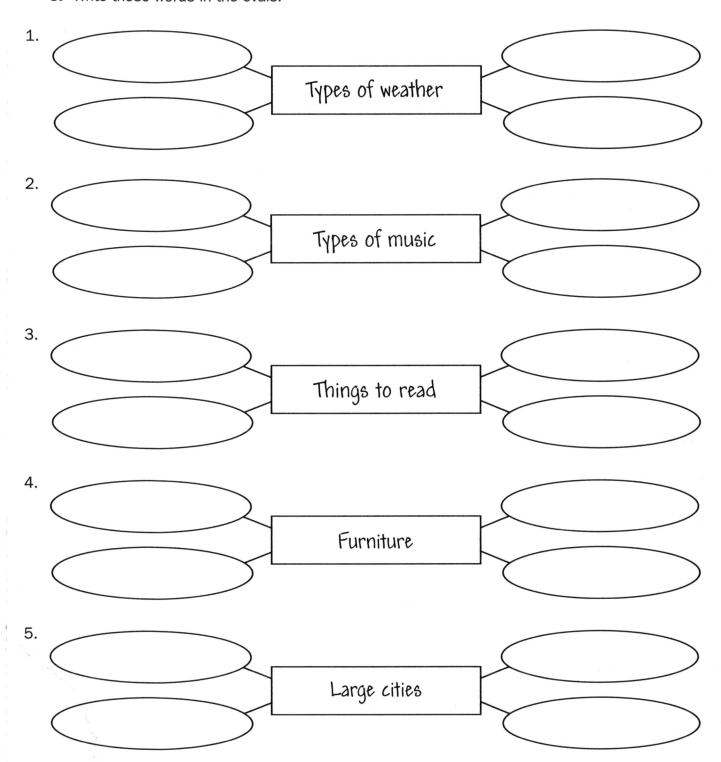

Name ___________________________

Academic Vocabulary	
category	element
challenge	exact
compare	trait
conflict	

The Challenge: Academic Vocabulary Review

A. Circle the word that best matches each definition.

1. a group of things that have something in common (**category** / **trait**)
2. a problem or disagreement (**conflict** / **element**)
3. a quality or characteristic of something (**presentation** / **trait**)
4. something that is accurate and specific (**exact** / **conflict**)
5. an important part of something (**category** / **element**)
6. when you think about how two things are alike and different (**compare** / **challenge**)
7. something that tests your strength and skill (**element** / **challenge**)

B. Rewrite each sentence. Replace the underlined words with an Academic Vocabulary word.

1. Kate and Lilly had a <u>disagreement</u> about which game to play.

____

2. Family members often share certain <u>characteristics</u>.

____

3. Carlos wants to <u>see what is alike and different about</u> the two bikes.

____

4. Mrs. Patel forgot an <u>important part</u> of the story.

____

5. James has a watch that keeps <u>very accurate</u> time.

____

6. Grains and vegetables are two <u>groups</u> of food.

____

7. The Math Bee is a <u>difficult task</u> for students who are not good with numbers.

____

Name ______________________________

Critical Viewing Guide

Take Notes

A. View the video. Take notes on at least three things that you learned.

____
____
____
____
____
____
____
____

Analyze the Video

B. Review your notes to help answer these questions.

1. Write two sentences to explain what was in the video.

____
____
____

2. What was the most interesting thing you learned?

____
____
____

3. Why do you think characters in folk tales face **challenges**?

____
____
____
____
____

Learn Key Vocabulary

Name ______________________________

Rachel the Clever: Key Vocabulary

A. Study each word. Circle a number to rate how well you know it. Then complete the chart.

Rating Scale	1	2	3
	I have never seen this word before.	I am not sure of the word's meaning.	I know this word and can teach the word's meaning to someone else.

▲ Bugs Bunny is a very **clever** cartoon rabbit. He loves to play tricks on Elmer Fudd.

Key Words	Check Understanding	Deepen Understanding
1 clever (**klev**-ir) *adjective* Rating: 1 2 3	☐ sad or gloomy ☐ smart and tricky	List three people you think are clever. ______
2 judgment (**juj**-mint) *noun* Rating: 1 2 3	☐ an opinion ☐ a question	List three judgments you have made. ______
3 marry (**mair**-ē) *verb* Rating: 1 2 3	☐ make a family ☐ make new friends	List three things that happen when two people marry. ______
4 obey (ō-**bā**) *verb* Rating: 1 2 3	☐ break a rule ☐ follow a rule	List three rules you obey at school. ______

Name ______________________________

Did You Know?

The expression "**proud** as a peacock" means to brag or be arrogant. This refers to the long, colorful feathers that a male peacock expands like a fan.

Key Words	Check Understanding	Deepen Understanding
5 possession (pu-**zesh**-un) *noun* **Rating: 1 2 3**	☐ something you want to buy ☐ something you own	List three of your possessions. ________
6 proud (**prowd**) *adjective* **Rating: 1 2 3**	☐ feel good ☐ feel nervous	List three things that make you feel proud. ________
7 release (ri-**lēs**) *verb* **Rating: 1 2 3**	☐ catch ☐ let go	List three things you have released. ________
8 riddle (**rid**-ul) *noun* **Rating: 1 2 3**	☐ a puzzle ☐ a sport	List three reasons that people like riddles. ________

B. Use at least two Key Vocabulary words. Write about someone you think is clever and why.

____

____

____

Name ____________________

Analyze Character

A. As you read the play, complete Character Charts about the king and Rachel. Think about how their actions influenced the plot.

Character: the king

Traits	Motives	Actions
clever	wants someone as clever as he is	
proud		

B. Character:

Traits	Motives	Actions

Name ______________________________

Rachel the Clever

Key Vocabulary	
clever	possession
judgment	proud
marry	released
obey	riddles

A. Read the paragraph.
Write a Key Vocabulary word in each blank.
Reread the paragraph to make sure the words make sense.

It was time for the king to ____________. He searched for a woman with a mind as ____________ as his own. One day, the king heard the innkeeper talking about his daughter Rachel. He was very ____________ of her intelligence. Rachel had to solve ____________ to show the king that she was smart. The king chose Rachel as his wife. He asked her never to disagree with any ____________ at court, or she would be ____________ from the palace. Rachel said she would ____________ the rule. One day, Rachel disagreed with one of the king's decisions. She was asked to leave and take only her dearest ____________. Therefore, Rachel gave the king a sleeping potion and took him away!

B. Write complete sentences to answer these questions about "Rachel the Clever."

1. Why is it good to be **clever**?

____

____

____

____

____

____

2. If you were the king, would you be angry with Rachel? Explain your answer.

____

____

____

____

____

____

Vocabulary Study

Name ______________________________

Use Synonyms

Follow the steps below to complete the Synonym Scales.

1. Think of two synonyms for each underlined word.
2. Write the synonyms in order on the Synonym Scale from weakest to strongest.
3. Use a print or online thesaurus to help you find synonyms for words you do not know.

1. When I eat a peanut butter and jelly sandwich, I chew hard because the peanut butter is sticky.

   ______________ ______________ ______________

2. I want a shiny new bicycle.

   ______________ ______________ ______________

3. When Esteban had the flu, he was too sick to go to school.

   ______________ ______________ ______________

4. After the little girl fell on the ground, we could hear her sob.

   ______________ ______________ ______________

5. The glass will break into a million pieces if you drop it on the floor.

   ______________ ______________ ______________

6. In this movie, the two enemies shout at each other.

   ______________ ______________ ______________

7. The baby learned how to walk across the room.

   ______________ ______________ ______________

8. It felt very cold outside because it was a blustery day.

   ______________ ______________ ______________

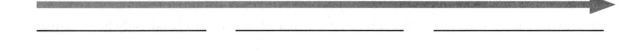

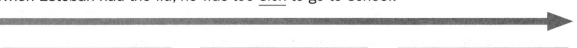

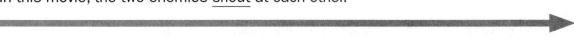

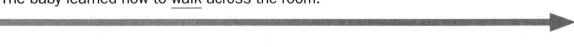

Name ______________________________

Rachel the Clever: Academic Vocabulary Review

Academic Vocabulary

affect	illustrate
challenge	similar
element	trait
exact	

A. Use each Academic Vocabulary word in a sentence. You may choose to use two words in one sentence.

1. ______________________________
2. ______________________________
3. ______________________________
4. ______________________________
5. ______________________________
6. ______________________________
7. ______________________________

B. Circle the word that best fits into each sentence.

1. One important (**element** / **exact**) of tennis is good footwork.
2. John and Nikki share a (**trait** / **similar**) taste in music.
3. Please tell me the (**exact** / **similar**) time you arrive.
4. A diagram is a good way to (**illustrate** / **affect**) how to build a birdhouse.
5. If you don't get enough sleep, it can (**affect** / **illustrate**) how you feel.
6. One important (**trait** / **challenge**) in an athlete is good sportsmanship.
7. A marathon is a difficult (**challenge** / **affect**) for even the best runners.

Name ____________________

Critical Viewing Guide

Take Notes

A. View the images. Take notes on at least three things that you learned.

____
____
____
____
____
____
____
____

Analyze the Images

B. Review your notes to help answer these questions.

1. Write two sentences to explain what was in the images.

____
____
____

2. What was the most interesting thing you learned?

____
____
____

3. Think about what it would be like to live in a different time and place. What kinds of **challenges** might you face?

____
____
____
____

Name ______________________________

A Contest of Riddles: Key Vocabulary

▲ It is important to express **knowledge** of your topic during a presentation. It is not a time for **nonsense**.

A. Study each word. Circle a number to rate how well you know it. Then complete the chart.

Rating Scale	1	2	3
	I have never seen this word before.	I am not sure of the word's meaning.	I know this word and can teach the word's meaning to someone else.

Key Words	Check Understanding	Deepen Understanding
1 choice (chois) *noun* Rating: 1 2 3	Circle the synonym for **choice**. **decision** **rule**	Tell about a difficult choice you made. ______
2 contest (kahn-test) *noun* Rating: 1 2 3	Circle the synonym for **contest**. **game** **meeting**	What contest would you like to enter? Why? ______
3 excellent (ek-su-lint) *adjective* Rating: 1 2 3	Circle the synonym for **excellent**. **awful** **wonderful**	What is an excellent movie you have seen? Explain. ______
4 interpret (in-tur-prit) *verb* Rating: 1 2 3	Circle the synonym for **interpret**. **explain** **question**	Give an example of a time when you need someone to interpret something. ______

Name ______________________________

"Little Red Riding Hood" is an **excellent** fairy tale, but the **outcome** can frighten some children. ▶

Key Words	Check Understanding	Deepen Understanding
5 knowledge (**nah**-lij) *noun* Rating: 1 2 3	Circle the synonym for **knowledge**. **secret** **understanding**	What do you have knowledge about? Explain. ________
6 nonsense (**nahn**-sens) *noun* Rating: 1 2 3	Circle the synonym for **nonsense**. **foolishness** **wisdom**	What do you think is nonsense? Explain. ________
7 outcome (**owt**-kum) *noun* Rating: 1 2 3	Circle the synonym for **outcome**. **prediction** **result**	What outcome do you want for a competition you are following? ________
8 response (ri-**spons**) *noun* Rating: 1 2 3	Circle the synonym for **response**. **test** **answer**	What response would you give to a cry for help from a stranger? Explain. ________

B. Use at least two Key Vocabulary words. Write about a time you won a contest or solved a difficult problem.

____

____

____

Prepare to Read

Name ______________________________

Analyze Elements of Drama

A. As you read each scene of "A Contest of Riddles," identify the elements of drama and write them in the first column. Then use the second column to record what you learn about the play from each element.

Drama Chart

Element of Drama	What I Learn
• Scene 1 description	• It is morning. The king and queen are talking in the garden when the princess comes in.
• Scene 2 description	

Name ________________________________

A Contest of Riddles

Key Vocabulary

choice	knowledge
contest	nonsense
excellent	outcome
interpret	response

A. Read the paragraph.
Write a Key Vocabulary word in each blank.
Reread the paragraph to make sure the words make sense.

In an Abron village many years ago, a girl could not choose her own husband. Her parents made this ____________ for her. A princess thought the rule was ____________ and did not like it. She liked riddles, so she and her father held a ____________ to find the best riddler for her to marry. Many riddlers came to the princess to test their ____________. Several riddlers often had an incorrect answer, or ____________, for her riddles. Finally, a master entered with a servant. The servant was able to ____________ the answers for his master. After the princess realized the servant was answering the questions, she had an ____________ idea. She and the servant took turns solving riddles. At first, her parents and his master would not give permission for them to be married. However, the final ____________ was that the princess and the servant became husband and wife.

B. Write complete sentences to answer these questions about "A Contest of Riddles."

1. How do the King and Queen feel when the princess solves the riddle from the Yam Vendor?

____

____

____

____

____

2. How do **contests** show our strengths and weaknesses?

____

____

____

____

____

Vocabulary Study

Name ______________________________

Use Synonyms and Antonyms

Follow the steps below to complete the Synonym-Antonym Scales.

1. Read each sentence. Think about the underlined word.
2. Write the underlined word on the middle line.
3. Write an antonym and a synonym for the word. Use a thesaurus if you need help.

1. The chair felt firm when I sat down on it.

______________ ______________ ______________

2. Some of my friends like to go to the movies.

______________ ______________ ______________

3. I left the door open because I was expecting company.

______________ ______________ ______________

4. On rainy days, Lucinda likes to jump in the puddles.

______________ ______________ ______________

5. My teacher asked me not to shout my answer across the room.

______________ ______________ ______________

6. I was thrilled because I finished my homework and could watch my favorite television show.

______________ ______________ ______________

7. Val was uncertain about how to put together the shelf.

______________ ______________ ______________

8. The rag felt damp because it was left outside in the rain.

______________ ______________ ______________

Name ______________________________

Academic Vocabulary	
challenge	role
element	similar
exact	trait

A Contest of Riddles: Academic Vocabulary Review

A. Use your own words to write what each Academic Vocabulary word means.

1. **challenge** ______________________________

2. **role** ______________________________

3. **similar** ______________________________

B. Read the paragraph. Replace each bold phrase with the correct Academic Vocabulary word.

Maria and her twin sister, Olga, have many ______________ (**almost the same**) ______________ (**characteristics**). They both have brown hair. They both have hazel eyes. They are both tall. It can be a real ______________ (**difficulty**) to tell them apart. The twins also share many interests. They both like to sing. They both love animals. However, Maria and Olga are not ______________ (**identical**) copies of each other. Maria likes to swim and play softball. Olga likes to paint and play soccer. There are also different ______________ (**parts**) to their personalities. Maria's ______________ (**position**) is to be the calm one. Olga can sometimes be unreasonable. Their differences can sometimes cause them to disagree. Olga and Maria are no different from many other sisters!

from *The Hobbit*

Riddles in the Dark

by J.R.R Tolkien

1 Deep down here by the dark water lived old Gollum, a small slimy creature. I don't know where he came from, nor who or what he was. He was Gollum—as dark as darkness, except for two big round pale eyes in his thin face. He had a little boat, and he rowed about quite quietly on the lake; for lake it was, wide and deep and deadly cold. He paddled it with large feet dangling over the side, but never a ripple did he make. Not he. He was looking out of his pale lamp-like eyes for blind fish, which he grabbed with his long fingers as quick as thinking. He liked meat too. Goblin he thought good, when he could get it.

2 He was watching Bilbo now from the distance with his pale eyes like telescopes. Bilbo could not see him, but he was wondering a lot about Bilbo, for he could see that he was no goblin at all.

3 Gollum got into his boat and shot off from the island, while Bilbo was sitting on the brink **altogether flummoxed** and at the end of his way and his wits. Suddenly up came Gollum and whispered and hissed:

4 "Bless us and splash us, my precioussss! I guess it's a choice feast; at least a tasty **morsel** it'd make us, gollum!" And when he said *gollum* he made a horrible swallowing noise in his throat. That's how he got his name, though he always called himself 'my precious.'

5 **The hobbit** jumped nearly out of his skin when the hiss came in his ears, and he suddenly saw the pale eyes sticking out at him.

6 "Who are you?" he said, **thrusting** his dagger in front of him.

7 "What iss he, my preciouss?" whispered Gollum (who always spoke to himself through never having anyone else to speak to). This is what he had come to find out, for he was not really very hungry at the moment, only curious; otherwise he would have grabbed first and whispered afterwards.

8 "I am Mr. Bilbo Baggins. I have lost the dwarves and I have lost the wizard, and I don't know where I am; and I don't want to know, if only I can get away."

Cultural Background

Imaginary creatures like goblins are common in fairy tales and traditional stories in many cultures.

In Other Words

altogether flummoxed completely confused
morsel bit of food
The hobbit A small, imaginary creature of the forest; Bilbo
thrusting pushing

"What's he got in his handses?" said Gollum, looking at the sword, which he did not quite like.

10 "A sword, a blade which came out of Gondolin!"

11 "Ssss," said Gollum, and became quite polite. "Praps ye sits here and chats with it a bitsy, my preciousss. It like **riddles**, praps it does, does it?" He was anxious to appear friendly, at any rate for the moment, and until he found out more about the sword and the hobbit, whether he was quite alone really, whether he was good to eat, and whether Gollum was really hungry.

12 "Very well," said Bilbo, who was anxious to agree, until he found out more about the creature, whether he was quite alone, whether he was fierce or hungry, and whether he was a friend of the goblins.

13 "You ask first," he said, because he had not had time to think of a riddle.

14 So Gollum hissed:

What has roots as nobody sees,
Is taller than trees,
Up, up it goes,
And yet never grows?

15 "Easy!" said Bilbo. "Mountain, I suppose."

16 "Does it guess easy? It must have a competition with us, my preciouss! If precious asks, and it doesn't answer, we eats it, my preciousss. If it asks us, and we doesn't answer, then we does what it wants, eh? We shows it the way out, yes!"

17 "All right!" said Bilbo, not daring to disagree, and nearly bursting his brain to think of riddles that could save him from being eaten.

Thirty white horses on a red hill,
First they champ,
Then they stamp,
Then they stand still.

18 That was all he could think of to ask—the idea of eating was **rather** on his mind. It was rather an old one, too, and Gollum knew the answer as well as you do.

19 "**Chestnuts, chestnuts**," he hissed. "Teeth! teeth! my preciousss; but we has only six!" Then he asked his second:

Voiceless it cries,
Wingless flutters,
Toothless bites,
Mouthless mutters.

20 "Half a moment!" cried Bilbo, who was still thinking uncomfortably about eating. Fortunately he had once heard something rather like this before, and getting his wits back he thought of the answer. "Wind, wind of course," he said, and he was so pleased that he made up one on the spot.

A box without hinges, key, or lid,
Yet golden treasure inside is hid,

he asked to gain time, until he could think of a really hard one. This he thought a **dreadfully** easy chestnut, though he had not asked it in the usual words. But it proved a **nasty poser** for Gollum. He hissed to himself, and still he did not answer; he whispered and spluttered.

Key Vocabulary
• **riddle** *n.*, a confusing question

In Other Words
rather really
Chestnuts, chestnuts Riddles, riddles
dreadfully very
nasty poser tricky puzzle

"If precious asks, and it
doesn't answer, we eats it,
my preciousss."

21 But suddenly Gollum remembered **thieving** from nests long ago, and sitting under the river bank teaching his grandmother, teaching his grandmother to suck—"Eggses" he hissed. "Eggses it is!" Then he asked:

This thing all things devours:
Birds, beasts, trees, flowers;
Gnaws iron, bites steel;
Grinds hard stones to meal;
Slays king, ruins town,
And beats high mountain down.

22 Poor Bilbo sat in the dark thinking of all the horrible names of all the giants and ogres he had ever heard told of in tales, but not one of them had done all these things. He had a feeling that the answer was quite different and that he **ought to** know it, but he could not think of it. He began to get frightened, and that is bad for thinking. Gollum began to get out of his boat. He flapped into the water and paddled to the bank; Bilbo could see his eyes coming towards him. His tongue seemed to stick in his mouth; he wanted to shout out: "Give me more time! Give me time!" But all that came out with a sudden squeal was: "Time! Time!"

23 Bilbo was saved by pure luck. For that of course was the answer.

In Other Words
thieving stealing
ought to should

Name ______________________________

Read for Understanding

A. From what kind of text is this passage taken? How do you know?

____

B. Write a sentence that tells the topic of the selection.

____

Reread and Summarize

C. On **Practice Book** pages 64–67, circle the 3–5 most important words in each section. Make notes about why you chose each word. Why is the word important?

1. Section 1: (paragraphs 1–4)

____

____

2. Section 2: (paragraphs 5–13)

____

____

3. Section 3: (paragraphs 14–19)

____

____

4. Section 3: (paragraphs 20–23)

____

____

D. Use your topic sentence from above and your notes to write a summary of the selection.

____

____

____

Name ______________________________

Reread and Analyze

E. Analyze how the author develops the setting for the story.

1. Reread paragraph 1 on **Practice Book** page 64. What does the author show you about the setting through this description? Underline words and phrases to support your answers. Use evidence from the text to support your answer.

____

____

____

2. Underline other words and phrases on **Practice Book** pages 64–67 that help you analyze the setting. Explain what each shows about the setting.

____

____

F. Analyze how the characters interact with the setting.

1. Read paragraphs 1–3 on **Practice Book** page 64. What do Gollum's and Bilbo's actions in this setting tell you about them? Underline the words and phrases that support your answer. Use evidence from the text to support your answer.

____

____

____

2. Underline other words on **Practice Book** pages 64–67 to analyze characters' actions that give clues about the setting. Explain what it shows about the setting.

____

____

Name ______________________________

Reread and Analyze

G. Analyze how the author gives information about the characters through their actions.

1. Reread paragraph 7 on **Practice Book** page 64. What does the author show you about Gollum through his actions here? Underline words and phrases to support your answers. Explain how the text evidence supports your answer.

____

____

____

2. Underline an action on **Practice Book** pages 64–67, that shows what Bilbo is like. Explain what it shows about Bilbo.

____

____

H. Analyze how the author gives information about the characters as they interact through dialogue.

1. Read paragraphs 13–17 on **Practice Book** page 66. What does the author show you about Bilbo through this dialogue? Underline the words and phrases that support your answer. Explain how the text evidence supports your answer.

____

____

____

2. In the **Practice Book**, underline other dialogue that shows what Gollum is like. Explain what it shows about Gollum.

____

____

Name ________________

Discuss and Write

I. Synthesize your ideas about how characters interact with the setting and each other in a story.

1. With the class, discuss how the author gave information about the characters and setting by showing the interactions between them. List the interactions you discuss.

____

____

____

2. Choose one of the interactions that you listed. Write a paragraph about how the author used this interaction to develop the story. Use the questions below to organize your thoughts.

   - What did this interaction show about a character or the setting?
   - What description supports this interaction? Give 2 examples.
   - What dialogue supports this interaction? Give 2 examples.
   - How important was this interaction to the story? Why?

____

____

____

____

Connect with GUIDING QUESTION

J. Discuss the Guiding Question: How should people use their talents?

1. How are Gollum, Bilbo, and other characters you know from fantasies alike and different?

____

2. How can you tell that Gollum is more confident he will win the contest?

____

____

3. What is the author's message about using one's talents?

____

____

____

Unit 2 Review

Name ______________________________

Academic Vocabulary	
affect	exact
category	illustrate
challenge	role
compare	similar
conflict	trait
element	

Academic Vocabulary Review

A. Circle the word that best fits into each sentence.

1. To play the lead (**element** / **role**) in the school play can be a (**challenge** / **category**).
2. I could not find my coat because they all look (**compare** / **similar**).
3. Can you (**identify** / **exact**) which backpack is yours?
4. This detailed painting will be used to (**conflict** / **illustrate**) the folk tale.
5. Speaking clearly is an important (**affect** / **element**) of a good speech.

B. Use your own words to write what each Academic Vocabulary word means.

Word	My Definition
1. **affect**	
2. **conflict**	
3. **exact**	
4. **illustrate**	

C. Answer the questions in complete sentences.

1. What is your favorite **category** of music? What is one **trait** you like about it?

____

____

2. Name two sports that are **similar**. Tell how they are alike.

____

____

3. **Compare** two kinds of fruit. Which do you like better and why?

____

____

Name ______________________________

Key Vocabulary Review

A. Read each sentence. Circle the word that best fits into each sentence.

1. When you (**approach** / **assume**) something, you go near it.
2. You (**notice** / **practice**) to get better at something.
3. A (**riddle** / **weight**) makes you think.
4. You do better when your friends (**encourage** / **obey**) you.
5. A (**possession** / **choice**) is something you own.
6. You can (**release** / **interpret**) a bird into the wilderness.
7. To (**notice** / **release**) something, you have to see or hear it.
8. A (**riddle** / **response**) is an answer.

B. Use your own words to write what each Key Vocabulary word means. Then write a synonym for each word.

Word	My Definition	Synonym
1. **assume**		
2. **awkward**		
3. **clever**		
4. **contest**		
5. **excellent**		
6. **interpret**		
7. **nonsense**		
8. **outcome**		

Name ______________________________

Unit 2 Key Vocabulary

approach	choice	excellent	marry	outcome	release
assume	clever	interpret	nonsense	possession	response
attention	contest	judgment	notice	practice	riddle
awkward	encourage	knowledge	obey	proud	weight

C. Answer the questions in complete sentences.

1. Tell about a time when you felt **proud**.

____

____

2. What is important to give your **attention** to? Explain.

____

____

3. Why do people lift **weights**?

____

____

4. Why is it important to **obey** laws?

____

____

5. Why is it sometimes difficult to make a **choice**?

____

____

6. Are all **judgments** fair? Explain.

____

____

7. What happens when two people **marry**?

____

____

8. What **knowledge** should an athlete have?

____

____

Name ______________________________

Mind Map

Use the Mind Map to show some of the different **chapters** in your life. Show important events from past and present **chapters** in your life and what you want for a future **chapter**.

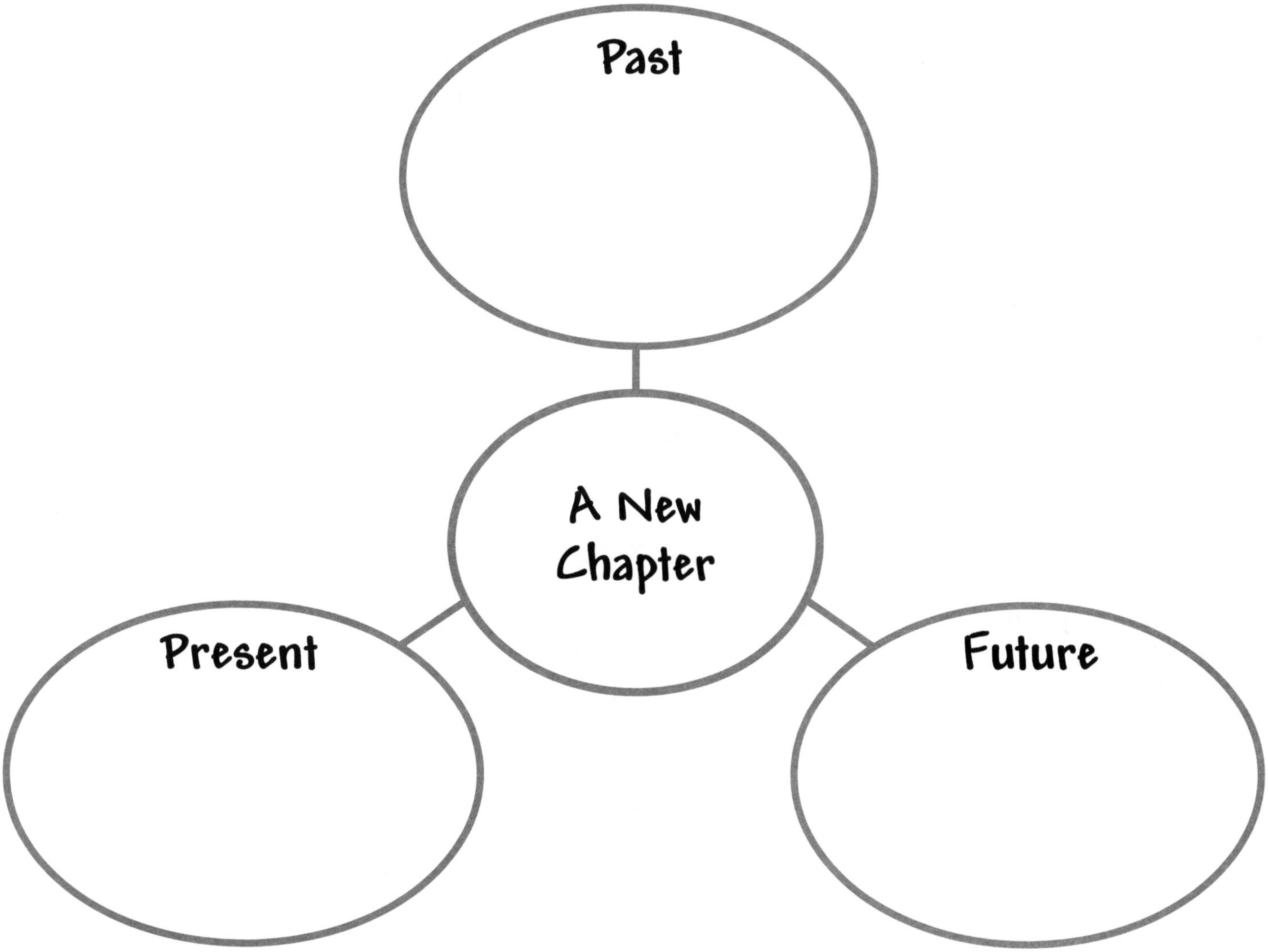

Academic Vocabulary

Think about a **chapter** in a book. Why do you think authors often use **chapters**? Use the word **chapter** in your answer.

____

____

____

____

Name ______________________________

Analyzing Interactions:
Cause and Effect and Sequence

A. Read the passage. Look for clues that show the interactions among individuals, ideas, and events.

> Around 1682 William Penn signed a peace treaty with the Delaware Tribe. This treaty guaranteed Native Americans ownership of their land and freedom of religion. William Penn earned the trust and respect of the Native Americans. He traveled throughout Native American territory in peace.

Describe Penn's interactions with the Delaware Tribe. How was Penn treated by the Native Americans?

____

____

____

B. Read the passage. Look for clues that show the interactions among individuals, ideas, and events.

> William Penn was born in England in 1644. He became a Quaker when he was in his early twenties. Since there was no religious freedom in England, Penn was frequently persecuted for his beliefs. In 1681, Penn was given land in the New World by King Charles II. In 1682, Penn decided to go to America, where he established the colony of Pennsylvania. It was intended to be a place where people could enjoy freedom of religion.

Describe the series of events that led to the establishment of Pennsylvania. How did events in England influence Penn's actions?

____

____

____

Academic Vocabulary

Think about an interaction you had with someone today. **Analyze** and explain how that interaction influenced other events in your day.

____

____

____

Focus on Vocabulary

Name ________________________________

Some Word Parts
Prefix: *en-* means "cause to"
Prefix: *un-* means "not"
Suffix: *-able* means "can be done"
Suffix: *-al* means "process of"
Suffix: *-ness* means "state of"

Use Word Parts

Read the passage. Follow these steps to figure out the meaning of each underlined word.

1. Look closely at the word to see if you know any of the parts.
2. Cover any prefixes or suffixes. Look at the base word. Think about the meaning of the base word.
3. Uncover any prefixes or suffixes and determine their meanings.
4. Put the meanings of the word parts together. Be sure the meaning of the word makes sense in the text.

Follow the directions above. Write the meaning of each underlined word.

> I came to the United States from El Salvador when I was eight years old. I was unsure of many English words, and I didn't know the games my new classmates enjoyed playing. However, the students in my class were very nice. They taught me how to play the games, and I taught them a few new games, too. We played at lunch and after dismissal from school.
>
> Now, I'm older and have learned many new things about the United States. Today my teacher said that a new student will join our class next week. I am filled with happiness because I know exactly what to do. I will help the new student feel comfortable just like my friends did for me.

1. **unsure** ________________________________
2. **enjoyed** ________________________________
3. **dismissal** ________________________________
4. **happiness** ________________________________
5. **comfortable** ________________________________

Academic Vocabulary

If I go on a nature walk in the forest, I might **identify** ________________________________

____

____

________________________________.

Build Background

Name ____________________

Critical Viewing Guide

Take Notes

A. View the video. Take notes on at least three things that you learned.

____

____

____

____

____

____

____

____

Analyze the Video

B. Review your notes to help answer these questions.

1. Write two sentences to explain what was in the video.

____

____

____

2. What was the most interesting thing you learned?

____

____

____

3. What **chapter** in the history of Vietnam would you like to know more about? Why?

____

____

____

____

____

Learn Key Vocabulary

Name ______________________________

The Lotus Seed: Key Vocabulary

A. Study each word. Circle a number to rate how well you know it. Then complete the chart.

Rating Scale	1	2	3
	I have never seen this word before.	I am not sure of the word's meaning.	I know this word and can teach the word's meaning to someone else.

▲ When we **arrived** at the garden, we saw many flowers in **bloom**.

Key Words	Check Understanding	Deepen Understanding
1 arrive (u-rîv) *verb* Rating: 1 2 3	When you **arrive**, you stay home. Yes No	When you arrive late to school, you have to ______ .
2 bloom (blüm) *verb* Rating: 1 2 3	Flowers often **bloom** in the spring. Yes No	When a flower blooms, it ______ .
3 chapter (chap-tur) *noun* Rating: 1 2 3	A **chapter** is part of a book. Yes No	A chapter of my life has been ______ .
4 emperor (em-pur-ur) *noun* Rating: 1 2 3	An **emperor** is a leader. Yes No	Some responsibilities of an emperor are ______ .

Name ______________________

Keepsakes help us **remember** **special** times and people from the past. ▶

Key Words	Check Understanding	Deepen Understanding
5 forget (fur-**get**) *verb* Rating: 1 2 3	When you **forget** something, you know it. Yes No	I sometimes forget ______________________.
6 remember (ri-**mem**-bur) *verb* Rating: 1 2 3	When you **remember** something, you think about it. Yes No	It is important to remember ______________________.
7 special (**spe**-shul) *adjective* Rating: 1 2 3	If something is **special**, it is ordinary. Yes No	Something that is special to me is ______________________.
8 throne (thrōn) *noun* Rating: 1 2 3	Anyone can sit on a **throne**. Yes No	Thrones are for______________________.

B. Use at least two of the Key Vocabulary words. Write about a special time in your life.

____

____

____

Prepare to Read

Name ____________________________________

Analyze Plot

Complete the Sequence Chain as you read "The Lotus Seed." Think about the interactions between the characters and the events in the story.

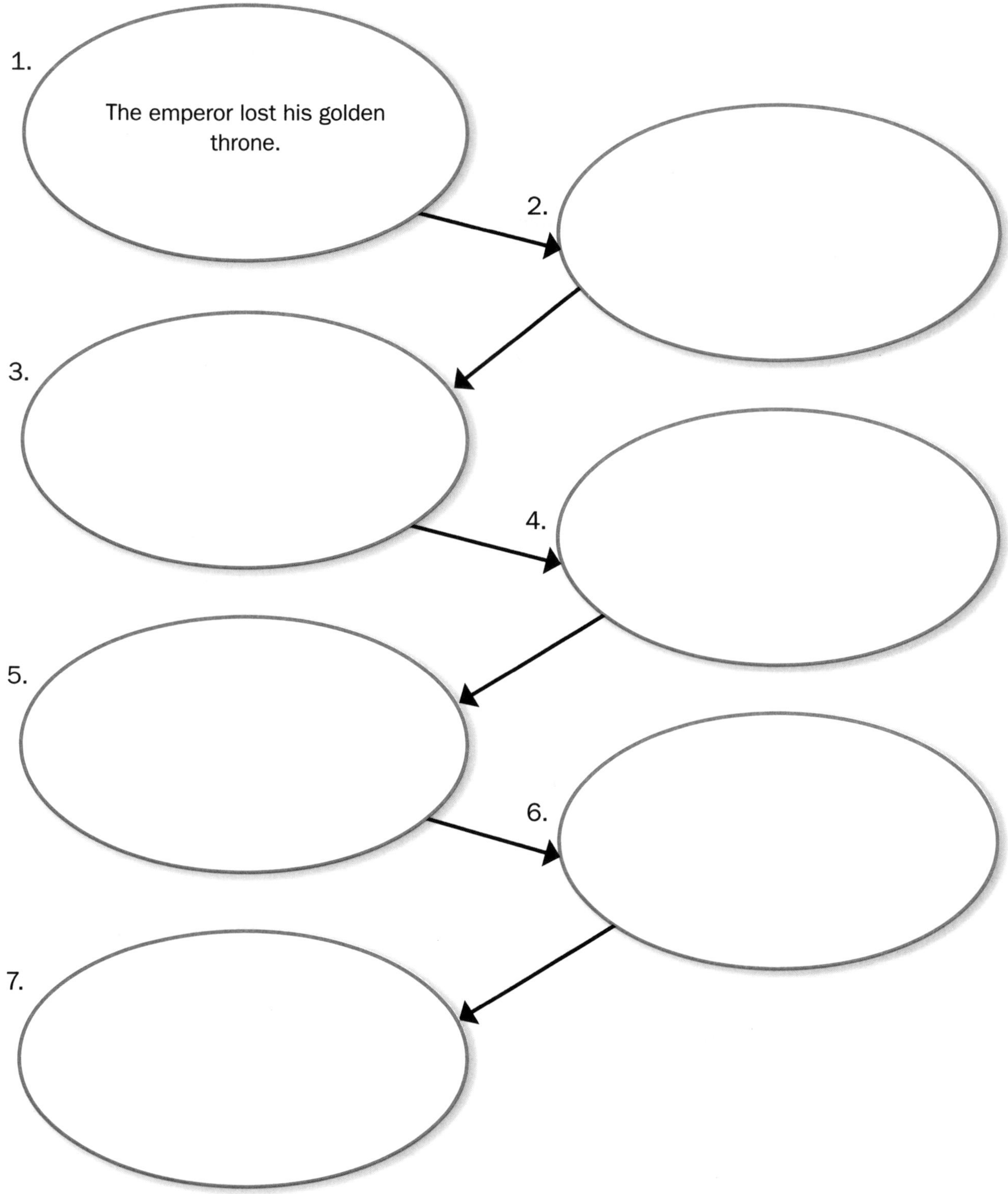

Name ______________________________

The Lotus Seed

Key Vocabulary	
arrived	forget
blooming	remember
chapter	special
emperor	throne

A. Read the paragraph.
Write a Key Vocabulary word in each blank.
Reread the paragraph to make sure the words make sense.

My grandmother ____________ in this country many years ago. Even so, she will never ____________ her homeland. She says, "I ____________ the smell of the beautiful flowers ____________ in the garden. I can picture the ____________ sitting on his ____________ in his elegant robes. Who would want to lose such ____________ memories? It was an amazing ____________ in my life."

B. Write complete sentences to answer these questions about "The Lotus Seed."

1. Why was the lotus seed so important to Bá?

____

____

____

____

____

____

____

2. How might the story of the lotus seed live on for generations?

____

____

____

____

____

____

____

Vocabulary Study

Name ______________________

Prefix	Meaning
de-	oposite
en-	cause to
re-	again
un-	not

Use Prefixes

Write the prefix and the base word with its meaning. Then write a sentence using each word. Be careful, not all of these words have a real prefix.

1. Cover up part of the word that you think is the prefix.
2. If you can't identify the word part that is left, it is not a true prefix.

1. **untrue** ______________________

   Sentence: ______________________

2. **enclose** ______________________

   Sentence: ______________________

3. **read** ______________________

   Sentence: ______________________

4. **regain** ______________________

   Sentence: ______________________

5. **untangle** ______________________

   Sentence: ______________________

6. **envelope** ______________________

   Sentence: ______________________

7. **entrust** ______________________

   Sentence: ______________________

8. **deliver** ______________________

   Sentence: ______________________

9. **deconstruct** ______________________

   Sentence: ______________________

Name ____________________

Academic Vocabulary

analyze	identify
chapter	sequence

The Lotus Seed: Academic Vocabulary Review

A. Write the Academic Vocabulary word next to its definition.

Definition	Word
1. to recognize something or discover it	
2. to study something closely	
3. the order in which events happen	
4. one part of something	

B. Read each sentence. Circle the word that best fits into each sentence.

1. The scientist will (**sequence** / **analyze**) the material in her laboratory.
2. The plot of a story is its (**sequence** / **chapter**) of events.
3. Mia is able to (**analyze** / **identify**) a rose just by its smell.
4. Tony read the first (**analyze** / **chapter**) of his book.

C. Use the words **analyze** and **identify** in a sentence.

____

____

____

____

____

____

Name ___________________________

Critical Viewing Guide

Take Notes

A. View the video. Take notes on at least three things that you learned.

____

____

____

____

____

____

____

____

Analyze the Video

B. Review your notes to help answer these questions.

1. Write two sentences to explain what was in the video.

____

____

____

2. What was the most interesting thing you learned?

____

____

____

3. Imagine you are writing a **chapter** about an immigrant's life. What is the title of your chapter? Why?

____

____

____

____

Name ______________________

▲ **Immigrants** have many things to **adjust** to.

Immigrants Today: Key Vocabulary

A. Study each word. Circle a number to rate how well you know it. Then complete the chart.

Rating Scale	1	2	3
	I have never seen this word before.	I am not sure of the word's meaning.	I know this word and can teach the word's meaning to someone else.

Key Words	Check Understanding	Deepen Understanding
❶ **adjust** (ud-**just**) *verb* **Rating:** 1 2 3	☐ adapt to something ☐ remember where you put something	Tell about a time when you had to adjust to something. ______
❷ **community** (ku-**myü**-nut-ē) *noun* **Rating:** 1 2 3	☐ a place where people live and work ☐ a place where you can see rare art	Describe the community you live in. ______
❸ **foreign** (**for**-in) *adjective* **Rating:** 1 2 3	☐ from nearby ☐ from somewhere else	Tell about a foreign place you know or have heard about. ______
❹ **immigrant** (**im**-i-grint) *noun* **Rating:** 1 2 3	☐ a person who comes to a place ☐ a person who is local	What are some reasons immigrants might come to the United States? ______

Name ______________________

Did You Know?

There are many types of **museums** in the world. There are museums for art, history, science, technology, and even special museums for children.

Key Words	Check Understanding	Deepen Understanding
5 local (**lō**-cul) *adjective* **Rating: 1 2 3**	☐ far away ☐ nearby	What local places do you go to? Why? ______
6 museum (myü-**zē**-um) *noun* **Rating: 1 2 3**	☐ a place to see valuable objects ☐ a place to see a movie	What type of museum would you like to go to? Why?
7 poverty (**pah**-vur-tē) *noun* **Rating: 1 2 3**	☐ having a lot of money ☐ having little money	What are some difficulties for people living in poverty?
8 preserve (pri-**zurv**) *verb* **Rating: 1 2 3**	☐ keep something ☐ get rid of something	Tell about something that is important to preserve.

B. Use at least two of the Key Vocabulary words. Write about a time when you had to adjust to a new situation.

____

____

____

Prepare to Read

Name ______________________________

Analyze Interactions Among Ideas

As you read "Immigrants Today," complete the Cause-Effect Chart to show how ideas influence individuals and events.

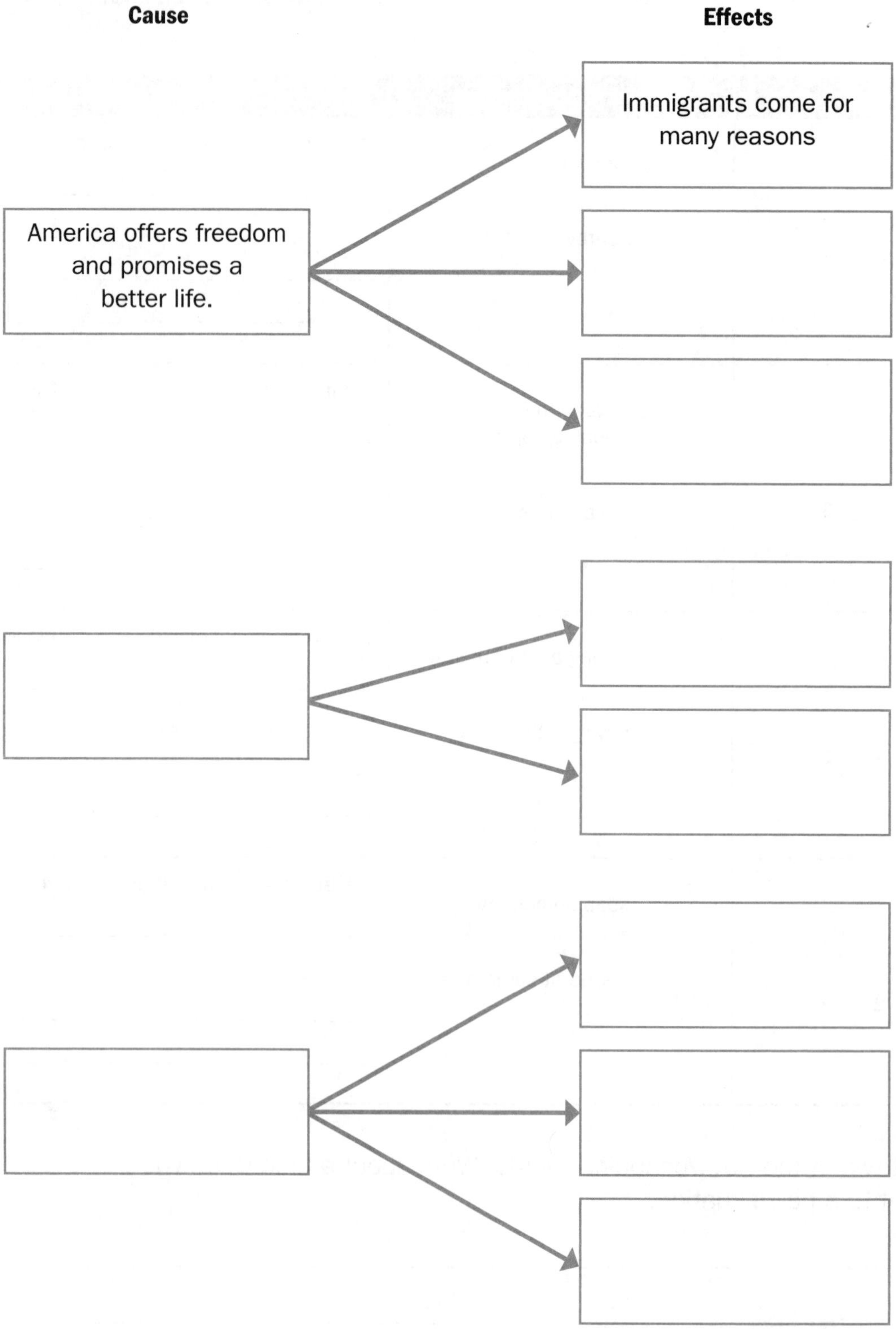
Cause
Effects
Immigrants come for many reasons
America offers freedom and promises a better life.

Selection Review

Name ______________________________

Immigrants Today

Key Vocabulary	
adjust	**local**
community	**museum**
foreign	**poverty**
immigrant	**preserve**

A. Read the paragraph.
Write a Key Vocabulary word in each blank.
Reread the paragraph to make sure the words make sense.

My neighbor is an ______________ from a ______________ country. It has taken her a while to ______________ to our way of life. She came from a small farming ______________ in Laos. She remembers what it is like to live in ______________. Now she works downtown at the art ______________. She is the ______________ expert on Hmong needlework. She shows people treasures from her homeland which helps ______________ her culture.

B. Write complete sentences to answer these questions about "Immigrants Today."

1. How can people from **foreign** countries **preserve** their culture when they move to the United States?

____

____

____

____

____

____

____

2. How does the mix of cultures in the United States make it easier for **immigrants** to **adjust**?

____

____

____

____

____

____

____

Vocabulary Study

Name ______________________________

Use Prefixes and Suffixes

Prefix	Meaning
im-	into; not
over-	too much; above
Suffix	**Meaning**
-al	process of; having characteristics of
-ful	full of, filling

Follow the steps below to identify the word parts in each word.

1. Cover up the prefix or suffix. Write the base word and its meaning.
2. Write the prefix or suffix and write the meaning that works best.
3. Write a sentence using the word to see if it makes sense.

1. **immobile** ______________________________

   Sentence: ______________________________

2. **overtired** ______________________________

   Sentence: ______________________________

3. **imperfect** ______________________________

   Sentence: ______________________________

4. **wishful** ______________________________

   Sentence: ______________________________

5. **emotional** ______________________________

   Sentence: ______________________________

6. **accidental** ______________________________

   Sentence: ______________________________

7. **overwork** ______________________________

   Sentence: ______________________________

8. **harmful** ______________________________

   Sentence: ______________________________

Academic Vocabulary

Name ______________________________

Academic Vocabulary	
analyze	data
chapter	identify
connect	

Immigrants Today: Academic Vocabulary Review

A. Draw a line to match each Academic Vocabulary word with its meaning.

Word	Definition
1. **chapter**	factual information
2. **connect**	to study something closely
3. **data**	one part of something
4. **identify**	to show how things are related
5. **analyze**	to recognize or discover something

B. Write an Academic Vocabulary word to complete each sentence.

1. Nutrition experts ________________ a balanced diet with better health.
2. A map can help you ________________ your location.
3. We entered all the ________________ into the computer program.

C. Use each word in a sentence.

1. **chapter** ____

____

2. **analyze** ____

____

Name ____________________

Critical Viewing Guide

Take Notes

A. View the video. Take notes on at least three things that you learned.

Analyze the Video

B. Review your notes to help answer these questions.

1. Write two sentences to explain what was in the video.

2. What was the most interesting thing you learned?

3. What did the video tell about a **chapter** in Sudanese history?

Learn Key Vocabulary

Name ___________________________

Brothers in Hope: Key Vocabulary

▲ Farmers use a lot of energy and **effort** to **tend** to their crops.

A. Study each word. Circle a number to rate how well you know it. Then complete the chart.

Rating Scale	1	2	3
	I have never seen this word before.	I am not sure of the word's meaning.	I know this word and can teach the word's meaning to someone else.

Key Words	Check Understanding	Deepen Understanding
1 cross (kros) *verb* **Rating: 1 2 3**	When you **cross** something, you go under it. **Yes** **No**	List three things that people cross. ______
2 dangerous (dān-jur-us) *adjective* **Rating: 1 2 3**	If something is **dangerous**, you don't need to worry about it. **Yes** **No**	List three things that are dangerous. ______
3 education (ej-u-kā-shun) *noun* **Rating: 1 2 3**	Schools offer an **education** to students. **Yes** **No**	List three reasons that a good education is important. ______
4 effort (e-furt) *noun* **Rating: 1 2 3**	It takes **effort** to learn a foreign language. **Yes** **No**	List three things that take effort. ______

Name ______________________________

In the early 1900s, many immigrants made a **dangerous journey** to America. They came to **improve** their lives. ▶

Key Words	Check Understanding	Deepen Understanding
5 emerge (i-**murj**) *verb* **Rating: 1 2 3**	When you **emerge**, you go into something. **Yes** **No**	List three places that animals emerge from. ________
6 improve (im-**prüv**) *verb* **Rating: 1 2 3**	When you **improve** something, you make it worse. **Yes** **No**	List three ways you would improve your community.___
7 journey (**jur**-nē) *noun* **Rating: 1 2 3**	We stay at home on a **journey**. **Yes** **No**	List three journeys you would like to take. ________
8 tend (**tend**) *verb* **Rating: 1 2 3**	When we **tend** to something, we take care of it. **Yes** **No**	List three ways that parents tend to their babies.

B. Use at least two of the Key Vocabulary words. Write about people who took a journey to a new home to improve their lives.

____

____

____

Name ______________________________

Compare Fiction and Nonfiction

A. Read the passage from "Refugees Find New Lives" and write down facts from the article in the first column. Then read the excerpt from "Brothers in Hope." Write down related facts and literary details from this passage. As you read "Brothers in Hope," continue to look for historical facts and fictional details that the author adds to the story.

"Refugees Find New Lives"	Brothers in Hope
• In 1987, soldiers attacked Wal's village while he was away tending his family's herd of cattle.	• I was far from home tending my animals when my village was attacked.

B. Compare the facts in "Refugees Find New Lives" to the facts in "Brothers in Hope." What kinds of facts does the nonfiction author give? How is the language different?

____

____

____

C. What kinds of details does the fiction author add? How does the fictional story help you understand what happened to the boy?

____

____

____

Selection Review

Name ______________________________

Brothers in Hope

Key Vocabulary

cross	emerged
dangerous	improve
education	journey
effort	tended

A. Read the paragraph.
Write a Key Vocabulary word in each blank.
Reread the paragraph to make sure the words make sense.

When Garang left his village, he did not know that his ____________ would take him thousands of miles. If he had known how ____________ it would be or how much ____________ it would take, he might have given up. It took courage for Garang to ____________ the desert, the river, and the ocean. The boys he ____________ owed him their lives. With love and ____________, Garang helped them ____________ their lives. They ____________ from the ordeal even stronger than they were before.

B. Write complete sentences to answer these questions about "Brothers in Hope."

1. How did the words of Garang's father help give him courage?

____

____

____

____

____

____

2. Imagine you are Garang. How would you keep from giving up?

____

____

____

____

____

____

Vocabulary Study

Name ______________________

Use Word Parts: Roots

Root	Meaning
cept	to take; hold; grasp
civ	citizen
cog	to know
famil	family
fin	to end
frig	cool
par	arrange; prepare; get ready; set
port	to carry
simil	together, likeness
viv	life

Follow the steps below to figure out the meaning of each word.

1. A root is a word part that needs to have a prefix and/or suffix added to it. Look at some words that are formed when you connect prefixes or suffixes.
2. For each word, write the root and its meaning. Look at the meaning of each prefix or suffix that is given.
3. Then write the meaning of each word. Check your answer in a dictionary.

1. **except** **ex-:** out of ______________________

   Meaning: ______________________

2. **revive** **re-:** again ______________________

   Meaning: ______________________

3. **transport** **trans-:** across ______________________

   Meaning: ______________________

4. **similarity** ______________________ **-ar:** being **-ity:** state of

   Meaning: ______________________

5. **refrigerator** **re-:** again ______________________ **-erator:** one that does

   Meaning: ______________________

6. **partial** ______________________ **-ial:** of or relating to

   Meaning: ______________________

7. **finish** ______________________ **-ish:** being or relating to

   Meaning: ______________________

8. **civilian** ______________________ **-ian:** one who is

   Meaning: ______________________

Name ______________________________

Academic Vocabulary

analyze	connect
chapter	identify
compare	role

Brothers in Hope: Academic Vocabulary Review

A. Use your own words to tell what each Academic Vocabulary word means.

1. **analyze** ______________________________
2. **chapter** ______________________________
3. **compare** ______________________________
4. **connect** ______________________________
5. **identify** ______________________________
6. **role** ______________________________

B. Complete the sentences.

1. The **role** of a teacher is ______________________________

______________________________.

2. When you **compare** two things, you ______________________________

______________________________.

3. An easy way to **identify** a zebra is to ______________________________

______________________________.

4. When you **connect** ideas, you ______________________________

______________________________.

5. To **analyze** something well, you ______________________________

______________________________.

6. Books are divided into **chapters** because ______________________________.

The New Colossus

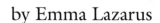

by Emma Lazarus

Not like the brazen giant of Greek fame,
With conquering limbs astride from land to land;
Here at our sea-washed, sunset gates shall stand
A mighty woman with a torch, whose flame
Is the imprisoned lightning, and her name
Mother of Exiles. From her **beacon-hand**
Glows world-wide welcome; her mild eyes command
The air-bridged harbor that twin cities frame.

"Keep, ancient lands, your **storied pomp**!" cries she
With silent lips. "Give me your tired, your poor,
Your huddled masses **yearning** to breathe free,
The **wretched refuse of your teeming shore**.
Send these, the homeless, **tempest-tost** to me,
I lift my lamp beside the golden door!"

Historical Background

The Colossus of Rhodes was an ancient statue of a Greek giant. The statue was destroyed in 226 BC.

In Other Words

beacon-hand hand that holds the guiding light
storied pomp extravagant ceremonies
yearning desiring
wretched refuse of your teeming shore hopeless and unwanted citizens from crowded countries
tempest-tost the people affected by hard times

The poem, "The New Colossus" was written about the Statue of Liberty in New York harbor. ▶

Name ______________________

Read for Understanding

A. What kind of text is this? How do you know?

____

____

B. Write a sentence that tells the topic of the selection.

____

Reread and Summarize

C. On **Practice Book** page 100, circle the 3–5 most important words in each section. Make notes about why you chose each word. Why is the word important in the section?

1. Section 1: (lines 1–5)

____

____

2. Section 2: (lines 6–8)

____

____

3. Section 3: (lines 9–14)

____

____

D. Use your topic sentence from above and your notes to write a summary of the selection.

____

____

____

Name ______________________

Reread and Analyze

E. Analyze how the author uses personification to help you understand the meaning of a poem.

1. Reread lines 1–4 on **Practice Book** page 100. How does the writer's use of personification help you understand the meaning of the poem's title? Underline words and phrases to support your answers. Use evidence from the text to support your answer.

____

____

____

2. Underline another example of personification on **Practice Book** page 100 that helps readers see the Statue of Liberty in human qualities and understand what she represents. Use evidence from the text to support your answer.

____

____

F. Analyze how the author uses alliteration to emphasize important words and ideas in the poem.

1. Read lines 6–7 on **Practice Book** page 100. How does the writer add meaning to these words through the use of alliteration? Underline the words and phrases that support your answer. Use evidence from the text to support your answer.

____

____

____

2. In the **Practice Book,** underline other words that show where the author uses rhythm or alliteration to emphasize certain words and add meaning. Use evidence from the text to support your answer.

____

____

Name ____________________

Discuss and Write

G. Synthesize your ideas about how the author conveys emotion and adds meaning to the poem.

1. With the class, discuss how the writer uses poetic elements to convey emotion and add meaning. List the elements you discuss.

____

____

2. Choose one of the poetic elements that you listed. Write a paragraph about how the writer uses this element to show how the poet connects the Statue of Liberty to immigrants and the idea of freedom. Use the questions below to organize your thoughts.
   - What poetic element does the writer use?
   - How does this element help you understand what the Statue of Liberty represents?
   - How does this element help you understand how people feel about the Statue of Liberty?
   - Was the writer's use of poetic elements effective? Why?

____

____

____

____

Connect with GUIDING QUESTION

H. Discuss the Guiding Question: How does our past impact our future?

1. What or who is an exile? Why is the Statue of Liberty called the Mother of Exiles?

____

____

2. How did the past impact the future in this poem?

____

____

____

Unit 3 Review

Name ______________________________

Academic Vocabulary

analyze
chapter
connect
data
identify
role
sequence

Academic Vocabulary Review

A. Use four Academic Vocabulary words to complete the paragraph.

It is not easy to prepare for the lead ____________ in a play. Every day I ____________, or study, my notes carefully and memorize my lines. I must remember to say them in the right order, or ____________. I want to help the audience ____________ their lives to the life of my character.

B. Read each statement. Circle **Yes** or **No** to answer.

1. **Data** includes personal opinions. **Yes** **No**
2. You **identify** a problem when you first recognize it. **Yes** **No**
3. Doctors **connect** exercise with better health. **Yes** **No**
4. A book usually contains only one **chapter**. **Yes** **No**

C. Answer the questions. Use complete sentences.

1. What **role** does television play in your life? Explain.

____

____

2. What **data** would you include in a speech about the importance of recycling? Explain why?

____

____

3. **Identify** two reasons why schools should provide healthier meals to students at lunch.

____

____

4. What **sequence** do you follow to get ready for school in the morning?

____

____

Name ______________________________

Key Vocabulary Review

A. Read each sentence. Circle the word that best fits into each sentence.

1. When a flower (**blooms** / **arrives**), the bud opens into a flower.
2. A (**journey** / **museum**) can sometimes take you very far away.
3. (**Immigrants** / **Thrones**) move to a new country.
4. A holiday is a (**foreign** / **special**) day.
5. Mom often (**forgets** / **improves**) where she left her keys.
6. You can see art at a (**journey** / **museum**).
7. (**Local** / **Foreign**) people sometimes come to the United States to visit.
8. Living in (**poverty** / **communities**) is difficult.

B. Use your own words to write what each Key Vocabulary word means. Then write a synonym for each word.

Word	My Definition	Synonym
1. **adjust**		
2. **arrive**		
3. **cross**		
4. **effort**		
5. **emerge**		
6. **emperor**		
7. **local**		
8. **throne**		

Name ____________________

Unit 1 Key Vocabulary

adjust	**community**	**effort**	**forget**	**local**	**remember**
arrive	**cross**	**emerge**	**immigrant**	**museum**	**special**
bloom	**dangerous**	**emperor**	**improve**	**poverty**	**tend**
chapter	**education**	**foreign**	**journey**	**preserve**	**throne**

C. Answer the questions in complete sentences.

1. Tell about a **chapter** you found difficult to read. What did you do to help you read it?

____

____

2. Describe a **dangerous** situation and how you can avoid it.

____

____

3. Tell about your favorite place or event in your **community**.

____

____

4. What do you think is the best way to get an **education**?

____

____

5. Describe something that you think is important to **preserve**.

____

____

6. What is a good way to **remember** something important?

____

____

7. Describe how someone might **tend** to a garden.

____

____

8. What is a skill that you would like to **improve**? Why?

____

____

Name ______________________________

Mind Map

Use the Mind Map to show your ideas about the human body. As you read the selections in this unit, add new ideas you learn about the human body.

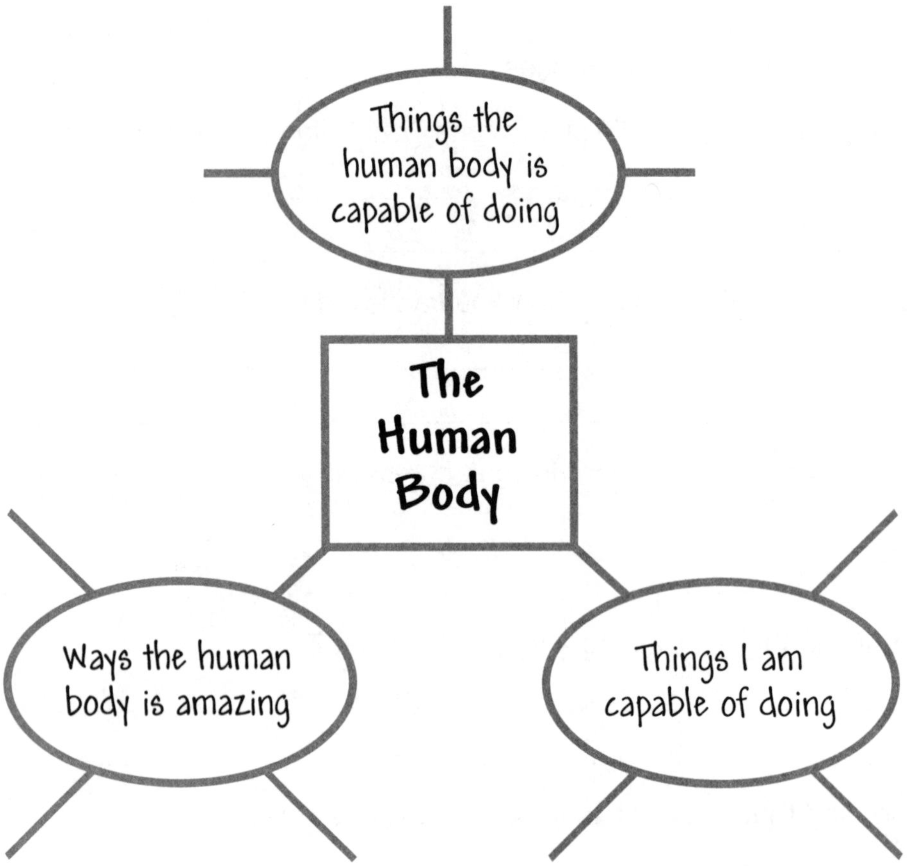

Academic Vocabulary

Think about something you are **capable** of doing. Why is it important to be **capable** of something? Use the word **capable** in your answer.

____

____

____

____

Focus on Reading

Name ______________________

Text Structure: Main Idea and Chronological Order

A. Read the passage. Look for clues that tell you what kind of text structure is used to organize the writing.

A Healthy Resolution

Many people make a resolution to eat well so they can be healthy. Kim decided to change what she ate. First, she plans her menus for the week. She eats three meals a day, starting with breakfast. Between meals she has a healthy snack such as nuts. Then for lunch and dinner, she includes a variety of colorful vegetables such as broccoli, peppers, and spinach each day. Desserts are always fresh fruits.

Circle the text structure used. **Chronological Order** **Main Idea**

Tell how you know. ______________________

____

B. Read the passage. Look for clues that tell you what kind of text structure is used to organize the writing.

Healthy Diet Plan

There are basic things you should do when starting a healthy diet. Make sure to eat a variety of foods. Eat plenty of high-fiber foods such as fruits, vegetables, whole grains, and beans. Limit sugary foods, foods made with white flour, and salty snacks. Drink water and other healthy beverages such as milk.

Circle the text structure used. **Chronological Order** **Main Idea**

Tell how you know. ______________________

____

Academic Vocabulary

Write a description of your diet. Identify whether you organized your **topic** using main idea or chronological order. ______________________

____

____

____

Name ____________________

Use Context Clues

Helpful Signal Words
is called
is someone
like
or
such as

Read the passage. Follow these steps.

1. Notice how the underlined words are used in the sentences.
2. Look for signal words to help identify clues to the words' meanings.
3. Decide if the clue is a restatement, a definition, or an example.

Follow the directions above. Write the meaning of each underlined word.

The Olympic games originated, or began, in Greece thousands of years ago. Only men and boys could participate in the sporting events. The contemporary, or current, Olympic games began in 1896. Males and females from continents such as North America, Asia, and Africa compete. Each sporting event has a winner, who earns a gold medal. Officials tally how many medals each country wins. To tally is to count things up.

Did you know that there is an Olympic sport that is comprised of, or includes, animals? This event is horseback riding. During show jumping, the horse and its rider must jump over about fifteen obstacles. An obstacle is an object that gets in the way of movement. Penalties are acquired, or received, if the horse knocks over a stone or falls into the water while jumping.

1. **originated** ____________________
2. **contemporary** ____________________
3. **continents** ____________________
4. **tally** ____________________
5. **is comprised of** ____________________
6. **obstacles** ____________________
7. **acquired** ____________________

Academic Vocabulary

Write a sentence that describes the word *athlete*. Use **context** clues.

____

____

____

Name ______________________

Critical Viewing Guide

Take Notes

A. View the images. Take notes on at least three things that you learned.

____
____
____
____
____
____
____
____

Analyze the Images

B. Review your notes to help answer these questions.

1. Write two sentences to explain what was in the images.

____
____
____

2. What was the most interesting thing you learned?

____
____
____

3. How do body systems help make athletes **capable** of doing well in sports?

____
____
____
____
____

Learn Key Vocabulary

Name ______________________________

The Human Machine: Key Vocabulary

▲ Competitive swimmers **examine** their strokes and study how to get **oxygen** efficiently as they swim.

A. Study each word. Circle a number to rate how well you know it. Then complete the chart.

Rating Scale	1	2	3
	I have never seen this word before.	I am not sure of the word's meaning.	I know this word and can teach the word's meaning to someone else.

Key Words	Check Understanding	Deepen Understanding
1 cell (sel) *noun* Rating: 1 2 3	**Cells** are part of our bodies. Yes No	How could a scientist examine a cell? ______________
2 circulate (sur-kū-lāt) *verb* Rating: 1 2 3	Things that **circulate** eventually return to where they started. Yes No	When is a time that you might circulate around a room? ______________
3 examine (ig-zam-un) *verb* Rating: 1 2 3	When you **examine** something, you ignore it. Yes No	Tell about something that you have examined closely. ______________
4 involve (in-vahlv) *verb* Rating: 1 2 3	All students **involve** themselves in school activities. Yes No	What school activity would you like to involve yourself in? Why? ______________

Name ______________________________

Did You Know?

Vessel can also mean a ship or large boat. Like vessels in our body, a large boat can carry things from one place to another.

Key Words	Check Understanding	Deepen Understanding
❺ **organ** (**or**-gun) *noun* Rating: 1 2 3	Our bodies have one **organ**. Yes No	What are some organs in your body? What do they do? ______
❻ **oxygen** (**ahk**-si-jun) *noun* Rating: 1 2 3	We breathe in **oxygen**. Yes No	How do we get oxygen into our bodies? ______
❼ **system** (**sis**-tum) *noun* Rating: 1 2 3	Trees have a **system** of roots that get water from the ground. Yes No	When do people follow a system to get something done? ______
❽ **vessel** (**ves**-ul) *noun* Rating: 1 2 3	Our bodies have blood **vessels**. Yes No	Why are vessels important? ______

B. Use at least two of the Key Vocabulary words. Write about a time you went to the doctor.

____

____

____

Prepare to Read

Name ______________________________

Text Structure: Main Idea and Details

A. Read the passage on page 269. Complete the Main Idea Chart for this section.

Main Idea:
Our bodies are made up of tiny parts called cells.

Detail:

Detail:

B. Choose one body system in the selection to analyze. First, identify the topic of the section you chose. As you read the section, complete the Main Idea Chart.

Main Idea:

Detail:

Detail:

Detail:

C. Explain how this section of the text contributes to the main idea of the whole article.

____

____

____

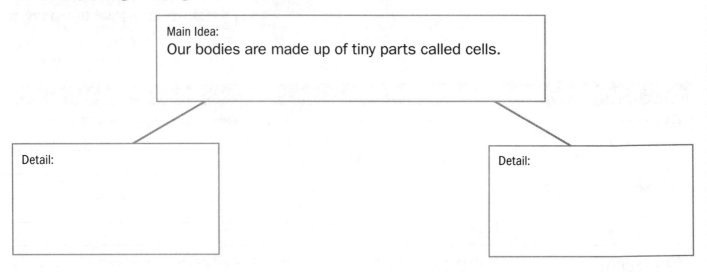

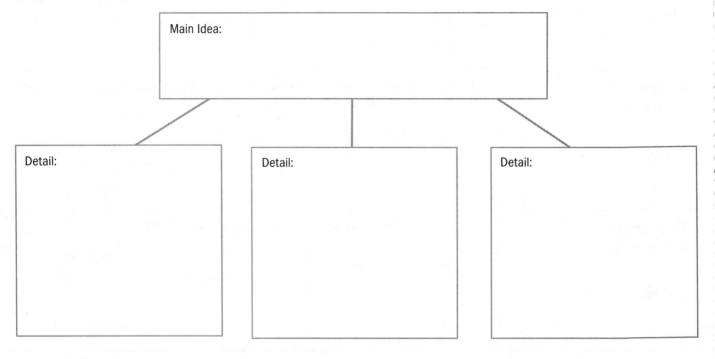

Selection Review

Name ______________________________

The Human Machine

Key Vocabulary	
cells	**organs**
circulates	**oxygen**
examine	**systems**
involved	**vessels**

A. Read the paragraph.
Write a Key Vocabulary word in each blank.
Reread the paragraph to make sure the words make sense.

Are you sick? You should get a doctor ____________. The doctor can ____________ you at a check-up. The doctor checks ____________ such as the heart and lungs. He or she can run tests to see how your ____________ are working. A doctor looks at ____________ under a microscope to see if you have an infection. He or she listens to your heart as your blood ____________ through your blood ____________. The doctor listens to your lungs to hear you breathe in ____________. He or she prescribes rest, exercise, or medicine to make you feel well again.

B. Write complete sentences to answer these questions about "The Human Machine."

1. What do you think is the most amazing thing about how your body works?

____

____

____

____

____

____

2. What can you do to keep your **organs** healthy?

____

____

____

____

____

____

Vocabulary Study

Name ______________________________

Use Context Clues: Definition and Restatement

Follow the steps below to figure out the meaning of each word or phrase.

1. Read the sentence. Look at the underlined word or words.
2. Look for clues that tell the meaning of the word or words.
3. Write the meaning.

1. The heart uses arteries, or blood vessels, to carry blood to and from the heart.

   arteries ______________________________

2. In medical school, students may be asked to dissect, or take apart, an animal's heart or lungs.

   dissect ______________________________

3. The stomach is an important organ because it stores and digests food.

   stomach ______________________________

4. Cardiovascular exercise is exercise that uses large muscles, such as your legs, and works your heart and lungs.

   cardiovascular exercise ______________________________

5. Doctors often use a microscope, a device used to look at things too small to be seen by the naked eye.

   microscope ______________________________

6. A ligament is a tissue that connects bones to other bones in your body.

   ligament ______________________________

7. A dietician, a person who is an expert on food and nutrition, can help you find out which foods are healthy and which foods are not.

   dietician ______________________________

8. A bone fracture is a condition where the bone is cracked or broken.

   fracture ______________________________

Name ____________________

Academic Vocabulary	
capable	organize
context	topic

The Human Machine: Academic Vocabulary Review

A. Use your own words to tell what each Academic Vocabulary word means. Then write a synonym for each word.

Word	My Definition	Synonym
1. **capable**		
2. **context**		
3. **organize**		
4. **topic**		

B. Read each statement. Circle **Yes** or **No** to answer.

1. The **topic** of a speech is its subject. **Yes** **No**
2. It is best to look in a dictionary to find the **context** of a word. **Yes** **No**
3. One way to **organize** laundry is to separate the light from the dark clothes. **Yes** **No**
4. If you need help with a special job, you should choose someone **capable**. **Yes** **No**

C. Answer the questions in complete sentences.

1. Give an example of something you **organize** at home. Tell how you **organize** it.

____

____

2. What **topic** would you discuss if you had to give a speech to the class?

____

____

Build Background

Name ______________________________

Critical Viewing Guide

Take Notes

A. View the video. Take notes on at least three things that you learned.

____

____

____

____

____

____

____

____

Analyze the Video

B. Review your notes to help answer these questions.

1. Write two sentences to explain what was in the video.

____

____

____

2. What was the most interesting thing you learned?

____

____

____

3. Explain why someone with an unhealthy heart might not be **capable** of doing some things.

____

____

____

____

____

Learn Key Vocabulary

Name ________________________________

The Beat Goes On: Key Vocabulary

A. Study each word. Circle a number to rate how well you know it. Then complete the chart.

Rating Scale	1	2	3
	I have never seen this word before.	I am not sure of the word's meaning.	I know this word and can teach the word's meaning to someone else.

Playing a sport helps to keep our **muscles** strong and our bodies **healthy.** ▶

Key Words	Check Understanding	Deepen Understanding
1 artery (**art**-u-rē) *noun* **Rating:** 1 2 3	☐ a type of blood vessel ☐ a type of lung	How do your arteries keep you alive? ______
2 healthy (**hel**-thē) *adjective* **Rating:** 1 2 3	☐ being fit and well ☐ being sick and weak	What can we do to stay healthy? ______
3 muscle (**mus**-ul) *noun* **Rating:** 1 2 3	☐ a vessel ☐ an organ	What can we do to make our muscles stronger? ______
4 pump (**pump**) *verb, noun* **Rating:** 1 2 3	☐ to pull something toward you ☐ to push liquid from one place to another	When do people need to pump water? ______

Name ______________________________

Did You Know?
The first human heart **transplant** was performed in South Africa in 1967.

Key Words	Check Understanding	Deepen Understanding
5 section (sek-shun) *noun* Rating: 1 2 3	☐ part of something ☐ all of something	Describe the sections of your community. ______
6 transplant (trans-plant) *noun, verb* Rating: 1 2 3	☐ something that is moved from one place and put in another place ☐ the lower area of the heart	Describe something you have transplanted. ______
7 vein (vān) *noun* Rating: 1 2 3	☐ a muscle ☐ a vessel	What do the veins you can see under your skin look like? ______
8 ventricle (ven-tri-kul) *noun* Rating: 1 2 3	☐ part of the heart ☐ part of the stomach	Why are ventricles important? ______

B. Imagine you are a doctor performing a heart transplant. Use at least two Key Vocabulary words to describe the procedure.

____

____

____

Prepare to Read

Name ______________________________

Text Structure: Main Idea and Details

A. As you read, "The Beat Goes On," look for the main idea and details in each section of the text. Then summarize each section.

Main Idea and Details	Summary
The heart works hard pumping blood.	The heart works hard pumping blood to keep the body healthy.

B. Explain how the author **organized** each section to develop ideas about the importance of the heart and heart problems.

____

____

____

Name ______________________________

,he Beat Goes On

Key Vocabulary

arteries	sections
healthy	transplant
muscle	veins
pumping	ventricle

A. Read the paragraph.
Write a Key Vocabulary word in each blank.
Reread the paragraph to make sure the words make sense.

A ____________ heart keeps blood ____________ through your body. There are four ____________, or chambers, in a heart. ____________ are in the top two chambers and carry blood away from your heart. ____________ are in the bottom chambers and carry "used" blood back to your heart. A heart attack can damage your heart ____________. The right or left ____________ can lose its power to pump. If this happens, you might need a heart ____________ to replace the organ and save your life.

B. Write complete sentences to answer these questions about "The Beat Goes On."

1. How do you think smoking affects how your heart and lungs work?

____

____

____

____

____

____

____

2. Why is it important to let your family know you want to be an organ donor?

____

____

____

____

____

____

____

Vocabulary Study

Name ______________________________

Use Context Clues: Synonyms and Antonyms

Follow the steps below to figure out the meaning of each word.

1. Read each sentence.
2. Look for synonyms or antonyms that can be used as context clues.
3. Write the meaning for each underlined word or words.

1. The brain has four lobes, or sections.

   lobes ______________________________

2. If you injure your knee, it may not heal before the game.

   injure ______________________________

3. The doctor restricted me from playing soccer, so I am not allowed to play in the game.

   restricted ______________________________

4. You must increase your level of physical activity, or movement, to decrease the amount of fat in your body.

   physical activity ______________________________

5. I sprained, or twisted, my ankle and needed to use crutches to walk.

   sprained ______________________________

6. You can stay passive, or you can become active.

   passive ______________________________

7. We should sterilize the bandages by cleaning them with intense heat.

   sterilize ______________________________

8. An acute cough occurs suddenly, while a chronic cough occurs over time.

   acute ______________________________

9. The doctor will bind, or bandage, my wound.

   bind ______________________________

Name ______________________

Academic Vocabulary	
capable	organize
context	topic

eat Goes On: Academic Vocabulary Review

raw a line to match each Academic Vocabulary word with its meaning.

Word	Definition
1. **capable**	surrounding text that helps explain the meaning of a word
2. **context**	something that you write or talk about
3. **organize**	to arrange things in a certain order
4. **topic**	when you have the qualities needed to do something

B. Rewrite each sentence. Replace the underlined words with an Academic Vocabulary word.

1. Derek placed the books into two separate categories: fiction and nonfiction.

____

2. Carmen chose stem cell research as the subject of her report.

____

3. Sanjay reread the surrounding text to better understand the new word.

____

4. Olivia did not want to compete in a swim meet until she felt ready.

____

C. Use two Academic Vocabulary words in a sentence.

____

____

____

Build Background

Name ____________________

Critical Viewing Guide

Take Notes

A. View the images. Take notes on at least three things that you learned.

____

____

____

____

____

____

____

____

Analyze the Images

B. Review your notes to help answer these questions.

1. Write two sentences to explain what was in the images.

____

____

____

2. What was the most interesting thing you learned?

____

____

____

3. Why is it important to be **capable** of overcoming failure?

____

____

____

____

____

Name ______________________________

Feet, Two Left Hands, Left on the Bench: Key Vocabulary

dy each word. Circle a number to rate how well you know it. hen complete the chart.

▲ Both teams are **determined** to play well so they can enjoy the **glory** of winning.

Rating Scale	1	2	3
	I have never seen this word before.	I am not sure of the word's meaning.	I know this word and can teach the word's meaning to someone else.

Key Words	Check Understanding	Deepen Understanding
1 accept (ak-**sept**) *verb* Rating: 1 2 3	Circle the synonym for **accept**. **admit** **reject**	List other words that describe *accept*. ______
2 assignment (u-**sīn**-mint) *noun* Rating: 1 2 3	Circle the synonym for **assignment**. **job** **disaster**	List other words that describe *assignment*. ______
3 clueless (**klü**-lis) *adjective* Rating: 1 2 3	Circle the synonym for **clueless**. **certain** **confused**	List other words that describe *clueless*. ______
4 determined (di-**tur**-mind) *adjective* Rating: 1 2 3	Circle the synonym for **determined**. **committed** **tired**	List other words that describe *determined*. ______

Name ____________________

Public safety campaigns, such as Smoky Bear, can help people prevent or **survive** natural **disasters**. ▶

Key Words	Check Understanding	Deepen Understanding
5 disaster (diz-as-tur) *noun* Rating: 1 2 3	Circle the synonym for **disaster**. **mess** **award**	List other words that describe *disaster*. ____
6 glory (glor-ē) *noun* Rating: 1 2 3	Circle the synonym for **glory**. **success** **disappointment**	List other words that describe *glory*. ____
7 realize (rē-u-līz) *verb* Rating: 1 2 3	Circle the synonym for **realize**. **forget** **understand**	List other words that describe *realize*. ____
8 survive (sur-vīv) *verb* Rating: 1 2 3	Circle the synonym for **survive**. **endure** **stop**	List other words that describe *survive*. ____

B. Imagine you have been assigned to deal with a **disaster**. Use at least two Key Vocabulary words to describe the situation.

____

____

____

Name ______________________________

cture: Chronological Order

lete the Sequence Chain as you read "Two Left Feet."

1. In second grade, Lubar joins the after-school football team.
2.
3.
4.
5.
6.
7.
8.

B. The author is writing about his own experiences playing sports. How did he use chronological order to organize these events?

____

____

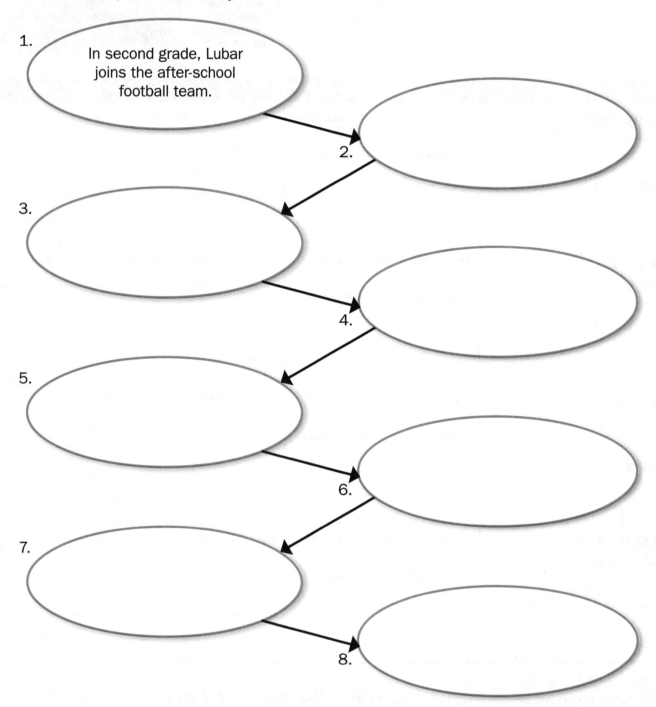

Name ______________________________

Two Left Feet, Two Left Hands, and Too Left on the Bench

Key Vocabulary

accepted	disaster
assignment	glory
clueless	realize
determined	survived

A. Read the paragraph.
Write a Key Vocabulary word in each blank.
Reread the paragraph to make sure the words make sense.

Sometimes, no matter how ____________ you are, you fail. It did not take long for David Lubar to ____________ this. In school sports, he suffered some bad starts that led to one ____________ after another. He was hopeless at football and ____________ at basketball. His only moment of ____________ was a kickball accident! He was the last player to get an ____________ on any team, but he ____________ it as something he would just have to live with. And guess what? He ____________ to tell other people that they'll live through it, too.

B. Write complete sentences to answer these questions about "Two Left Feet, Two Left Hands, and Too Left on the Bench."

1. How might the author feel about sports if he had not found karate?

____

____

____

____

____

2. Which sport would you like to be able to play well? Explain your answer.

____

____

____

____

____

ulary Study

Name ____________________

xt Clues: Examples

the steps below to figure out the meaning of each word.

Read each sentence.
. Use context clues to figure out the meaning of each underlined word.
3. Write the meaning of each word.

1. A referee is an official who watches a game. For example, he decides if the players break any rules.

   referee ____________________

2. Players on the same team wear identical uniforms, such as orange shirts and shorts, during a game.

   identical ____________________

3. Jessie walked up the wooden steps to the stage, or platform, to accept his award.

   stage ____________________

4. I tried to hit the target, which was a bull's eye, in gym class.

   target ____________________

5. The person who throws the javelin, which is like a spear, the farthest distance will win.

   javelin ____________________

6. The players drank a lot of liquids like water and juice.

   liquids ____________________

7. When he rides a bike, Neil wears protective gear. For instance, he has a helmet and knee pads.

   gear ____________________

8. The most productive member of the basketball team scores at least 30 points every game and keeps the other team from scoring.

   productive ____________________

Academic Vocabulary

Name ______________________________

Two Left Feet: Academic Vocabulary Review

Academic Vocabulary	
capable	sequence
context	topic
element	

A. Write the Academic Vocabulary word next to its definition.

1. a basic part of something ______________________________
2. surrounding text that helps explain the meaning of a word ______________________________
3. the order in which events happen ______________________________
4. the subject that you talk or write about ______________________________
5. when someone has the qualities needed to do something ______________________________

B. Read each sentence. Circle the word that best fits into each sentence.

1. The (**context** / **topic**) of the sentence made the unfamiliar word more clear.
2. The speaker knew a lot about the (**sequence** / **topic**).
3. The young child was (**capable** / **context**) of tying his own shoelaces.
4. The dancers' routine was a (**topic** / **sequence**) of complicated steps.

C. Write an Academic Vocabulary word to complete each sentence.

1. Reed chose a ________________ for his science project.
2. The ________________ of the sentence did not help us understand the word. We had to look it up in the dictionary.
3. Instructions usually follow a step-by-step ________________.
4. Alexis is ________________ of doing the work without help.
5. An important ________________ in sportsmanship is respect for the other players.

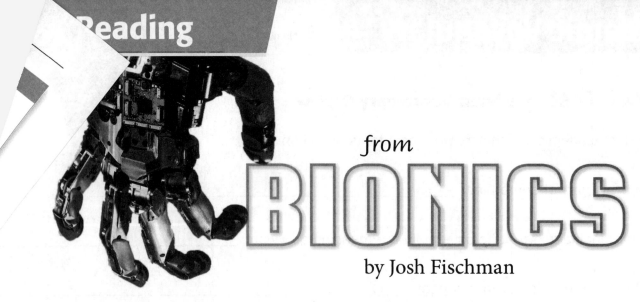

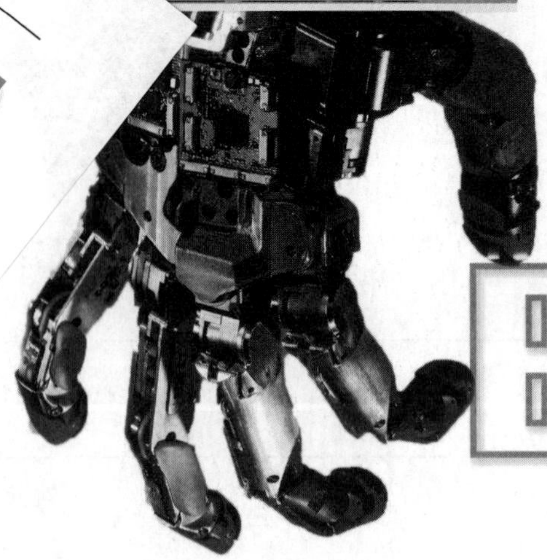

from BIONICS

by Josh Fischman

1 Amanda Kitts crouches down to talk to a small girl, putting her hands on her knees.

2 "The robot arm!" several kids cry.

3 A boy reaches out, hesitantly, to touch her fingers. What he brushes against is flesh-colored plastic, fingers curved slightly inward. Underneath are three motors, a metal frame, and a network of sophisticated electronics. The **assembly** is topped by a white plastic cup midway up Kitts's biceps. It encircles a stump that is almost all that remains from the arm she lost in a car accident in 2006.

4 "I don't really think about it. I just move it," says the 40-year-old.

5 Kitts is **living proof** that, even though the flesh and bone may be damaged or gone, the nerves and parts of the brain that once controlled it live on. In many patients, the nerves sit there waiting to communicate—dangling telephone wires, separated from a handset. With **microscopic electrodes and surgical wizardry**, doctors have begun to connect these parts in other patients to devices such as cameras and microphones and motors. As a result, the blind can see, the deaf can hear, and Amanda Kitts can fold her shirts.

6 Kitts is one of "Tomorrow's People," a group whose missing or ruined body parts are being replaced by devices embedded in their nervous **systems**. These devices respond to commands from their brains. The machines they use are called neural prostheses or—as scientists have become more comfortable with a term made popular by science fiction writers—bionics.

7 As scientists have learned that it's possible to link machine and mind, they have also learned how difficult it is to maintain that connection. If the cup atop Kitts's arm shifts just slightly, for instance, she might not be able to close her fingers. Still, bionics represents a big leap forward, helping researchers to give people back much more of what they've lost than was ever possible before.

8 Todd Kuiken, a physician and **biomedical engineer**, was the person responsible for the "bionic arm." He knew that nerves in an amputee's stump could still carry signals from

Key Vocabulary

- **system** *n.*, a group of things that work together to make one working unit

In Other Words

assembly device; machine
living proof a human example
microscopic electrodes and surgical wizardry highly advanced materials and methods
biomedical engineer person who designs artificial body parts

the brain. He also knew that a computer in a **prosthesis** could direct electric motors to move the limb. The problem was making the connection. Nerves **conduct** electricity, but they can't be spliced together with a computer cable. (Nerve fibers and metal wires don't get along well. And an open wound where a wire enters the body could lead to infections.)

9 Kuiken needed **an amplifier to boost the** signals from the nerves to avoid the need for a direct splice. He found one in **muscles**. When muscles contract they give off an electrical burst strong enough to be detected by an electrode placed on the skin. He developed a technique to reroute **severed** nerves from their old, damaged spots to other muscles. Those muscles could give their signals the proper boost.

10 In October 2006 Kuiken set about rewiring Amanda Kitts. The first step was to save major nerves that once went all the way down her arm. A surgeon rerouted those nerves to different areas of her upper-arm muscles. For months, the nerves grew into their new homes.

11 Then Kitts was fitted with her first bionic arm. Now the challenge was to change signals from her muscles into commands to move the elbow and hand. A microprocessor in the prosthesis had to be programmed to find the right signal and send it to the right motor.

12 "It wasn't easy at first," Kitts says. "I would try to move it, and it wouldn't always go where I wanted." But she worked at it, and the more she used the arm, the more lifelike the motions felt. What Kitts would really like now is sensation. That could come next.

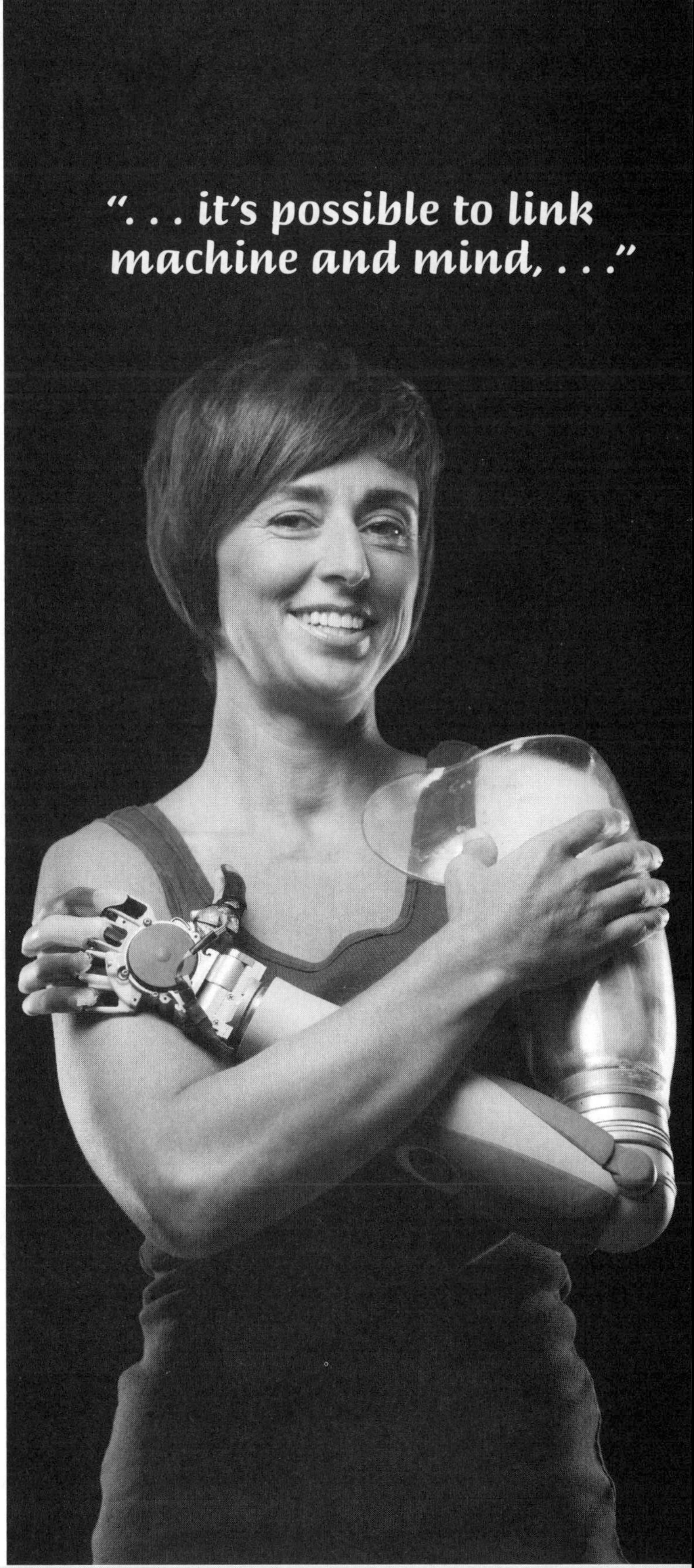
". . . it's possible to link machine and mind, . . ."

Key Vocabulary

- **muscle** *n.*, a body tissue that produces movement

In Other Words

prosthesis machine-made body part
conduct help move
an amplifier to boost the something to make louder or stronger
severed cut

Closing In On a Lifelike Limb

The abilities of today's Proto 1 Bionic Arm will triple in the next prototype.

Human Arm
22+ Movements

From the shoulder to a finger's last joint, an arm has at least 22 points of movement. Nerves carry the brain's instructions from the spinal cord to the muscles.

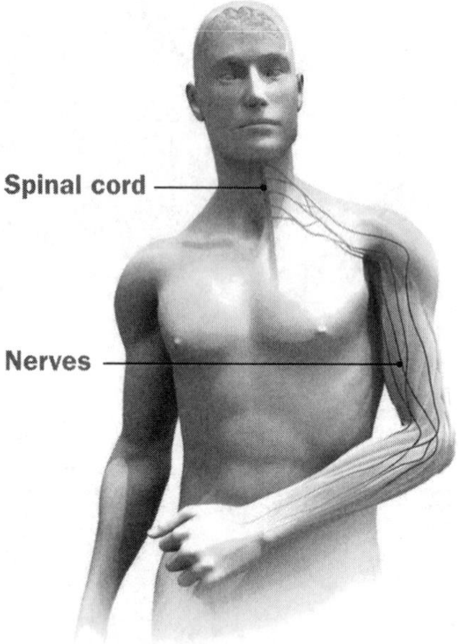

Traditional Prosthesis
3 Movements

The pincer-hand prosthesis has cables that move when the chin or other arm presses levers on a harness. It is the only device available to most amputees.

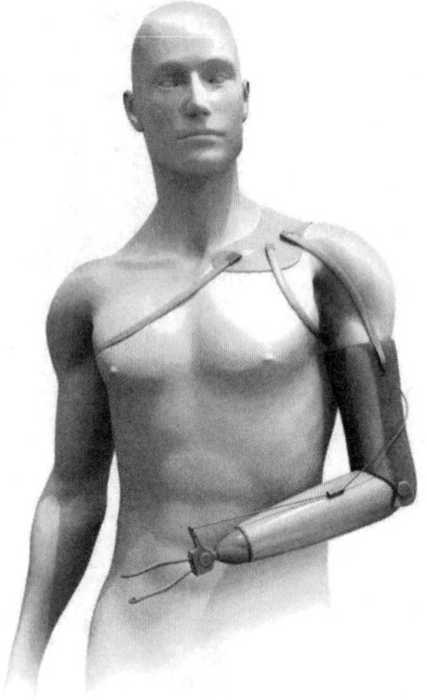

Proto 1
7 Movements

Nerves that once reached the lower arm are rerouted into other muscles. Electrodes placed on those muscles capture the brain's commands and send them by wires in the prosthesis.

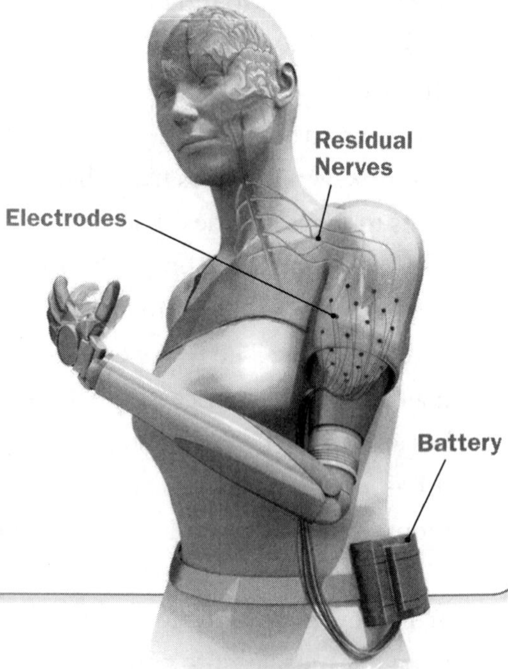

Modular Design Placing the controller in the palm lets the prosthesis work for both full and partial amputations.

Sensory Data Fingertip nodes will detect pressure, vibration, and temperature. The data will be sent to the brain.

There are 17 hand motions.

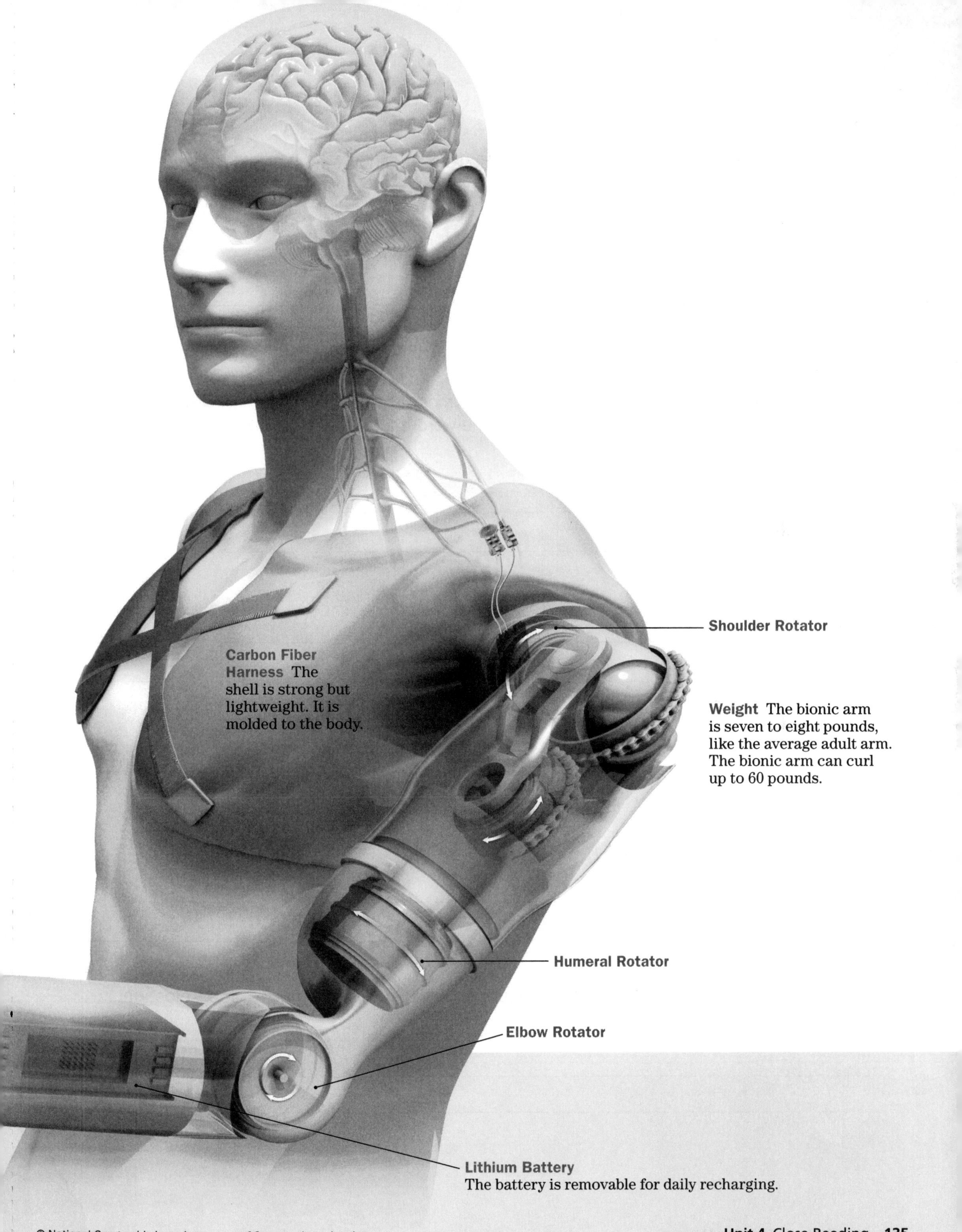
Shoulder Rotator
Carbon Fiber Harness The shell is strong but lightweight. It is molded to the body.
Weight The bionic arm is seven to eight pounds, like the average adult arm. The bionic arm can curl up to 60 pounds.
Humeral Rotator
Elbow Rotator
Lithium Battery
The battery is removable for daily recharging.

Name ______________________________

Read for Understanding

A. From what kind of text is this passage taken? How do you know?

____

B. Write a sentence that tells the topic of the selection.

____

Reread and Summarize

C. On **Practice Book** pages 133–136, circle the 3–5 most important words in each section. Make notes about why you chose each word. Why is the word important?

1. Section 1: (paragraphs 1–6)

____

____

2. Section 2: (paragraphs 7–9)

____

____

3. Section 3: (paragraphs 10–12)

____

____

4. Section 4: (diagram on pages 135–136)

____

____

D. Use your topic sentence from above and your notes to write a summary of the selection.

____

____

____

Name ______________________________

Reread and Analyze

E. Analyze how the author presents main ideas to convey important information in "Bionics."

1. Reread paragraphs 1–5 on **Practice Book** page 133. What is the main idea of this section? Underline words and phrases to support your answers. Use evidence from the text to support your answer.

____

____

____

2. Choose another section of text on **Practice Book** pages 133–136 and determine the main idea. Figure out what this section is mostly about.

____

____

F. Analyze how the author uses details to explain a main idea.

1. Read the last sentence in paragraph 5 on **Practice Book** page 133. How does this detail help you understand the main idea of the paragraph? Underline the words and phrases that support your answer. Use evidence from the text to support your answer.

____

____

____

2. In the **Practice Book**, underline details that explain the main idea that it is possible to link machine to mind. Describe how these details explain this idea.

____

____

Reread and Analyze

G. Analyze how the author uses headings and diagrams to help explain a main idea.

1. Reread the title and headings in the diagram on **Practice Book** pages 135–136. What main idea does the writer explain with these details? Underline words and phrases to support your answers. Use evidence from the text to support your answer.

______

______

______

2. Underline another detail that supports this main idea in the diagram on **Practice Book** pages 133–136 that shows how technology helps scientists make these limbs more lifelike.

______

______

H. Analyze how the author uses procedural order to organize supporting details in a passage.

1. Read the first sentence in paragraph 10 on **Practice Book** page 134. How does the organization of the details that follow help you understand this main idea? Underline the words and phrases that support your answer. Explain how the text evidence supports your answer.

______

______

______

2. In the **Practice Book**, underline other details that support this main idea. Explain why the writer arranged these details in procedural order.

______

______

Name ______________________________

Discuss and Write

I. Synthesize your ideas about how the author uses main idea and details to organize his information for readers.

1. With the class, discuss how the writer used the main idea and details to organize the information about bionic body parts. List the ideas you discuss.

____

____

2. Choose an idea that you listed. Write a paragraph about how main idea and details help you understand the topic. Use the questions below to organize your thoughts.

    - What was the main idea of this passage?
    - What details support this main idea? Give 2 examples.
    - How did the organization of these details help you understand this information?

____

____

____

Connect with GUIDING QUESTION

J. Discuss the Guiding Question: Why is the human body so amazing?

1. How do you think the author feels about bionic technology and the human body? Explain.

____

____

____

2. What surprised you about the information you learned?

____

____

3. Which do you think is more amazing—the technology used to make bionics or the human body? What from the selection makes you think this?

____

____

Name ______________________________

Academic Vocabulary

capable	organize
context	sequence
element	topic

Academic Vocabulary Review

A. Circle the Academic Vocabulary word that best fits into each sentence.

1. You can read the (**context** / **element**) of a sentence to learn more about a new word.
2. When you arrange art materials by their use, you (**organize** / **capable**) them.
3. The order in which objects are shown or listed is their (**context** / **sequence**).
4. (**Topic** / **Context**) is another word for subject.

B. Rewrite each sentence. Replace each underlined word with an Academic Vocabulary word.

1. The subject of his report will be of interest to other students.

   ____

2. From the word's position in the sentence, I can tell it means the opposite of "fearful."

   ____

3. The directions must be followed in the correct order.

   ____

4. I arrange the papers on my desk to keep things neat.

   ____

C. Complete the sentences.

1. It is important to **organize** your ideas when writing because ______________________

   ____.

2. One **topic** I would like to learn more about is ______________________

   ____.

3. When you study you feel more **capable** of making a good grade because ______________________

   ____.

4. The script is an important **element** in making a movie because ______________________

   ____.

Name ______________________________

Key Vocabulary Review

A. Read each sentence. Circle the word that best fits into each sentence.

1. A (**cell** / **organ**) is the smallest working part of a living thing.
2. (**Organs** / **Assignments**) are parts of our bodies.
3. A(n) (**transplant** / **artery**) is a type of blood vessel.
4. A (**muscle** / **ventricle**) is something you can feel and see in your arm.
5. When you (**survive** / **accept**), you get through something.
6. A flood is a natural (**disaster** / **assignment**).
7. We breathe in (**oxygen** / **glory**).
8. A (**ventricle** / **disaster**) is part of the heart.

B. Use your own words to write what each Key Vocabulary word means. Then write a synonym for each word.

Word	My Definition	Synonym
1. **assignment**		
2. **circulate**		
3. **clueless**		
4. **examine**		
5. **glory**		
6. **pump**		
7. **realize**		
8. **section**		

Name ______________________________

Unit 4 Key Vocabulary

accept	**circulate**	**examine**	**muscle**	**realize**	**transplant**
artery	**clueless**	**glory**	**organ**	**section**	**vein**
assignment	**determined**	**healthy**	**oxygen**	**survive**	**ventricle**
cell	**disaster**	**involve**	**pump**	**system**	**vessel**

C. Answer the questions in complete sentences.

1. Describe something you do that you would like to **involve** others in.

____

____

2. What do some people do that stops them from being **healthy**? Explain.

____

____

3. Tell about something that people can **transplant**.

____

____

4. What is something that you **accept**?

____

____

5. Tell about someone you know or have heard about who is **determined** to do something.

____

____

6. What do **veins** do? Why are they important?

____

____

7. Tell about a **system** that helps you make or do something.

____

____

8. Describe a **vessel** and what it does.

____

____

Name ____________________

Mind Map

Use the Mind Map to show what might happen when you **encounter** a new culture. As you read the selections in this unit, add new ideas about **encountering** a new culture.

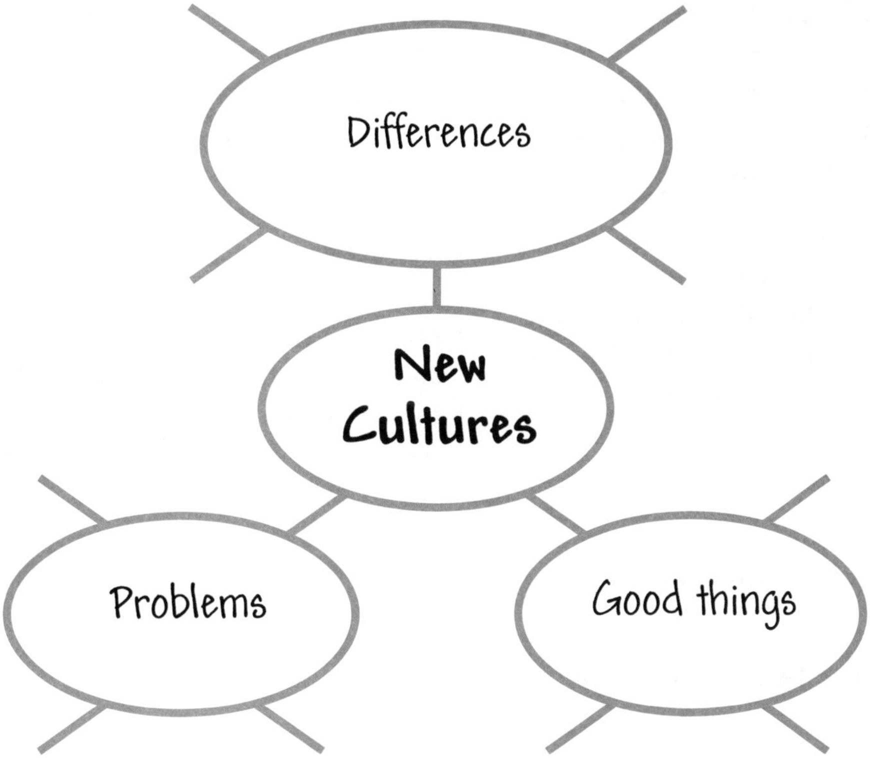

Academic Vocabulary

Think about an **encounter** with a friend. What might you talk about when you **encounter** a friend? Use the word **encounter** in your answer.

___

___

___

___

Name ______________________________

Compare Fiction and Nonfiction

A. Read each passage. Determine if it is fiction or nonfiction and circle the correct response.

Henry Hudson's Third Voyage

Henry Hudson was an English explorer. In 1609, The Dutch East India Company hired him to find a passage to China. Hudson sailed northeast from Holland, but found that way was blocked by ice. When there was talk of mutiny among the crew, he decided to try another route. He sailed his ship, the *Half Moon*, west to the New World.

Hudson's River

When Hudson reached the New World, he found a wide river. He sailed up the river to Albany, New York, and then turned back. That river is named after him, the Hudson River.

Fiction Nonfiction

An Inexperienced Sailor

Thomas shivered. The *Half Moon* had been sailing for over a month now. The air was colder, and the ice grew thicker every day. Even an inexperienced sailor like himself knew the ship could not go much farther. Thomas rubbed his hands together, daydreaming about a nice warm bed and dry clothes. No wonder there had been talk of mutiny. Just last night, he'd overheard a conversation that disturbed him greatly. The sailors said that Captain Hudson was no longer fit to lead the expedition. Thomas shivered again, this time with fear. He hoped that the captain would give up the idea of a passage to China and sail for home.

Fiction Nonfiction

B. Compare the factual details that are included in the two passages.

____

____

____

Academic Vocabulary

Contrast the differences between the two passages. What kinds of fictional details does the author add to the story?

____

______________________________.

______________________________.

Focus on Vocabulary

Name ______________________________

Go Beyond the Literal Meaning

Figurative Language

A **simile** compares two things that are alike using *like*, *as*, or *than*.
A **metaphor** compares two things without using *like*, *as*, or *than*.
Personification gives human qualities to things that are not human.
In an **idiom**, the words together mean something different than the words by themselves.

Read the passages. Follow these steps.

1. Look at each underlined phrase.
2. Think about the types of figurative language. For metaphors and similes, ask yourself what two things are being compared. For personification, picture what the writer is saying. For idioms, look at the other words around the phrase.
3. Use the chart or check the dictionary if you need to.

Follow the directions above. Label the phrase as a simile, a metaphor, personification, or an idiom. Write the meaning of the phrase.

> There are many things to do in the Caribbean. Snorkeling is a popular underwater sport. People search for sea creatures that are as colorful as a rainbow. Jamaica is one of the Caribbean's most popular destinations. It sparkles like a diamond in the Caribbean Sea. Jamaican food is one of the reasons this island is such a hot spot. Jamaican people use many spices in their food. Jerk is a spicy sauce that is usually added to meat. This sauce gives tourists a real kick!

As colorful as a rainbow is an example of ______________________________.

It means ______________________________.

Sparkles like a diamond is an example of ______________________________.

It means ______________________________.

Hot spot is an example of ______________________________.

It means ______________________________.

Gives tourists a real kick is an example of ______________________________.

It means ______________________________.

Academic Vocabulary

It is important to learn the **definition** of words you do not know because ______________________________

____

____

______________________________.

Name ______________________________

Critical Viewing Guide

Take Notes

A. View the images. Take notes on at least three things that you learned.

____

____

____

____

____

____

____

____

Analyze the Images

B. Review your notes to help answer these questions.

1. Write two sentences to explain what was in the images.

____

____

____

2. What was the most interesting thing you learned?

____

____

____

3. What did the images tell about an important **encounter**?

____

____

____

____

____

Learn Key Vocabulary

Name ______________________

It is a **custom** in the Caribbean to play music on steel drums. Musicians **welcome** visitors with beautiful island songs. ▶

Encounter: Key Vocabulary

A. Study each word. Circle a number to rate how well you know it. Then complete the chart.

Rating Scale	1	2	3
	I have never seen this word before.	I am not sure of the word's meaning.	I know this word and can teach the word's meaning to someone else.

Key Words	Check Understanding	Deepen Understanding
❶ **custom** (**kus**-tum) *noun* Rating: 1 2 3	Shaking hands is a **custom** in the United States. **Yes** **No**	Describe a custom in your family. ______
❷ **desire** (di-**zī**-ur) *verb* Rating: 1 2 3	If you **desire** something, you do not want it. **Yes** **No**	What is something you desire? ______
❸ **dream** (**drēm**) *noun* Rating: 1 2 3	A **dream** can be scary. **Yes** **No**	Describe your favorite dream. ______
❹ **encounter** (en-**kown**-tur) *noun* Rating: 1 2 3	An **encounter** with a wild animal can be dangerous. **Yes** **No**	Describe an encounter you have had with an animal. ______

Name ____________

The warm sun, blue water, and sandy **shores** of the Caribbean Islands feel like a **dream** come true for many visitors. ▶

Key Words	Check Understanding	Deepen Understanding
5 shore (shor) *noun* Rating: 1 2 3	All cities have a **shore**. Yes No	What are some things you might see at the shore?
6 stranger (strānj-ur) *noun* Rating: 1 2 3	A **stranger** is someone you know. Yes No	Tell about a time when you felt like a stranger.
7 warning (wor-ning) *noun* Rating: 1 2 3	A **warning** can keep us safe. Yes No	Describe a warning that helped you.
8 welcome (wel-kum) *verb* Rating: 1 2 3	When you **welcome** someone, you make the person feel uncomfortable. Yes No	When was the last time your family welcomed someone into your home?

B. Use at least two of the Key Vocabulary words. Write about a time you went to a new place.

Name ______________________________

Analyze Plot, Setting, and Character

A. As you read "The Encounter," look for historical and fictional details about the plot, characters, and setting. Complete the Details Chart.

Historical Details	Fictional Details
sailing ships	...three great-winged birds with voices like thunder rode wild waves into our bay

B. Choose one historical detail and one related fictional detail from the chart above. Tell why you think the author included each one and how these details affect the story.

____

____

____

____

____

Name ____________________________

Encounter

Key Vocabulary	
custom	shore
desires	strangers
dream	warning
encounter	welcome

A. Read the paragraph.
Write a Key Vocabulary word in each blank.
Reread the paragraph to make sure the words make sense.

A young boy wakes suddenly from a bad ____________. He goes to the beach and sees ships heading for the ____________. ____________ get off the ships. The boy warns his chief not to ____________ them to their land. The chief ignores the boy's ____________ and trades gifts with the visitors because this is his people's ____________. The boy knows that this ____________ is the beginning of the end for his people and their way of life. He wants to save his people, but no matter how much he ____________ it, no one will listen to him.

B. Write complete sentences to answer these questions about "Encounter."

1. Why did the adults **welcome** the **strangers** and trust them?

____

____

____

____

____

____

2. If you had an **encounter** like the one in the story, would you **welcome** the **strangers**? Why or why not?

____

____

____

____

____

____

____

Vocabulary Study

Name ______________________

Analyze Personification

Follow the steps below.

1. Read each sentence.
2. Think about the image that comes to your mind.
3. Write the meaning of each sentence.

1. Snow blanketed the playground in white.

____

2. The leaves raced to the ground in the windstorm.

____

3. The wind whispered a pleasant poem as it moved through the forest.

____

4. The windows complained loudly when Mom opened them in the summer.

____

5. The earthquake made a hole in the ground and swallowed the houses.

____

6. The rain pounded on the rooftop.

____

7. The mountain stared down at us as we began our hike.

____

8. The hungry waves gobbled up our sandcastle.

____

9. The cornstalks waved “hello” when I approached the garden.

____

10. The clouds ran across the sky after the storm.

____

Academic Vocabulary

Name ____________________

Academic Vocabulary	
analyze	encounter
contrast	image
definition	response

Encounter: Academic Vocabulary Review

A. Draw a line to match each Academic Vocabulary word with its meaning.

Word
1. **analyze**
2. **contrast**
3. **definition**
4. **encounter**
5. **image**
6. **response**

Definition
the meaning of a word
an answer
to study closely
a meeting
to tell how things are different
a picture of something

B. Read each sentence. Circle the Academic Vocabulary word that best fits into each sentence.

1. Some words have more than one (**contrast** / **definition**).
2. Our team (**analyzes** / **contrasts**) games so we can play better.
3. The director (**contrasted** / **analyzed**) our best show with our worst.
4. Marion had no (**encounter** / **response**) to the difficult question.
5. The scary book created frightening (**definitions** / **images**) in my mind.
6. I was nervous about my (**encounter** / **image**) with the principal.

C. Imagine you have an **encounter** with a bear. What would your **response** be? Use complete sentences.

____

____

____

____

Name ______________________________

Critical Viewing Guide

Take Notes

A. View the video. Take notes on at least three things that you learned.

____
____
____
____
____
____
____
____

Analyze the Video

B. Review your notes to help answer these questions.

1. Write two sentences to explain what was in the video.

____
____
____

2. What was the most interesting thing you learned?

____
____
____

3. Explain why an **encounter** between two different cultures could cause problems.

____
____
____
____

Learn Key Vocabulary

Name ______________________________

Culture Clash: Key Vocabulary

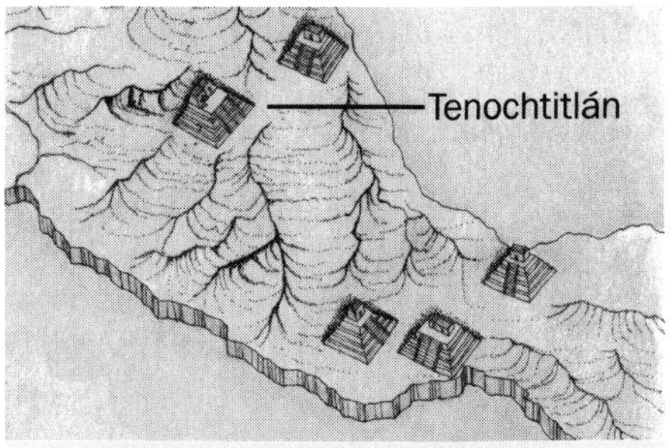

▲ Tenochtitlán was the **capital** city of the Aztec **Empire**. The city was **conquered** by Spain in 1521.

A. Study each word. Circle a number to rate how well you know it. Then complete the chart.

Rating Scale	1	2	3
	I have never seen this word before.	I am not sure of the word's meaning.	I know this word and can teach the word's meaning to someone else.

Key Words	Check Understanding	Deepen Understanding
❶ **blend** (**blend**) *verb* Rating: 1 2 3	☐ mix something together ☐ win control of something	List three things you blend together to make cookies. ____________
❷ **capital** (**kap**-ut-ul) *noun* Rating: 1 2 3	☐ a government ☐ a city	List three capitals. ____________
❸ **conflict** (**kahn**-flikt) *noun* Rating: 1 2 3	☐ an agreement ☐ a problem	List three possible results of a conflict. ____________
❹ **conquer** (**kahn**-kur) *verb* Rating: 1 2 3	☐ win control ☐ lose a battle	List three reasons that some groups of people try to conquer other groups. ____________

Name ______________________________

> **Did You Know?**
> The word **empire** comes from the Latin word *imperium,* meaning "military command."

Key Words	Check Understanding	Deepen Understanding
5 culture (**kul**-chur) *noun* **Rating:** 1 2 3	☐ a place ☐ a way of life	List three examples of your family's culture. ______
6 defeat (di-**fēt**) *noun* **Rating:** 1 2 3	☐ a gain ☐ a loss	List three situations that might feel like a defeat.
7 empire (em-**pī**-ur) *noun* **Rating:** 1 2 3	☐ a country ruled by a government ☐ a country ruled by one person	List three countries that are NOT empires. ______
8 ruler (**rü**-lur) *noun* **Rating:** 1 2 3	☐ a person ☐ a place	List three rulers that you have learned about. ______

B. Use at least two of the Key Vocabulary words. Tell about a country you would like to visit.

____

____

____

____

Prepare to Read

Name ______________________________

Compare a Topic

A. As you read “Culture Clash” and “Mexico City,” record the information in each article about the Aztecs and the city of Tenochtitlán. Use the bottom row to show similarities in each article.

“Culture Clash”	**“Mexico City”**
Includes sensory details about the ancient city.	Lists places in the city.
Compare Texts	

B. Choose one comparison you made. Explain the information each author included and why you think each emphasized certain information.

____

____

____

____

____

Selection Review

Name ________________________________

Key Vocabulary	
blend	cultures
capital	defeat
conflict	empire
conquer	ruler

Culture Clash

A. Read the paragraph.
Write a Key Vocabulary word in each blank.
Reread the paragraph to make sure the words make sense.

In 1519, Spaniards marched into the city of Tenochtitlán, the Aztec ____________. Their goal was to ____________ the city and take control of the entire Aztec ____________. First they captured Moctezuma, the mighty Aztec ____________. Then they used disease and starvation to ____________ the Aztec people. After two years of fighting and ____________, the Aztec surrendered. Although the Aztec lost their battle with the Spaniards, their presence in Mexico remains strong. The ____________ of Aztec and Spanish ____________ that exists in Mexico today helps make it a fascinating country.

B. Write complete sentences to answer these questions about "Culture Clash."

1. What might have happened if the Spaniards had not infected the Aztec with smallpox?

____

____

____

____

____

____

2. What do you think Mexico City would look like today if the Spaniards had not **conquered** the Aztec?

____

____

____

____

____

____

Vocabulary Study

Name ______________________________

Understand Idioms

Follow the steps below.

1. Read each sentence.
2. Think about the image you picture for each underlined idiom.
3. Write how the image helped you understand the idiom.

1. The train was up and running early this morning.

____

____

2. He beat around the bush, because he did not want to tell his friend he could not go to the concert.

____

____

3. My friend got a kick out of the movie he saw on Friday night.

____

____

4. I have to hit the hay early on school nights.

____

____

5. The athlete lost the race, but her coach told her to keep her chin up because she had tried her best.

____

____

6. The college student did not study very much, so he had to burn the midnight oil before the test.

____

____

7. I do not want to go outside because it is raining cats and dogs.

____

____

8. The child did not go to school because he was feeling under the weather.

____

____

Name ______________________________

Academic Vocabulary	
definition	image
encounter	source
compare	

Culture Clash: Academic Vocabulary Review

A. Use your own words to tell what each Academic Vocabulary word means.

Word	My Definition
1. **definition**	
2. **encounter**	
3. **compare**	
4. **image**	
5. **source**	

B. Rewrite each sentence. Replace each underlined word or phrase with an Academic Vocabulary word.

1. Reviewers <u>analyze the similarities between</u> this movie and an earlier version of it.

   ____

2. I used many <u>books and magazine articles</u> to research my paper.

   ____

3. Synonyms are words that have a similar <u>meaning</u>.

   ____

4. I created some wonderful <u>pictures</u> as I read the poem.

   ____

5. We had a successful <u>meeting</u> with the doctor.

   ____

Name ______________________________

Critical Viewing Guide

Take Notes

A. View the video. Take notes on at least three things that you learned.

____

____

____

____

____

____

____

____

Analyze the Video

B. Review your notes to help answer these questions.

1. Write two sentences to explain what was in the video.

____

____

____

2. What was the most interesting thing you learned?

____

____

____

3. What was the effect of Columbus's **encounter** with America?

____

____

____

____

____

Name ______________________________

When Cultures Meet: Key Vocabulary

A. Study each word. Circle a number to rate how well you know it. Then complete the chart.

Rating Scale	1	2	3
	I have never seen this word before.	I am not sure of the word's meaning.	I know this word and can teach the word's meaning to someone else.

▲ Native Americans made **tools** from the antlers and bones of large animals. They used them as farming **tools** to grow **crops**.

Key Words	Check Understanding	Deepen Understanding
❶ contact (**kahn**-takt) *noun* **Rating: 1 2 3**	If you are in **contact** with someone, you never talk to that person. **Yes No**	I stay in contact with my friends by ______________________________.
❷ crop (**krop**) *noun* **Rating: 1 2 3**	One carrot is a **crop**. **Yes No**	A crop that grows in my area is ______________________________.
❸ forever (for-**e**-vur) *adverb* **Rating: 1 2 3**	**Forever** is a long time. **Yes No**	Something I want to have forever is ______________________________.
❹ route (**rowt**) *noun* **Rating: 1 2 3**	A **route** helps you get somewhere. **Yes No**	Something that helps me follow a route is ______________________________.

Name ______________________________

When European **settlers** began to hunt buffalo for food and sport, the once-great buffalo herds were changed **forever**. ▶

Key Words	Check Understanding	Deepen Understanding
5 settler (set-lur) *noun* **Rating: 1 2 3**	A **settler** has always lived in the same place. **Yes** **No**	A settler might move to a new place to ____________________________________.
6 spread (spred) *verb* **Rating: 1 2 3**	Some illnesses can **spread**. **Yes** **No**	Some things you can spread on toast are ____________________________________.
7 starve (starv) *verb* **Rating: 1 2 3**	When you **starve,** you have enough to eat. **Yes** **No**	Some people starve because ____________________________________.
8 tool (tül) *noun* **Rating: 1 2 3**	You need more than one **tool** to build a house. **Yes** **No**	Tools help us ____________________________________.

B. Imagine you are a settler. Use at least two of the Key Vocabulary words to write about your life.

____

____

____

Prepare to Read

Name ____________________

Analyze Text Features

A. As you read "When Cultures Meet," compare and contrast the information in the text with the information given in text features such as illustrations, maps, charts, and diagrams. Complete a Comparison Chart. In the left and right columns, write information given only by the text or a feature. Then write the information that is the same for both in the middle column.

Text	Both	Text Features
page 384: Each culture had its own language and way of life.	Many different Native American cultures were present in the Americas.	page 385:
page 386:		page 386:
page 388:		page 388:
page 389:		page 389:
page 392:		page 392:
page 394:		page 394:

Name ______________________________

When Cultures Meet

Key Vocabulary	
contact	settlers
crops	spread
forever	starve
routes	tools

A. Read the paragraph.
Write a Key Vocabulary word in each blank.
Reread the paragraph to make sure the words make sense.

As more and more ____________ came to the New World, Native Americans had to learn how to deal with them. ____________ between the two groups was not always friendly, but they made the best of the situation. Native Americans traded seeds for ____________ and showed the newcomers how to ____________ the seeds across the land. Together they produced healthy ____________ so no one would ____________ over the long, cold winters. Over time the Europeans created ____________ across the entire United States. The Native American way of life changed ____________.

B. Write complete sentences to answer these questions about "When Cultures Meet."

1. Why do many cultural changes have to do with food?

____

____

____

____

____

____

2. How did Native Americans influence cultures in Europe?

____

____

____

____

____

____

Name ______________________________

Analyze Idioms

Follow the steps below to understand idioms.

1. Read each sentence.
2. Think about the connotative meaning of the idiom.
3. Write the meanings of the underlined phrases. Use context clues.

1. She was getting very angry, so I told her to take it easy.

____

2. The boss asked his employees to keep him up-to-date.

____

3. She was two-faced and told her friends' secrets.

____

4. I thought she was pulling my leg when she said she won the lottery.

____

5. I can never make up my mind when it is time to pick a movie.

____

6. I said I would keep an eye out for my neighbor's lost cat.

____

7. My little brother was getting on my nerves because he kept unplugging my video game.

____

8. After five hours of basketball, we decided to call it a day.

____

9. Jack knew the names of all fifty states. The test would be a piece of cake.

____

Name ____________________

When Cultures Meet: Academic Vocabulary Review

Academic Vocabulary	
analyze	definition
compare	encounter
context	feature
contrast	

A. Write each Academic Vocabulary word next to the correct definition.

Definition	Word
1. to tell how things differ	
2. a meeting	
3. to study closely	
4. the meaning of a word	
5. a separate but important part of something	
6. the surrounding text that explains the meaning of a word	
7. to tell how things are the same	

B. Write an Academic Vocabulary word to complete each sentence.

1. James and Maya ________________ the socks to see if they are the same color.
2. Cheryl asked the teacher to repeat the ________________ of the vocabulary word.
3. The remote control is a helpful ________________ of the television.
4. During our ________________ with the pop star, we got his autograph.
5. To understand a word, it helps to read it in its ________________ .
6. Can you ________________ the results of the survey and give me a detailed report?
7. It is easy to ________________ the twins because they have very different personalities.

C. Write one sentence to **compare** cats and dogs.

____

FROM

The Log of Christopher Columbus

BY CHRISTOPHER COLUMBUS

translated by Robert Fuson

Saturday, 13 October 1492

1 After sunrise people from San Salvador again began to come to our ships in boats fashioned in one piece from the trunks of trees. These boats are wonderfully made, considering the country we are in, and every bit as fine as those I have seen in Guinea. They come in all sizes. Some can carry 40 or 50 men; some are so small that only one man rides in it. The men move very swiftly over the water, rowing with a blade that looks like a **baker's peel**. They do not use **oarlocks**, but dip the peel in the water and push themselves forward. If a boat capsizes they all begin to swim, and they rock the boat until about half of the water is splashed out. Then they bail out the rest of the water with gourds that they carry for that purpose.

2 The people brought more balls of spun cotton, spears, and parrots. Other than the parrots, I have seen no beast of any kind on this island.

3 I have been very attentive and have tried very hard to find out if there is any gold here. I have seen a few natives who wear a little piece of gold hanging from a hole made in the nose. By signs, if I interpret them correctly, I have learned that by going to the south, or rounding the island to the south, I can find a king who possesses a lot of gold and has great containers of it. I have tried to find some natives who will take me to this great king, but none seems **inclined** to make the journey.

4 Tomorrow afternoon I intend to **go to the SW**. The natives have indicated to me that not only is there land to the south and SW, but also to the NW. I shall go to the SW and look for gold and precious stones. Furthermore, if I understand correctly, it is from the NW that **strangers** come to fight and capture the people here.

5 This island is fairly large and very flat. It is green, with many trees and several bodies of water. There is a very large lagoon in the middle of the island and there are no mountains. It is a pleasure to gaze upon this place because it is all so green, and the weather

Key Vocabulary

- **stranger** *n.*, an unknown person

In Other Words

baker's peel wooden board with a long handle
oarlocks brackets to hold the oars in place
inclined to want
go to the SW explore the sea to the southwest

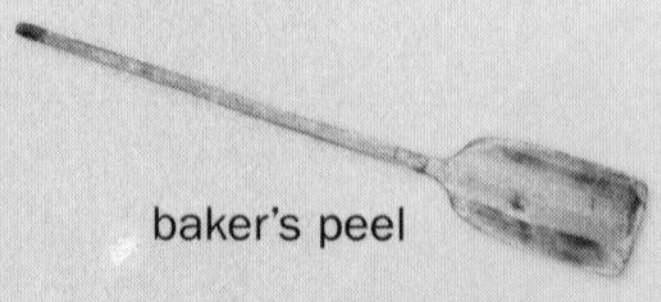

is delightful. In fact, since we left the Canaries, God has not failed to provide one perfect day after another.

6 I cannot get over the fact of how **docile** these people are. They have so little to give but will give it all for whatever we give them, if only broken pieces of glass and **crockery**. One seaman gave three Portuguese *ceitis* (not even worth a penny!) for about 25 pounds of spun cotton. I probably should have forbidden this exchange, but I wanted to take the cotton to Your Highnesses, and it seems to be in abundance. I think the cotton is grown on San Salvador, but I cannot say for sure because I have not been here that long. Also, the gold they wear hanging from their noses comes from here, but in order not to lose time I want to go to see if I can find the island of Japan.

"I have tried very hard to find out if there is any gold here."

Critical Viewing Compare how the artist shows the two groups. What can you infer from what he chose to paint?

The Landing of Christopher Columbus in the New World, 1821, Frederick Kemmelmeyer, oil on canvas

Geographical Background

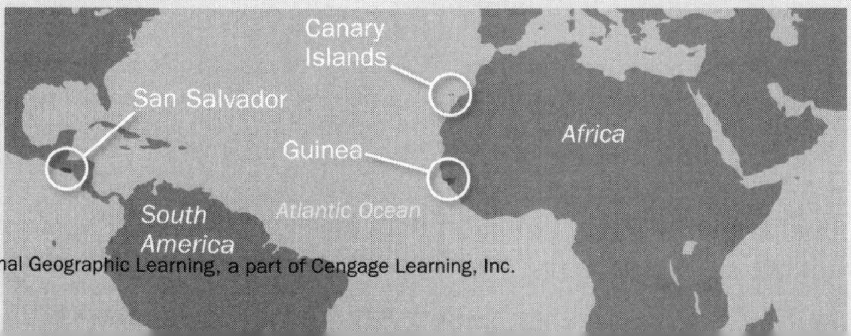

In Other Words
docile calm, agreeable
crockery pottery; dishes

Name ______________________________

Read for Understanding

A. From what kind of text is this passage taken? How do you know?

____

____

B. Write a sentence that tells the topic of the selection.

____

____

Reread and Summarize

C. On **Practice Book** pages 168–169, circle the 3–5 most important words in each section. Make notes about why you chose each word. Why is the word important in the section?

1. Section 1: (paragraphs 1–2)

____

____

2. Section 2: (paragraphs 3–4)

____

____

3. Section 3: (paragraphs 5–6)

____

____

D. Use your topic sentence from above and your notes to write a summary of the selection.

____

____

____

Name ____________________

Reread and Analyze

E. Analyze how the Columbus's descriptions of his interactions with the natives influenced his ideas about them and their culture.

1. Reread paragraphs 1 and 2 on **Practice Book** page 168. What does Columbus learn about the culture of this island? Underline words and phrases to support your answers. Use evidence from the text to support your answer.

____

____

____

2. Underline another detail about Columbus's encounters on **Practice Book** pages 168–169 that you have read in the text. Explain how this information influences Columbus's view of the natives.

____

____

F. Analyze how cause-and-effect relationships can show how individuals influence events.

1. Read paragraphs 3 and 4 on **Practice Book** page 168. How does Columbus's details about the natives help you understand the purpose of his expedition? How do his interactions with the natives of San Salvador affect his future plans? Underline the words and phrases that support your answer. Use evidence from the text to support your answer.

____

____

____

2. In the **Practice Book,** underline other examples of interactions that help you understand how Columbus's ideas and actions are affected by his contact with the natives of San Salvador.

____

____

Name ____________________

Discuss and Write

G. Synthesize your ideas about how writers show the interactions between individuals, ideas, and events.

1. With the class, discuss how writers can show how interactions between individuals affect ideas and events. List the examples you discuss.

____

____

____

2. Choose one of the examples that you listed. Write a paragraph about how the writer describes the interactions between individuals, ideas, and events. Use the questions below to organize your thoughts.
   - What do you learn about the individuals?
   - How does the writer's description of interactions between individuals help you understand the events and ideas in this log?

____

____

____

Connect with GUIDING QUESTION

H. Discuss the Guiding Question: What happens when cultures meet?

1. Why does Columbus call these people "docile"?

____

____

2. What do the people's actions tell you about their culture?

____

____

3. What does Columbus's interactions with the people tell you about him?

____

____

Unit 5 Review

Name ______________________________

Academic Vocabulary Review

Academic Vocabulary

analyze	definition	response
compare	encounter	source
context	feature	
contrast	image	

A. Use five Academic Vocabulary words to complete the paragraph.

Some words have more than one meaning, or ____________. It is important to ____________ the text to find out which definition works. The surrounding words, or ____________, can help. A dictionary is another reliable ____________ of information. It might even help you form a mental ____________ of the word.

B. Read each statement. Circle **Yes** or **No** to answer.

1. When you tell how two things are the same, you **contrast** them. **Yes** **No**
2. Your **response** is how you react to something. **Yes** **No**
3. When you **analyze** something, you are looking at its parts. **Yes** **No**

C. Answer the questions in complete sentences.

1. Why is it a good idea to **compare** the prices of similar items at a store?

____

____

2. In your opinion, what is the most important **feature** of a television? Explain.

____

____

3. Would you like to have an **encounter** with someone famous? Tell why or why not.

____

____

4. What is the best **response** to someone who insults you?

____

____

Name ______________________________

Key Vocabulary Review

A. Read each sentence. Circle the Key Vocabulary word that best fits into each sentence.

1. You can visit many government buildings in the (**capital** / **contact**).
2. A (**welcome** / **defeat**) can be difficult.
3. A strong leader ruled the (**empire** / **custom**).
4. (**Customs** / **Strangers**) are people you do not know.
5. Wheat is a plentiful (**crop** / **warning**) in the Midwest.
6. Colds can (**blend** / **spread**) quickly when people work closely together.
7. You can (**starve** / **welcome**) if you don't have enough food.
8. A (**route** / **dream**) happens when you sleep.

B. Use your own words to write what each Key Vocabulary word means. Then write a synonym for each word.

Word	My Definition	Synonym
1. **blend**		
2. **conquer**		
3. **contact**		
4. **custom**		
5. **desire**		
6. **route**		
7. **shore**		
8. **warning**		

Name ______________________________

Unit 5 Key Vocabulary

blend	**contact**	**defeat**	**encounter**	**settler**	**stranger**
capital	**crop**	**desire**	**forever**	**shore**	**tool**
conflict	**culture**	**dream**	**route**	**spread**	**warning**
conquer	**custom**	**empire**	**ruler**	**starve**	**welcome**

C. Answer the questions in complete sentences.

1. Tell about a **conflict** you have experienced.

____

____

2. What **culture** do you think is most interesting? Why?

____

____

3. If you were the **ruler** of the United States, what would you change?

____

____

4. If you were a **settler** who just arrived in a new place, what would you do first? Why?

____

____

5. What is a **tool** you have used and how did it help you?

____

____

6. What do you think it would it be like to live **forever**?

____

____

7. What can you do to make a new student to your school feel **welcome**?

____

____

8. Describe what an **encounter** with an alien might be like.

____

____

Name ____________________

Mind Map

Answer the questions in the Mind Map to show your ideas about the word **aid**.
As you read the selections in this unit, add new ideas you learn about the word **aid**.

What are kinds of aid?

Who gives aid?

Aid

Why do people need aid?

How are people aided?

Academic Vocabulary

Think about a time you might need to **aid** someone. Why is it important to **aid** others? Use the word **aid** in your answer.

____

____

____

____

Name ______________________________

Determine Author's Viewpoint

A. Read the fiction passage. Look at the words and phrases the author uses to help you figure out each character's viewpoint.

The Rescue

I was walking home from school when I hear something. I looked up and saw a kitten stuck in a the tree. It was meowing loudly. My heart broke. "You poor little thing! I'll get you some help," I called.

I went to my neighbor's house and asked for help. At first he was reluctant. "Kittens are trouble. If it found it's way up, it will find it's way down."

It took some convincing, but he finally got a ladder and helped me rescue the kitten.

Contrast the narrator's and the neighbor's viewpoints about kittens. What words and phrases help you distinguish between them?

____

____

____

B. Read the nonfiction passage. Use the author's word choice and details to determine the author's viewpoint.

Helping Victims of Disaster

When disaster first strikes, many of us say we want to help. However, just saying the words is not enough. Sympathy alone is not the answer. To truly help victims of a disaster, we must act on our words. Do something that is within your means, ability, or time: clean up, start repairs, give a donation, collect supplies, give assistance, or provide transportation. It's not what you do that is important, it's that you do something.

What is the author's viewpoint on helping victims of disaster? Tell how you know.

____

____

Academic Vocabulary

Write about how you might **aid** someone in need.

____

Focus on Vocabulary

Name ______________________________

Use Word Origins

Read the passages. Follow these steps.

1. Break the word into meaningful parts. If you cannot break the word into parts, it may be a borrowed word.
2. Focus on the root. Think about related words. Use the Roots Chart to find its meaning.
3. Put the meanings of all the word parts together.
4. See if the meaning makes sense in the sentence.

Roots Chart

Root	Origin	Meaning
aud	Latin	hear
log	Greek	reason, study
part	Latin	portion, part
phys	Greek	nature
poli	Greek	city
port	Latin	to carry

A. Follow the directions above. Write the meaning of each underlined word.

> Physicians and animals are partners in healing sick people. The love and companionship of a dog, cat, or bird can help sick people get better. A loving pet may be a logical way to help many people.

physicians ______________________________

partners ______________________________

logical ______________________________

B. Follow the directions above. Write the meaning of each underlined word.

> Many dogs can help people in danger. The police use search and rescue dogs to find people who are lost. The police also use dogs to help stop crime. Some dogs work at airports to help officials find items that are not allowed on airplanes. Dogs have such a good sense of smell. They also have excellent auditory skills, so they can hear sounds that people cannot.

police ______________________________

airports ______________________________

auditory ______________________________

Academic Vocabulary

The **original** reason for training a dog might be to do a trick, but a trained dog may also be able to

____

____

______________________________.

Name ______________________________

Critical Viewing Guide

Take Notes

A. View the video. Take notes on at least three things that you learned.

____
____
____
____
____
____
____
____

Analyze the Video

B. Review your notes to help answer these questions.

1. Write two sentences to explain what was in the video.

____
____
____
____

2. What was the most interesting thing you learned?

____
____
____

3. Explain some of the different ways dogs **aid** people.

____
____
____
____

Name ______________________________

Dogs at Work: Key Vocabulary

A. Study each word. Circle a number to rate how well you know it. Then complete the chart.

▲ **Obedient** animals can be **trained** to help people with special needs.

Rating Scale	1	2	3
	I have never seen this word before.	I am not sure of the word's meaning.	I know this word and can teach the word's meaning to someone else.

Key Words	Check Understanding	Deepen Understanding
❶ **dependable** (di-**pen**-du-bul) *adjective* **Rating:** 1 2 3	☐ can be trusted to do the right thing ☐ can make you laugh	List three people who are dependable. ____________
❷ **employee** (im-**ploi**-ē) *noun* **Rating:** 1 2 3	☐ a job ☐ a worker	List three places where employees work. ____________
❸ **job** (**job**) *noun* **Rating:** 1 2 3	☐ something you do for money ☐ something you do for fun	List three examples of jobs. ____________
❹ **obedient** (ō-**bē**-dē-int) *adjective* **Rating:** 1 2 3	☐ do what you're told ☐ help someone else	List three ways that you are obedient. ____________

Name ______________________

Did You Know?

Some flowers have **odors** that bees can "smell" from more than half a mile away.

Key Words	Check Understanding	Deepen Understanding
5 odor (ō-dur) *noun* **Rating: 1 2 3**	☐ an event ☐ a smell	List three things that have an odor. ____
6 search (surch) *verb, noun, adjective* **Rating: 1 2 3**	☐ to find something ☐ to look for something	List three examples of things people search for. ____
7 service (sur-vis) *noun* **Rating: 1 2 3**	☐ something you do to help someone ☐ something you do to keep going	List three examples of services your community provides.
8 train (trān) *verb* **Rating: 1 2 3**	☐ teach someone how to do something ☐ help someone search for something	List three things we can train a dog to do. ____

B. Use at least two of the Key Vocabulary words. Write about what it means to be a dependable employee.

____

____

____

Prepare to Read

Name ______________________________

Analyze Author's Purpose and Tone

A. As you read "Dogs at Work," look at the word choices made by the author. Complete the chart to help you analyze the author's tone and purpose.

Word Choice	Tone	Purpose
professional pooches, doggone dependable	informal: funny, light-hearted	to entertain, to interest

B. Explain how the author's word choice and tone support the author's purposes and viewpoint that dogs are valuable. Use details from the text to support your answer.

____

____

____

____

Selection Review

Name ______________________________

Dogs at Work

Key Vocabulary

dependable	**odors**
employees	**search**
jobs	**service**
obedient	**train**

A. Read the paragraph.
Write a Key Vocabulary word in each blank.
Reread the paragraph to make sure the words make sense.

Four-legged ____________ are some of the hardest workers you can find. The ____________ dogs do provide a ____________ to many humans. To ____________ for the work they will do, the dogs must be smart. They must learn to take orders, or be ____________. They must be faithful and trustworthy so that they will be ____________ in any situation. Drug-sniffing dogs must be good at smelling different ____________ when they ____________ through all kinds of items. If you want to hire the best, hire a dog!

B. Write complete sentences to answer these questions about "Dogs at Work."

1. What qualities does a **search** dog need?

____

____

____

____

____

____

2. How would you **train** a dog to help you with the **jobs** you need to do?

____

____

____

____

____

____

Vocabulary Study

Name ____________________

Use Words and Phrases from Mythology

Follow the steps below to figure out the meaning of each phrase from mythology.

1. Read each sentence.
2. Read the mythological connection and think about how it relates to the sentence.
3. Explain what the underlined words mean in each sentence.

1. Miranda was dressed to the nines for dinner at a fancy restaurant.

   Mythological Connection: The nine Muses were Greek goddesses who ruled over the arts.

   Meaning: ____________________

2. Scott wished he had the Midas touch as he looked at his collection of pennies.

   Mythological Connection: King Midas was a greedy man who asked the gods to make everything he touched turn to gold.

   Meaning: ____________________

3. He was green with envy as he watched his friend win a huge prize.

   Mythological Connection: The monster, Envy, captured people and infected them with poison. The poison was said to contain jealousy and anger.

   Meaning: ____________________

4. Jake opened Pandora's box when he told his friend a secret about his brother.

   Mythological Connection: Pandora received a box from the Greek god, Zeus, that spilled evil when she opened it.

   Meaning: ____________________

5. The illness was like a Trojan horse; once one person caught it, everyone else did, too.

   Mythological Connection: The people of Troy believed that a large wooden horse was a peace offering, so they brought it into their city. However, there were warriors hiding inside the horse.

   Meaning: ____________________

6. When my mother gets angry, she can give you a look that will turn you to stone.

   Mythological Connection: Anyone who looked directly at a Gorgon would be turned to stone.

   Meaning: ____________________

Academic Vocabulary

Name ______________________________

Academic Vocabulary

aid, purpose, characteristic, refer, original

Dogs at Work: Academic Vocabulary Review

A. Use your own words to tell what each Academic Vocabulary word means. Then write a synonym for each word.

Word	My Definition	Synonym
1. **aid**		
2. **characteristic**		
3. **original**		
4. **purpose**		
5. **refer**		

B. Read each statement. Circle **Yes** or **No** to answer.

1. It is kind to **aid** people who need help. **Yes** **No**
2. Loyalty is a **characteristic** of a good friend. **Yes** **No**
3. An **original** song is one of a kind. **Yes** **No**
4. The **purpose** of exercise is to improve your health. **Yes** **No**
5. To **refer** is to give support. **Yes** **No**

C. Answer the questions in complete sentences.

1. If you were going to **refer** someone for a job, what **characteristics** would you tell about them?

____

____

2. Name an object that has more than one **purpose**. What are two ways it can be used?

____

____

Build Background

Name ______________________________

Critical Viewing Guide

Take Notes

A. View the images. Take notes on at least three things that you learned.

____
____
____
____
____
____
____
____

Analyze the Images

B. Review your notes to help answer these questions.

1. Write two sentences to explain what was in the images.

____
____
____

2. What was the most interesting thing you learned?

____
____
____

3. How do rescue workers **aid** people? Give examples.

____
____
____
____
____

Learn Key Vocabulary

Name ____________________

Angels in the Snow: Key Vocabulary

A. Study each word. Circle a number to rate how well you know it. Then complete the chart.

Rating Scale	1	2	3
	I have never seen this word before.	I am not sure of the word's meaning.	I know this word and can teach the word's meaning to someone else.

▲ An owner and his seeing-eye dog make a great **team**. Crossing the street is not **difficult** with a little help.

Key Words	Check Understanding	Deepen Understanding
1 accident (**ak**-sud-ent) *noun* Rating: 1 2 3	An **accident** is an area. Yes No	Tell about an accident you have seen or heard about. What happened? ____
2 career (ku-**rēr**) *noun* Rating: 1 2 3	A **career** is a person's hobby. Yes No	Tell about a career you would like to have someday.
3 department (di-**part**-mint) *noun* Rating: 1 2 3	A **department** is part of a larger business. Yes No	Tell about a department in a store where you shop.
4 difficult (**dif**-i-kult) *adjective* Rating: 1 2 3	Doing something new can be **difficult**. Yes No	Tell about something difficult that you learned to do.

Name ______________________________

Emergency workers have **experience** helping people who have been in an **accident**. ▶

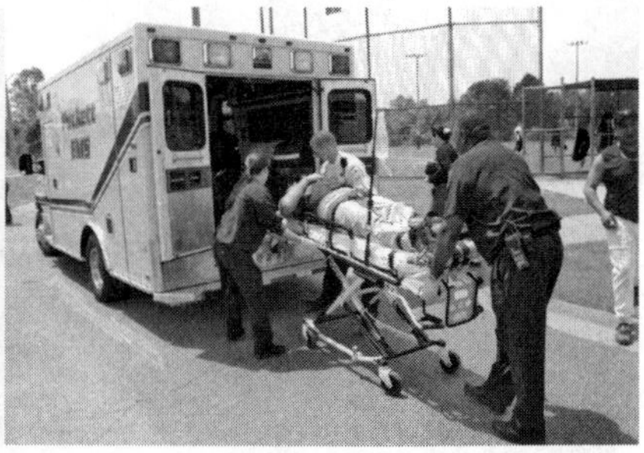

Key Words	Check Understanding	Deepen Understanding
5 emergency (i-**mur**-jen-sē) *adjective* **Rating: 1 2 3**	An ambulance is an **emergency** vehicle. **Yes** **No**	Describe an emergency service in your community. ____________________ ____________________ ____________________ ____________________
6 experience (ik-**spēr**-ē-uns) *noun* **Rating: 1 2 3**	It takes **experience** to be a great chef. **Yes** **No**	Tell about a time when your experience helped you do something. ____________________ ____________________ ____________________ ____________________
7 region (**rē**-jun) *noun* **Rating: 1 2 3**	A **region** is a group of people. **Yes** **No**	Tell about the region you live in. What is it like? ____________________ ____________________ ____________________ ____________________
8 team (**tēm**) *noun* **Rating: 1 2 3**	When you are on a **team**, you are alone. **Yes** **No**	Tell about a time when you were on a team. What was it like? ____________________ ____________________ ____________________ ____________________

B. Imagine you are an emergency worker. Use at least two of the Key Vocabulary words. Describe your job.

____

____

____

Name ______________________________

Analyze Author's Viewpoint

A. As you read "Angels in the Snow," look for words and phrases that tell you about the author's viewpoint. Complete the Two-Column Chart.

Words and Phrases	What I Learn About the Author's Viewpoint
Marteney stayed brave.	The author admired Marteney's actions.

B. How would you describe the author's overall viewpoint of the program that trains teenagers to provide emergency medical services? Use evidence from the text to support your answer.

____

____

____

Name ______________________________

Angels in the Snow

Key Vocabulary

accidents	emergency
careers	experiences
departments	region
difficult	teams

A. Read the paragraph.
Write a Key Vocabulary word in each blank.
Reread the paragraph to make sure the words make sense.

Aniak is a small city in a remote ____________ of central Alaska. The Dragon Slayers are ____________ of teens that are trained to help in urgent, or ____________, situations. They help the fire and police ____________ respond to calls. They face many challenging, or ____________, situations with courage and confidence. They are trained to rescue victims and give first aid at the scenes of ____________. The hands-on ____________ of the Dragon Slayers often lead to medical ____________ when they grow up.

B. Write complete sentences to answer these questions about "Angels in the Snow."

1. How do the Dragon Slayers help their community?

____

____

____

____

____

____

____

2. What do you think would be the hardest part of being a Dragon Slayer?

____

____

____

____

____

____

____

Name ______________________________

Use Greek, Latin, and Anglo-Saxon Roots

Root	Original Language	Meaning
bi	Latin	two
medic	Latin	physician; to heal
sophos	Greek	wise

Many English words have Greek, Latin, or Anglo-Saxon roots. Follow the steps below to figure out the meaning of each word.

1. Write the root of the word.
2. Use the chart to find the meaning of the root.
3. Write the meaning of the whole word.

1. The doctor prescribed a medicine for my allergies.

____

____

2. The man planted a bicolored flower in his backyard.

____

____

3. Aristotle was a great Greek philosopher and teacher.

____

____

4. The school will have their biannual Parents' Math Night next week.

____

____

5. The woman was very sophisticated and had traveled around the world.

____

____

6. The child rode his bicycle up the hill.

____

____

Name ______________________________

Academic Vocabulary	
aid	original
communicate	perspective

Angels in the Snow: Academic Vocabulary Review

A. Use the Academic Vocabulary words to complete the paragraph.

Each person has his or her own ____________, or way of thinking about things. The ideas we have are ____________ because they belong to us alone. One reason we talk is to share our unique point of view. Our ideas can help, or ____________, others. For this reason, it is important to ____________ our thoughts clearly.

B. Answer the questions in complete sentences.

1. In what ways can you **aid** your neighbors?

____

____

2. How can you **communicate** feelings without using words?

____

____

3. How can you create **original** artwork?

____

____

4. What is your **perspective** on people who talk loudly?

____

____

C. Use two Academic Vocabulary words in a sentence.

____

____

____

Name ______________________________

Critical Viewing Guide

Take Notes

A. View the images. Take notes on at least three things that you learned.

____

____

____

____

____

____

____

____

Analyze the Images

B. Review your notes to help answer these questions.

1. Write two sentences to explain what was in the images.

____

____

____

____

2. What was the most interesting thing you learned?

____

____

____

3. What are some of the ways animals **aid** people in everyday life?

____

____

____

____

Learn Key Vocabulary

Name ______________________________

▲ In many parts of the world, **peasants** and farmers **continue** to use animals rather than tractors or machines.

Zlateh the Goat: Key Vocabulary

A. Study each word. Circle a number to rate how well you know it. Then complete the chart.

Rating Scale	1	2	3
	I have never seen this word before.	I am not sure of the word's meaning.	I know this word and can teach the word's meaning to someone else.

Key Words	Check Understanding	Deepen Understanding
❶ **blizzard** (**bli**-zurd) *noun* Rating: 1 2 3	☐ a storm ☐ a worker	In a blizzard, you should ______________________________.
❷ **confidence** (**kahn**-fu-dints) *noun* Rating: 1 2 3	☐ a bad feeling ☐ a good feeling	People feel confidence when ______________________________.
❸ **continue** (kun-**tin**-yü) *verb* Rating: 1 2 3	☐ keep doing something ☐ stop doing something	When you are learning something difficult, it is important to continue to ______________________________.
❹ **decide** (di-**sīd**) *verb* Rating: 1 2 3	☐ ask a question ☐ make a choice	Sometimes it's difficult to decide ______________________________.

Name ______________________________

A sled guide must **trust** his dogs if he goes out during a **blizzard.** ▶

Key Words	Check Understanding	Deepen Understanding
❺ **patiently** (pā-shint-lē) *adverb* **Rating:** 1 2 3	☐ to do something without getting upset ☐ to do something quickly	Sometimes we need to patiently ______________________________ .
❻ **peasant** (pe-zint) *noun* **Rating:** 1 2 3	☐ a waiter ☐ a farm worker	Peasants work very hard to ______________________________ .
❼ **shelter** (shel-tur) *noun* **Rating:** 1 2 3	☐ protects you ☐ conquers you	You need shelter when ______________________________ .
❽ **trust** (trust) *verb* **Rating:** 1 2 3	☐ teach someone ☐ believe in someone	We can usually trust ______________________________ .

B. Use at least two of the Key Vocabulary words. Write about a time when someone gave you confidence.

____

____

____

Prepare to Read

Name ______________________________

Analyze Plot and Theme

A. As you read "Zlateh the Goat," continue to identify elements of plot and complete the Plot Diagram to analyze how the theme develops.

Climax ______________________________

____

Complication: ______________________________

____

Complication: ______________________________

____

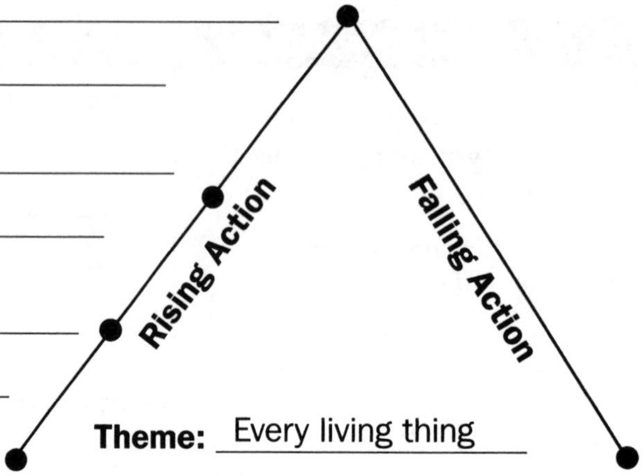

Theme: Every living thing has value.

Conflict: ______________________________

____

Resolution: ______________________________

____

B. Explain how these events help to develop the theme. Use examples from the text.

____

____

____

____

____

____

____

Selection Review

Name ______________________________

Key Vocabulary

blizzard	**patiently**
confidence	**peasants**
continued	**shelter**
decided	**trust**

Zlateh the Goat

A. Read the paragraph.
Write a Key Vocabulary word in each blank.
Reread the paragraph to make sure the words make sense.

At first I followed Aaron with complete faith and ____________. These ____________ sometimes have funny ideas, but most of the time you can ____________ them. When the ____________ blew in, I thought we would turn around, but we ____________. I was glad when Aaron finally made up his mind and ____________ to stop. The ____________ he made in the haystack was nice and cozy. We waited ____________ for the storm to pass, and then we went home. I had never been happier to be home!

B. Write complete sentences to answer these questions about "Zlateh the Goat."

1. What would have happened to Zlateh if the **blizzard** had not stopped the journey?

____

____

____

____

____

____

2. Why was Aaron's family relieved when he and Zlateh came home?

____

____

____

____

____

____

Vocabulary Study

Name ______________________________

Borrowed Words

Follow the steps below to figure out the meaning of each word.

1. Find each word in a dictionary.
2. Write the original language from which the word was borrowed.
3. Then use the word in a sentence.

1. **ballet** ______________________________

   Sentence: ______________________________

2. **macaroni** ______________________________

   Sentence: ______________________________

3. **gymnasium** ______________________________

   Sentence: ______________________________

4. **karate** ______________________________

   Sentence: ______________________________

5. **moustache** ______________________________

   Sentence: ______________________________

6. **marathon** ______________________________

   Sentence: ______________________________

7. **crayon** ______________________________

   Sentence: ______________________________

8. **calendar** ______________________________

   Sentence: ______________________________

9. **mosquito** ______________________________

   Sentence: ______________________________

Name ______________________________

Academic Vocabulary	
affect	original
aid	response

Zlateh the Goat: Academic Vocabulary Review

A. Use your own words to tell what each Academic Vocabulary word means.

1. **affect** ______________________________
2. **aid** ______________________________
3. **original** ______________________________
4. **response** ______________________________

B. Read each sentence. Circle the Academic Vocabulary word that best fits into each sentence.

1. Good weather always (**response** / **affects**) my mood.
2. Terrence shrugged his shoulders in (**aid** / **response**) to the question.
3. I thought my sweater was (**original** / **affect**) until I saw you with the same one.
4. Nurses (**aid** / **original**) people in a hospital.

C. Complete the sentences.

1. Fast music **affects** me because ______________________________

____

2. One **response** to someone who offers you help is ______________________________

____

3. One way to **aid your parents** is to ______________________________

____

4. People are inspired by **original** thought because ______________________________

____

A Conflict Close to Home

by Aziz Abu Sarah

1 A disaster can strike your nation, your state, or even the house of your next-door neighbor, but as long as it strikes someone else, it is still a distance away. Like many in Jerusalem, I grew up seeing many people die because of a "worthless conflict." I felt sad for them, but I **continued** to live my life just as before. My reaction was the same as others who see an **accident** on the side of the road, think "how sad," and drive on. However, my life changed forever the moment the disaster struck my house and my family, and the casualty was my brother.

2 In the spring of 1990, I shared a room with four of my brothers. One ordinary day I was woken at 5:00 a.m., as Israeli soldiers **burst** into my room. They asked us for our identity cards, and questioned the five of us. "Where were you yesterday? Did you throw stones?" They demanded the answers, and when they received none, they took my 18-year-old brother with them. My mother pleaded desperately with the soldiers but in the end they took Tayseer with them. She would not hold him again until eleven months later, when he was released from prison.

3 Tayseer was kept without trial. He was **interrogated** and beaten for fifteen days until he admitted that he had thrown stones at Israeli cars. During the eleven months he was imprisoned, we met him three times. Although we spoke with him through two fences, it was obvious that with each visit his health was **deteriorating** from the beatings. Finally, in the late days of March, he was released from prison. His condition was critical, and he was throwing up blood. We rushed him to the hospital.

4 Tayseer held on for about three weeks, before dying after surgery. I was 10 years old at that time, and Tayseer had been closest to me in age and closest to me as a friend and brother. I could not accept his death. He had helped me with homework. He **had accompanied** me on my first day of school.

5 I became extremely bitter and angry. Even at ten I understood that his death was not natural, and someone was responsible. I grew up with anger burning in my heart. I wanted justice. I wanted revenge.

6 In my high school years I started writing for a youth magazine. I was a consistent writer

Key Vocabulary

- **continue** *v.*, to keep happening
- **accident** *n.*, an unexpected event that causes injury

In Other Words

burst came quickly
interrogated questioned
deteriorating getting worse
had accompanied came with

and wrote about two articles a week. I wrote with anger and bitterness, and used my anger to spread hatred against the other side. My success soon earned me the position of editor at the magazine. However, the more I wrote the more empty and angry I became. Eventually I grew tired of the anger, so I quit the magazine and tried to move out of the country.

7 I failed to get anywhere. After graduating from high school I found myself stuck in Jerusalem. I had refused to learn Hebrew growing up: it was the "enemy's" language. Now, to attend university or get a good job I would have to compromise. I started studying in a Hebrew Ulpan, an institute for Jewish newcomers to Israel. It was the hardest experience I had faced yet, but its results were the best I have encountered. It was the first time I had sat in a room of Jews who were not superior to me. It was the first time I had seen faces different from the soldiers at the checkpoints. Those soldiers had taken my brother; these students were the same as me. My understanding of the Jewish people started to collapse after just a few weeks of the Ulpan. I found myself confused, thinking, "How can they be normal human beings, just like me?" I was amazed that I could build friendships with these students and share their struggles. We went out for coffee together. We studied together. Sometimes we even found that we shared the same interests. For me, this was a turning point in my life.

"Eventually I grew tired of the anger."

8 I came to understand that unfortunate things happen in our lives which are out of our control. A ten-year-old could not control the soldiers who took his brother. But now as an adult, I could control my response to these hurts. **They** had acted unjustly and murdered Tayseer, but I had the choice, and I still have the choice, of whether to follow in the same direction.

9 Each day I live I refuse to become like those soldiers fifteen years ago, and I choose to put aside the rage I worshipped as a teenager. I will always have this choice. It is a hard decision to abandon revenge, and an easy road to follow your feelings. Yet hatred **begets** hatred, and the same tools you use on the others will be used on you. As a result, each day I must choose again to love and forgive those around me.

10 As humans, we try to rationalize our hatred. In our minds we demonize the enemy, and discredit their humanity. This is the lie that fires the conflict between Israel and Palestine.

11 Maybe I will never see the world restored to perfect humanity, but I still feel obligated to believe that the tools for peace are not tools of violence and hatred. More than this, I feel obligated to use my pain to spread peace, rather than using it to fuel a hatred that would have eventually **consumed me**. I believe we are all obligated to do our best to create peace, and not wait until it **hits home**. After all, there is no good war or bad peace.

In Other Words

They The Israeli soldiers who captured my brother
begets creates more
consumed me taken over my life
hits home directly affects our families

Name ______________________________

Read for Understanding

A. From what kind of text is this passage taken? How do you know?

____

B. Write a sentence that tells the topic of the selection.

____

____

Reread and Summarize

C. On **Practice Book** pages 200–201, circle the 3–5 most important words in each section. Make notes about why you chose each word. Why is the word important in the section?

1. Section 1: (paragraphs 1–4)

____

____

2. Section 2: (paragraphs 5–6)

____

____

3. Section 3: (paragraphs 7–11)

____

____

D. Use your topic sentence from above and your notes to write a summary of the selection.

____

____

____

Name ______________________________

Reread and Analyze

E. Analyze how the writer shares personal experiences to communicate his viewpoint on an issue.

1. Reread paragraphs 2–5 on **Practice Book** page 200. What does the writer show you about his viewpoint by sharing this experience? Underline words and phrases to support your answers. Use evidence from the text to support your answer.

____

____

____

2. Underline another example of personal experience on **Practice Book** pages 200–201 that shows the writer's viewpoint. Explain how this experience shows his viewpoint.

____

____

F. Analyze how the author uses word choice to communicate his emotions and viewpoint on an issue.

1. Read the first four sentences in paragraph 7 on **Practice Book** page 201. What words and phrases does the writer use to communicate that his viewpoint is causing him problems? Underline the words and phrases that support your answer. Use evidence from the text to support your answer.

____

____

____

2. In the **Practice Book,** underline other words and phrases that communicate the writer's viewpoint. Explain what it shows about the changes to his viewpoint.

____

____

Name ______________________________

Discuss and Write

G. Synthesize your ideas about how an author has a purpose for writing and communicates his viewpoint to meet that purpose.

1. With the class, discuss how this author's purpose in writing is to use his viewpoint to teach a lesson. What lessons do you think he is trying to teach? List the ideas you discuss.

2. Choose one of the examples that you listed. Write a paragraph about how the writer supports this example with his own personal story. Use the questions below to organize your thoughts.
   - What had filled Aziz with so much anger and hatred as a teenager?
   - What happened that led him to let go of his anger and hatred?

Connect with GUIDING QUESTION

H. Discuss the Guiding Question: How do we come to the aid of one another?

1. Who did Aziz find was the same as he was?

2. Why did Aziz realize he needed to love and forgive?

3. How can Aziz's experiences aid other people?

Unit 6 Review

Name ____________________

Academic Vocabulary	
affect	perspective
aid	purpose
characteristic	refer
communicate	response
original	

Academic Vocabulary Review

A. Circle the Academic Vocabulary word that best fits into each sentence.

1. Every question deserves a (**response** / **purpose**).
2. A player's attitude can (**refer** / **affect**) the outcome of a game.
3. The (**characteristic** / **original**) automobile was much slower than cars today.
4. The (**purpose** / **aid**) of sleeping is to get rest.

B. Read each statement. Circle **Yes** or **No** to answer.

1. To **affect** is to make a request for something. **Yes** **No**
2. Painters can **communicate ideas** through their art. **Yes** **No**
3. A good way to **aid** people is to tease them. **Yes** **No**
4. When you **refer** to something, you criticize it. **Yes** **No**

C. Answer the questions in complete sentences.

1. What **response** can you give someone if you don't know the answer to a question?

____

____

2. What are some **characteristics** of a good doctor?

____

____

3. Why is it important to consider different **perspectives** when reading an article or story?

____

____

4. How can you **communicate** in a nice way that you need time alone?

____

____

Name ______________________________

Key Vocabulary Review

A. Read each sentence. Circle the Key Vocabulary word that best fits into each sentence.

1. When you are (**obedient** / **difficult**), you do what you are told.
2. A (**department** / **region**) is part of an organization.
3. An (**employee** / **emergency**) situation should be handled immediately.
4. When you (**search** / **train**) someone, you help them learn something new.
5. A (**job** / **peasant**) is usually poor.
6. A (**shelter** / **blizzard**) usually protects people.
7. You shouldn't go outside during a (**blizzard** / **job**).
8. If you're not finished with a task, you should (**trust** / **continue**) doing it.

B. Use your own words to write what each Key Vocabulary word means. Then write an example for each word.

Word	My Definition	Example
1. **career**		
2. **dependable**		
3. **difficult**		
4. **employee**		
5. **job**		
6. **odor**		
7. **patiently**		
8. **search**		

Name ______________________________

Unit 6 Key Vocabulary

accident	**continue**	**difficult**	**job**	**peasant**	**shelter**
blizzard	**decide**	**emergency**	**obedient**	**region**	**team**
career	**department**	**employee**	**odor**	**search**	**train**
confidence	**dependable**	**experience**	**patiently**	**service**	**trust**

C. Answer the questions in complete sentences.

1. When do you have **confidence**? Why?

____

____

2. Tell about a time when you had to **decide** about something.

____

____

3. Whom do you **trust**? Why?

____

____

4. If you saw a car **accident**, what would you do first? Explain.

____

____

5. What life **experience** do you have? Explain.

____

____

6. What **region** of the world would you like to live in? Why?

____

____

7. What **team** do you want to belong to? Why?

____

____

8. What **service** would you like to provide to your community? Explain.

____

____

Name ______________________________

Mind Map

Use the Mind Map to show your ideas about **bonds** formed through sports.
As you read the selections in this unit, add more effects that you think **bonds** formed through sports can create.

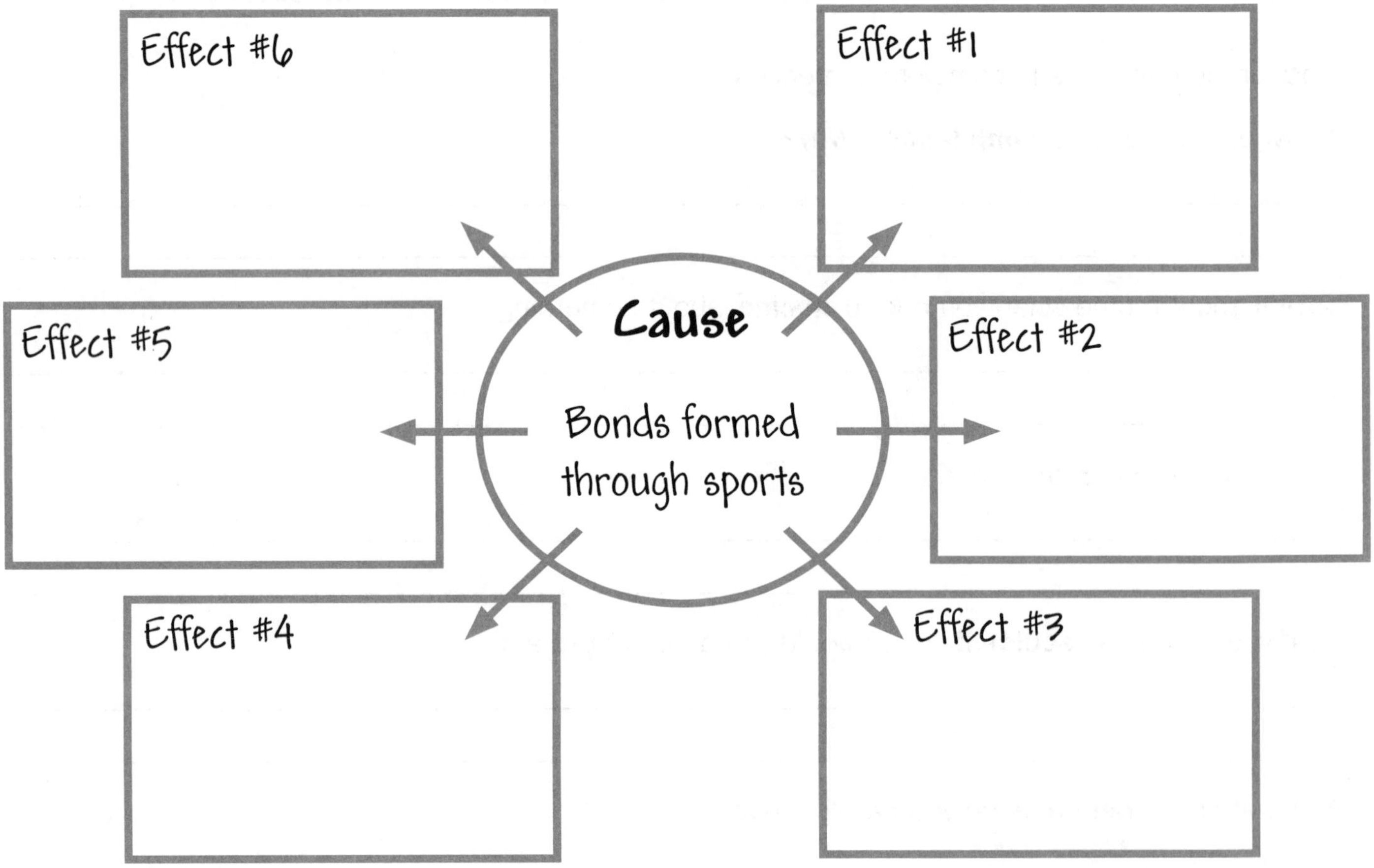

Academic Vocabulary

Think about someone you have a **bond** with. How did you form that **bond**?
Use the word **bond** in your answer.

____

____

____

____

Name ______________________________

Text Structure: Chronological Order

Read the passage. Underline the clues that show the organization.

Born in 1972, Mia Hamm was playing soccer by the time she was five years old. At the age of fifteen, she became the youngest player ever on the United States National Team. She played in games around the world.

After she played college soccer, Hamm felt it was time for a professional women's soccer league in the United States. She became a founding member of the Women's United Soccer Association (WUSA), which had its first game in 2001. In 2000, Hamm played on the U.S. Olympic team that won a silver medal. In 2004, her Olympic team won a gold medal.

Hamm holds many sports records, including the record as the world's all-time leading scorer in soccer. She is now recognized as one of the best soccer players this country has ever seen.

Reread the passage and answer the questions.

1. How is the passage organized? ______________________________

2. Tell how you know. ______________________________

3. What elements tell you that the passage is nonfiction? ______________________________

Academic Vocabulary

Write about a **goal** you or someone you know worked to achieve.

Focus on Vocabulary

Name ______________________________

Use Context Clues: Multiple-Meaning Words

Read the passages. Follow these steps.

1. Look at each underlined multiple-meaning word. Think about the topic of the passage.
2. Look for clues to the word's meaning in surrounding words and sentences.
3. Use a dictionary and the clues to decide which meaning makes sense.

A. Follow the directions above. Write the meaning of each underlined word.

> Do you want to learn how to play basketball? If you do, there are many things you should learn before getting on the court. First, you should understand the basic rules of the game. You should also learn about the different positions teammates can play. Then you should practice drills, such as dribbling, passing, and shooting. Soon, you'll be ready for your first competition.

court ______________________________

positions ______________________________

drills ______________________________

B. Follow the directions above. Write the meaning of each underlined word.

> Can you imagine running, biking, and swimming all in one race? This type of event is called a triathlon. Athletes begin by swimming many laps in a pool. Then, they jump out of the water and hop onto their bikes. After their long bike ride, they run a road race! Every athlete has special gear to use for each part of this very hard race.

laps ______________________________

gear ______________________________

hard ______________________________

Academic Vocabulary

Describe an exciting **situation** you might see at a sporting event. ______________________________

____

____

Build Background

Name ______________________________

Critical Viewing Guide

Take Notes

A. View the video. Take notes on at least three things that you learned.

____

____

____

____

____

____

____

____

Analyze the Video

B. Review your notes to help answer these questions.

1. Write two sentences to explain what was in the video.

____

____

____

2. What was the most interesting thing you learned?

____

____

____

3. Why is there a **bond** between baseball teams and their fans?

____

____

____

____

____

Name ______________________

▲ **Professional** baseball **leagues** **compete** in stadiums like this one.

Play Ball!: Key Vocabulary

A. Study each word. Circle a number to rate how well you know it. Then complete the chart.

Rating Scale	1	2	3
	I have never seen this word before.	I am not sure of the word's meaning.	I know this word and can teach the word's meaning to someone else.

Key Words	Check Understanding	Deepen Understanding
❶ **champion** (**cham**-pē-un) *noun* **Rating:** 1 2 3	☐ a loser ☐ a winner	List examples for the word *champion:* ______
❷ **compete** (kum-**pēt**) *verb* **Rating:** 1 2 3	☐ to participate in a contest ☐ to watch a contest	List examples for the word *compete:* ______
❸ **fan** (**fan**) *noun* **Rating:** 1 2 3	☐ a person who supports a team ☐ a person who competes on a team	List examples for the word *fan:* ______
❹ **league** (**lēg**) *noun* **Rating:** 1 2 3	☐ a competition ☐ a group of teams	List examples for the word *league:* ______

Name ____________________

Did You Know?
Many businesses in the United States used to **segregate** their African American customers from their white customers.

Key Words	Check Understanding	Deepen Understanding
❺ **pastime** (**pas**-tīm) *noun* **Rating: 1 2 3**	☐ an activity for pets ☐ an activity for fun	List examples for the word *pastime:* ____
❻ **popular** (**pop**-yu-lur) *adjective* **Rating: 1 2 3**	☐ frightening for many people ☐ liked by many people	List examples for the word *popular:* ____
❼ **professional** (pru-**fesh**-un-ul) *adjective* **Rating: 1 2 3**	☐ works for money ☐ works for free	List examples for the word *professional:* ____
❽ **segregate** (**se**-gri-gāt) *verb* **Rating: 1 2 3**	☐ put together ☐ keep apart	List examples for the word *segregate:* ____

B. Use at least two of the Key Vocabulary words. Write about a pastime you enjoy.

____

____

____

Prepare to Read

Name ______________________

Text Structure: Chronological Order

A. Look for the sequence of events as you read "Play Ball!" Complete the Time Line by adding the most important dates and events.

1861 — Civil War begins. Both sides play baseball.

____ — ______________________

____ — ______________________

____ — ______________________

____ — ______________________

____ — ______________________

____ — ______________________

____ — ______________________

____ — ______________________

____ — ______________________

____ — ______________________

B. Compare events recorded on your Time Line with the Time Line included at the end of "Play Ball." What kind of events did the author include?

____

____

____

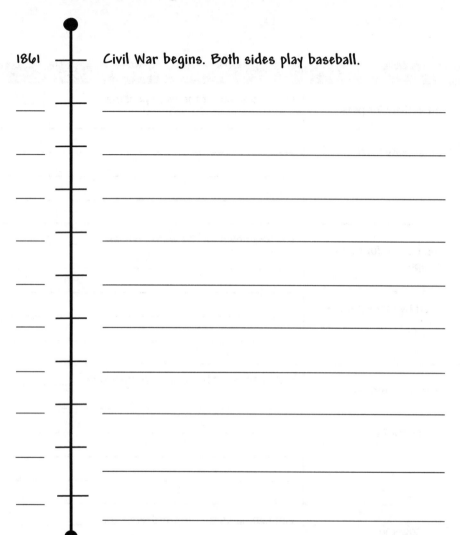

Name ______________________________

Play Ball!

Key Vocabulary	
champions	**pastime**
compete	**popular**
fans	**professional**
league	**segregated**

A. Read the paragraph.
Write a Key Vocabulary word in each blank.
Reread the paragraph to make sure the words make sense.

Baseball is known as "America's ____________." Since baseball began in the 1800s, life in America has changed. Life has changed for the ____________ watching the games and for the players on the field. For example, women began playing baseball during World War II when a separate baseball ____________ for women was formed. Over the years, many excellent African American players have also become ____________ in the record books. However, there was a time when the ____________ teams were ____________. In 1947, Jackie Robinson became the first African American to ____________ in professional baseball. Baseball has been ____________ since the Civil War and it will probably continue to be a favorite sport in the future.

B. Write complete sentences to answer these questions about "Play Ball!"

1. How has baseball changed since the 1800s?

____
____
____
____
____
____

2. How do you feel about America's **pastime**?

____
____
____
____
____

Name ______________________________

Use Multiple-Meaning Words Across Content Areas

Follow the steps below to write the correct definition of each multiple-meaning word.

1. Read each sentence and think about the topic. Look at the underlined word.
2. Look for words and phrases that may be clues to the word's meaning.
3. Use a dictionary and the clues to figure out the meaning that makes the most sense.
4. Write the correct meaning of the word.

1. The coiled wire springs up when released.

springs ______________________________

2. You should be careful while walking on bumpy streets or you may trip.

trip ______________________________

3. The waiter brought us our check so we could pay for lunch.

check ______________________________

4. The carpenter pounds on the nail with the hammer.

pounds ______________________________

5. The office worker found a file containing information about another company.

file ______________________________

6. The road angles to the right in one mile.

angles ______________________________

7. Bread and milk are staples that many people buy weekly.

staples ______________________________

8. The steep grade of the ramp made the toy car roll faster.

grade ______________________________

Name ______________________________

Academic Vocabulary	
bond	sequence
goal	situation
reflect	

Play Ball!: Academic Vocabulary Review

A. Draw a line to match each Academic Vocabulary word with its meaning.

Word	Definition
1. **bond**	the order in which events happen
2. **goal**	to form a close relationship
3. **reflect**	to be a sign of something
4. **sequence**	the context, or where something is placed
5. **situation**	a purpose

B. Use each Academic Vocabulary word in a sentence.

1. **bond** ______________________________

____

2. **goal** ______________________________

____

3. **reflect** ______________________________

____

4. **sequence** ______________________________

____

5. **situation** ______________________________

____

Build Background

Name ______________________________

Critical Viewing Guide

Take Notes

A. View the video. Take notes on at least three things that you learned.

____
____
____
____
____
____
____
____

Analyze the Video

B. Review your notes to help answer these questions.

1. Write two sentences to explain what was in the video.

____
____
____

2. What was the most interesting thing you learned?

____
____
____

3. What did the video tell you about the **bond** between athletes and society?

____
____
____
____

Learn Key Vocabulary

Name ______________________________

Roberto Clemente: Key Vocabulary

A. Study each word. Circle a number to rate how well you know it. Then complete the chart.

Rating Scale	1	2	3
	I have never seen this word before.	I am not sure of the word's meaning.	I know this word and can teach the word's meaning to someone else.

Jesse Owens was such a **mighty** athlete that he had the **honor** of winning four gold medals in one year. ▶

Key Words	Check Understanding	Deepen Understanding
1 celebrate (sel-u-brāt) *verb* Rating: 1 2 3	People **celebrate** special events. Yes No	Tell about something your family celebrates. ________
2 credit (kred-ut) *noun* Rating: 1 2 3	It feels good to get **credit** for something. Yes No	Tell about a time you got credit for something. ______
3 honor (ahn-ur) *noun* Rating: 1 2 3	It is an **honor** to get a bad grade. Yes No	Tell about an honor you can receive at school. ______
4 introduce (in-tru-düs) *verb* Rating: 1 2 3	We **introduce** friends who know each other well. Yes No	Tell about a time someone introduced you. ________

Name ______________________________

> **Did You Know?**
> Both the words **spirit** and *respiratory* come from the same Latin root, *spiritus*, meaning "breath."

Key Words	Check Understanding	Deepen Understanding
5 invitation (in-vu-**tā**-shun) *noun* **Rating: 1 2 3**	If you receive an **invitation** to an event, you will not be allowed in. **Yes** **No**	Tell about an invitation you or someone you know has received. ______
6 mighty (**mī**-tē) *adjective* **Rating: 1 2 3**	All people are **mighty**. **Yes** **No**	Tell about a mighty animal you admire and why. ______
7 respect (ri-**spekt**) *noun* **Rating: 1 2 3**	If you have **respect** for someone, you don't listen to that person. **Yes** **No**	Tell about someone who deserves respect. ______
8 spirit (**spir**-ut) *noun* **Rating: 1 2 3**	To do well in sports, it helps to have team **spirit**. **Yes** **No**	Tell about someone you know who has a fun-loving spirit. ______

B. Use at least two of the Key Vocabulary words. Write about how to show respect for a person.

____

____

____

Prepare to Read

Name ______________________________

Compare Media

A. Reread the last two paragraphs silently. Then listen as a partner reads them aloud. Record your reactions to reading the text and listening to it.

Look Into the Text

His first time at bat, he heard the announcer stumble through his Spanish name: "ROB, uh, ROE . . . BURRT, um let's see, TOE CLUH-MAINT?" It echoed in the near-empty stands. Roberto Clemente was his name, and this is pronounced "Roe-BEAR-toe Cleh-MEN-tay."

As if to introduce himself, Roberto *smacked* the very first pitch. But it went right up the infield and into the shortstop's glove. Still, Roberto ran like lightning--and beat the throw to first base.

The Pittsburgh fans checked their scorecards. Who was this guy, "Roberto Clemente"?

Experience Reading the Text	Experience Listening to the Text Read
As I read the text, the capital letters stood out. They show me how hard the announcer struggled to pronounce it.	Listening to my partner read the text, I can imagine how this sounded over a loudspeaker.
B	**B**

B. Read the following passage to yourself. Then listen to a partner read it aloud. Add your responses to the chart above.

The year was 1971. The Pirates were in the World Series again, playing against the Baltimore Orioles, who were favored to win.

All around America and Puerto Rico, people sat watching on RV as Roberto put on a one-man show. Stealing bases, hitting home runs, playing right field with a *fire* most fans had never seen before.

Finally, *finally*, it could not be denied: Roberto was the greatest all-around baseball player of his time, maybe of all time.

Name ______________________________

Roberto Clemente

Key Vocabulary

celebrated	invitation
credit	mighty
honor	respect
introduced	spirit

A. Read the paragraph.
Write a Key Vocabulary word in each blank.
Reread the paragraph to make sure the words make sense.

When Roberto Clemente accepted the ____________ to join the Pittsburgh Pirates, no one knew what a ____________, larger-than-life force he would become. When Clemente was ____________ to the crowd at his first Pirates game, he didn't get much of a response. It took a long time for Clemente to earn the fans' ____________ and get the full ____________ he deserved. He was awarded one ____________ after another, but what he wanted was acceptance. In 1971, Clemente's hard work paid off, and the fans ____________ his 3,000th hit with a game-stopping cheer. The ____________ of Roberto Clemente lives on in the hearts of his fans.

B. Write complete sentences to answer these questions about "Roberto Clemente."

1. Roberto Clemente died trying to help others. What does this tell you about his personality?

____

____

____

____

____

____

2. Clemente said, "If you don't try as hard as you can, you are wasting your life."
Do you agree or disagree? Why?

____

____

____

____

____

____

Vocabulary Study

Name ______________________________

Interpret Baseball Jargon

Use context clues to help you interpret the meaning of jargon.

1. Look for other words or phrases in the sentence that may be clues to the meaning of each underlined word or phrase.
2. Test the meaning in the sentence to see if it makes sense.
3. Use a dictionary if you need help. Then write the meaning of the underlined word or phrase.

1. The pitcher threw the ball so quickly, the batter whiffed.

   whiffed ______________________________

2. The batter hit a double into left field and then ran to second base.

   double ______________________________

3. The catcher has a bigger glove than the other players on the field.

   glove ______________________________

4. The pitcher did not have good control of his pitches and beaned three batters.

   beaned ______________________________

5. She hit the ball weakly and grounded out.

   grounded out ______________________________

6. The pitcher who started the game was tired, so the closer was brought in to relieve him.

   closer ______________________________

7. The pitcher stood on the mound ready to throw the ball.

   mound ______________________________

8. The batter cleared the bases when he hit the ball far into the outfield and three players scored.

   cleared the bases ______________________________

9. The batter foul-tipped the ball right into the catcher's glove.

   foul-tipped ______________________________

Name ______________________________

Academic Vocabulary	
bond	interpret
evidence	sequence
goal	situation

Roberto Clemente: Academic Vocabulary Review

A. Choose a synonym for each Academic Vocabulary word. Write the word in the chart below.

Word	Choose from These Words			Synonym
1. **bond**	break	connection	tease	
2. **evidence**	share	count	proof	
3. **goal**	aim	grade	job	
4. **interpret**	predict	show	blame	
5. **sequence**	support	group	order	
6. **situation**	room	circumstance	feature	

B. Read each statement. Circle **Yes** or **No** to answer.

1. The people most likely to **bond** are enemies. **Yes** **No**
2. It is best to support facts with **evidence**. **Yes** **No**
3. One **goal** of school is to learn. **Yes** **No**
4. You can **interpret** artwork in more than one way. **Yes** **No**
5. The **sequence** of events happens at the end of a story. **Yes** **No**
6. *Purpose* is another word for **situation**. **Yes** **No**

C. Use the following word pair in a sentence.

interpret **evidence**

____

____

____

Name ____________________

Critical Viewing Guide

Take Notes

A. View the video. Take notes on at least three things that you learned.

____
____
____
____
____
____
____
____

Analyze the Video

B. Review your notes to help answer these questions.

1. Write two sentences to explain what was in the video.

____
____
____

2. What was the most interesting thing you learned?

____
____
____

3. Why is a **bond** between a coach and an athlete important?

____
____
____
____

Learn Key Vocabulary

Name ________________________________

Raymond's Run: Key Vocabulary

▲ **Serious** athletes do **exercises** to build strength and flexibility.

A. Study each word. Circle a number to rate how well you know it. Then complete the chart.

Rating Scale	1	2	3
	I have never seen this word before.	I am not sure of the word's meaning.	I know this word and can teach the word's meaning to someone else.

Key Words	Check Understanding	Deepen Understanding
❶ **congratulate** (kun-**grach**-u-lāt) *verb* **Rating: 1 2 3**	☐ to say "good job" ☐ to say "good luck"	People congratulate you when ________________ .
❷ **energy** (**e**-nur-jē) *noun* **Rating: 1 2 3**	☐ the desire to quit something ☐ the power to do something	It takes a lot of energy to ________________ .
❸ **exercise** (**ek**-sur-sīz) *noun* **Rating: 1 2 3**	☐ an activity that keeps you healthy ☐ a break from walking	Exercise is good for ________________ .
❹ **gesture** (**jes**-chur) *noun* **Rating: 1 2 3**	☐ an action to show how you feel ☐ a strategy to win a game	Some gestures we use to communicate are ________________ .

Name ______________________________

> ***Did You Know?***
> When we clean a window so well that it squeaks, we say that it is "**squeaky** clean."

Key Words	Check Understanding	Deepen Understanding
● **honest** (**ahn**-ust) *adjective* **Rating:** 1 2 3	☐ telling stories ☐ telling the truth	It is important to be honest when ____.
● **interrupt** (in-tu-**rupt**) *verb* **Rating:** 1 2 3	☐ break into an activity ☐ begin an activity	It's OK to interrupt when ____.
● **serious** (**sir**-ē-us) *adjective* **Rating:** 1 2 3	☐ very important ☐ very interesting	I am serious about ____.
● **squeaky** (**skwē**-kē) *adjective* **Rating:** 1 2 3	☐ high-pitched noise ☐ deep, rumbling noise	If a door sounds squeaky, it ____.

B. Use at least two of the Key Vocabulary words. Write about why honesty is a good trait.

____

____

____

Prepare to Read

Name ______________________________

Determine Viewpoint

A. As you read the story, fill in the chart to show how the author develops Squeaky's viewpoint of her brother before, during, and after the race.

Character's Words and Actions	Character's Viewpoint
Minding Raymond is enough work.	Taking care of Raymond is a full-time job.

B. How does Squeaky's viewpoint about Raymond change as the story develops?

____

____

____

____

____

____

____

____

____

Name ______________________________

Raymond's Run

Key Vocabulary	
congratulate	honest
energy	interrupted
exercise	serious
gesture	squeaky

A. Read the paragraph.
Write a Key Vocabulary word in each blank.
Reread the paragraph to make sure the words make sense.

I ____________ the victory celebration to ____________ Hazel Elizabeth Deborah Parker with a nod in her direction. It was a simple ____________, but she knew what I meant. We are both ____________ about running. We both work hard. I remember seeing her one day before the race while she was doing a breathing ____________. She had plenty to say in her ____________ voice about the May Day race. To be completely ____________, I know she's the best. She always has that extra ____________ to carry her to the finish line. I still want to beat her someday!

B. Write complete sentences to answer these questions about "Raymond's Run."

1. How does Gretchen help Squeaky run as fast as she can?

____
____
____
____
____
____

2. How can you tell that Squeaky really respects Gretchen?

____
____
____
____
____
____

Vocabulary Study

Name ______________________________

Use Context Clues: Multiple-Meaning Words

Follow these steps for each item below.

1. Look at each underlined multiple-meaning word. Think about the topic of the sentence.
2. Look for clues to the word's meaning in surrounding words.
3. Use an online or print dictionary and the clues to decide which meaning makes sense.
4. Write the meaning of the word.

1. The camel carried a heavy load through the desert.

   load ______________________________

2. He brushed past the table, but somehow the glass fell over.

   brushed ______________________________

3. After withdrawing some money, his bank account balance was $200.

   balance ______________________________

4. He will press the wrinkles out of his clothes.

   press ______________________________

5. The basketball player was lean, tall, and fast.

   lean ______________________________

6. My mother asked me to strip the bed so she could wash the sheets.

   strip ______________________________

7. The men work in an underground mine that contains coal.

   mine ______________________________

8. Stanley bought a yard of string to tie the package.

   yard ______________________________

9. This issue of the magazine is the best one this year.

   issue ______________________________

Name ______________________________

Academic Vocabulary	
bond	goal
distinguish	situation
evaluate	

Raymond's Run: Academic Vocabulary Review

A. Use your own words to tell what each Academic Vocabulary word means.

Word	My Definition
1. **bond**	
2. **distinguish**	
3. **evaluate**	
4. **goal**	
5. **situation**	

B. Read each sentence. Circle the Academic Vocabulary word that best fits into each sentence.

1. The soldiers were in a dangerous (**situation** / **goal**).
2. Our coach's (**bond** / **goal**) was to give every player a position in the game.
3. I (**evaluated** / **bonded**) each product to choose the best one.
4. It was difficult to (**distinguish** / **evaluate**) between the two twin sisters.

C. Answer the questions in complete sentences.

1. How would you **distinguish** a safe bicycle from an unsafe bicycle?

____

____

____

2. What evidence might show that two people have **bonded** in friendship?

____

____

____

from

PRESSURE Is a Privilege

BY CHRISTINE BRENNAN

1 September 20, 1973. I was just starting my sophomore year in high school in the suburbs of Toledo, Ohio, when Billie Jean King played tennis hustler and **self-declared male chauvinist** Bobby Riggs in the "Battle of the Sexes." That was a very different time in our world. There were only three or four channels to pick from on the television dial, so when a big event was **aired**, the audience was huge and the impact was immediate.

2 Billie Jean's win was an historic moment witnessed by millions of people at the same time. We all watched as history was made. In the course of just a few hours, the perception of women in the United States changed forever.

3 Billie Jean ruled women's tennis in the late 1960s and early 1970s with a demeanor on court that was a startling departure from that of the more **demure** women who preceded her. It was great to see a female athlete who was so aggressive. As a young player myself, I wore a tennis dress that looked like the kind King wore, sleeveless with a zipper up the middle and a big striped collar. I was so enthusiastic about the sport that my family took a small black-and-white television set on vacation to northern Michigan every year so I wouldn't miss Wimbledon.

4 Women's and girls' sports were very different in those days. Although I was **the "tomboy" of** the neighborhood, playing and watching sports with the boys for weeks on end, there were no organized teams for me to join until my freshman year of high school. When I did get to play on a team, my experience was quite different from the boys'. Before field hockey games, we sometimes had to dash out and mow the grass on our field, then add the white lines. (Of course, the football field was in pristine condition three days before the next game.) We didn't have buses for our games and had to cancel softball games if we didn't have enough parents to drive us. And the cheerleaders for the boys' teams had better uniforms than we did.

5 This was the world of girls' and women's sports the day Billie Jean played Bobby. Our gym teacher and the coach of most of our girls' sports teams, Sandy Osterman, had us all worked up in the days leading to the match.

In Other Words

self-declared male chauvinist someone who said he was better than women
aired shown on TV
demure quiet, calm
the "tomboy" of a girl who behaved more like the boys in

Historical Background

Wimbledon is an international tennis tournament near London. It is one of the four major international tennis tournaments played each year. Champions at Wimbledon earn great prestige in the sport of tennis.

In gym class and at our practices, if a boy came by, Miss O yelled out, "We know who's going to win the big match!" There were side bets worth all of a few dollars between Miss O and her male coaching counterparts. "We'll see who wins," she'd say with a mischievous laugh.

6 I finished my homework early to watch the match that night. It was **a carnival atmosphere** when Billie Jean and Bobby came on the court. Years later, when I got to know Billie, she told me that she had been extremely nervous. But I never knew. On television, she looked calm and confident. Before the match started, my father and mother pointed out the subtlety behind Riggs's over-the-top bravado; while he was a blatant male chauvinist, they said he didn't seem to be a terrible guy. "He's acting bad, but in some ways, he's just playing along," my Dad said. "He's the perfect opponent for Billie Jean. He makes you want her to win even more."

"On television, she looked calm and confident."

7 As it was, I already wanted her to win very badly. Billie Jean was one of the very few female sports heroes I had. But there was no reason for me to worry that night. Billie Jean **routed** Bobby, 6-4, 6-3, 6-3, throwing her wood racket into the air as we cheered in the family room. It was the first time I had ever seen a woman beat a man at anything.

8 The next day at our lockers in the high school hallway, I spotted one of the star boy athletes in my grade, an athletic rival of mine who also was a good friend.

9 "We won," I said to him. "The girls won."

10 "Yeah, I know," he said, grimacing and walking away.

11 In the many years since, a few men have told me they thought it was one of the most **over-hyped** sports events of all time. I always disagree. "For you, maybe, but not for me," I tell them. I have talked to Billie Jean quite a few times in interviews, at dinners, at Wimbledon, even at a White House dinner, where, nearly two decades into my career, she pulled me aside to get my thoughts on the women's sports movement. I smiled about that later: there was Billie Jean King asking me for my opinion on the topic that she pioneered and forever changed for the better.

12 No matter when or where we talk, I always make sure to thank Billie Jean for what she did that night in Houston. It is surely overkill by now, but I cannot help it.

13 "What you meant to a fifteen-year-old girl in Toledo, Ohio . . . " I tell her.

14 I never complete the sentence. She knows.

In Other Words

a carnival atmosphere festive and thrilling
routed easily overpowered
over-hyped sensationalized

Name ______________________________

Read for Understanding

A. From what kind of text is this passage taken? How do you know?

____

B. Write a sentence that tells the topic of the selection.

____

Reread and Summarize

C. On **Practice Book** pages 232–234, circle the 3–5 most important words in each section. Make notes about why you chose each word. Why is the word important?

1. Section 1: (paragraphs 1–3)

____

____

2. Section 2: (paragraphs 4–5)

____

____

3. Section 3: (paragraphs 6–10)

____

____

4. Section 4: (paragraphs 11–14)

____

____

D. Use your topic sentence from above and your notes to write a summary of the selection.

____

____

____

Name ______________________

Reread and Analyze

E. Analyze how the author uses chronological order to connect events in the text.

1. Reread in paragraph 4 on **Practice Book** page 232. What time order words does the author use to help you understand the sequence of events? Underline the words and phrases that support your answer. Use evidence from the text to support your answer.

2. In the **Practice Book**, underline other time words and dates that show chronological order. Explain how they help you understand the sequence of events.

F. Analyze how the author uses chronological order to help you understand the setting in which the story takes place.

1. Reread paragraph 1 on **Practice Book** page 232. How does the narrator's use of dates and names help you understand the setting in which this event took place? Underline words and phrases to support your answers. Explain how the text evidence supports your answer.

2. Underline other dates, names, or details on **Practice Book** pages 232–234 that help you understand when this event took place. Explain how these details show chronological order.

Name ______________________

Discuss and Write

G. Synthesize your ideas about how the author connects events through chronological order.

1. With the class, discuss why you think the writer used chronological order to tell about women in sports. List the details you discuss.

____

____

2. Choose one of the details of chronological order that you listed. Write a paragraph to explain why you think the writer used chronological order to tell about women in sports. Use the questions below to organize your thoughts.

   - What is the key event in this selection?
   - Before this event, what was it like for women in sports? Give 2 examples.
   - After this event, how did things change for women in sports? Give 2 examples.
   - How does the chronological order help you understand the memoir's time and place?

____

____

____

____

Connect with GUIDING QUESTION

H. Discuss the Guiding Question: How do sports bring people together?

1. Why does the author call herself a "tomboy"?

____

2. How did the author know people didn't take women in sports seriously when she was in high school?

____

____

3. How did the big match bring people together?

____

____

Unit 7 Review

Name ______________________

Academic Vocabulary	
bond	interpret
distinguish	reflect
evaluate	sequence
evidence	situation
goal	

Academic Vocabulary Review

A. Circle the Academic Vocabulary word that best fits into each sentence.

1. A coach (**evaluates** / **reflects**) players who want to join the team.
2. Judges (**sequence** / **interpret**) laws when they decide a case.
3. A (**goal** / **situation**) helps people aim for success.
4. Polite behavior often (**reflects** / **bonds**) good manners.

B. Rewrite each sentence. Replace the underlined word or words with an Academic Vocabulary word.

1. I planned the <u>order</u> of events for my birthday party.

____

2. It is easy to <u>tell apart</u> the cats since one has a longer tail.

____

3. I share a <u>close relationship</u> with my cousin, despite living in different states.

____

4. The man had overwhelming <u>facts</u> to prove his statements were true.

____

C. Answer the questions in complete sentences.

1. How do your actions **reflect** your mood when you are happy?

____

____

2. What is one of your **goals** for the school year?

____

____

3. Give an example of someone in a serious **situation**. Explain.

____

____

Name ______________________________

Key Vocabulary Review

A. Read each sentence. Circle the Key Vocabulary word that best fits into each sentence.

1. When you have (**credit** / **energy**), you have physical power.
2. When you use your hands to communicate, you (**gesture** / **congratulate**).
3. Dad dislikes it when phone calls (**interrupt** / **introduce**) dinner.
4. Students should be (**squeaky** / **serious**) about learning.
5. Athletes (**compete** / **interrupt**) in sports.
6. Many professional sports teams are grouped into (**leagues** / **fans**).
7. A (**champion** / **professional**) works for money.
8. Sometimes the wheels on a bike can get (**squeaky** / **exercise**).

B. Use your own words to write what each Key Vocabulary word means.
Then write a synonym for each word.

Word	My Definition	Synonym
1. **champion**		
2. **fan**		
3. **honest**		
4. **honor**		
5. **mighty**		
6. **pastime**		
7. **popular**		
8. **segregate**		

Name ______________________________

Unit 7 Key Vocabulary

celebrate	**credit**	**gesture**	**introduce**	**pastime**	**segregate**
champion	**energy**	**honest**	**invitation**	**popular**	**serious**
compete	**exercise**	**honor**	**league**	**professional**	**spirit**
congratulate	**fan**	**interrupt**	**mighty**	**respect**	**squeaky**

C. Answer the questions in complete sentences.

1. Who is someone you'd like to be **introduced** to? Why?

____

____

2. If you could receive an **invitation** to any event in the world, what would it be? Why?

____

____

3. Why would you like people to give you their **respect**?

____

____

4. What **exercises** do you do to stay fit?

____

____

5. What do you give your family **credit** for doing? Explain.

____

____

6. How would you describe your **spirit**? Explain.

____

____

7. What is something you would like to **celebrate**? Explain.

____

____

8. If you could **congratulate** anyone in the world, who would it be? Explain.

____

____

Unit 8 Launch

Name ______________________________

Mind Map

Think of a global warning sign. Write it in the first box of the Mind Map. In the following boxes, write what you can do to change it and how the change can **benefit** the planet.

Global Warnings		Changes		Benefits
	→		→	

Academic Vocabulary

Think about how a clean environment can **benefit** you. What are some ways you can help keep the environment clean? Use the word **benefit** in your answer.

____

____

____

____

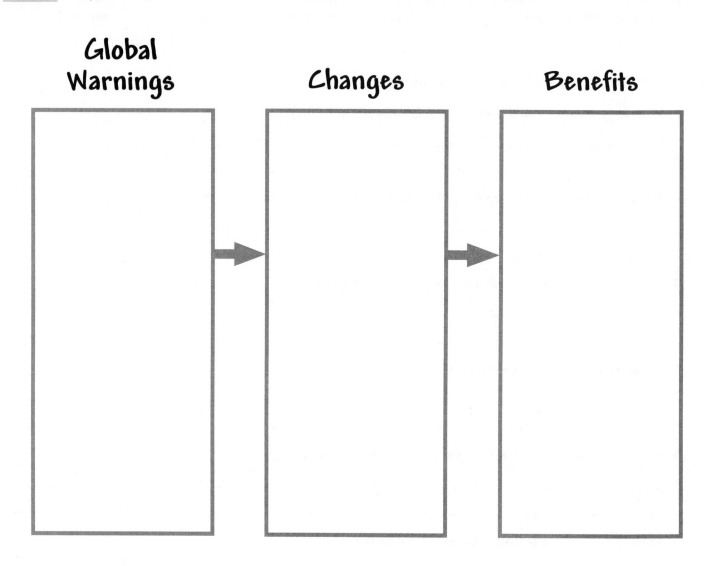

Name ______________________________

Analyze Argument

Read the passage. Underline the writer's **position** on protecting the environment. Look for evidence that supports the argument.

You can help protect the environment by making small changes in your daily life. The next time you shop for school supplies, think about the environment first. Look for products that are made from recycled materials. Recycled materials are materials that were originally used for one purpose but have been reused for a new purpose. You should avoid products that use harmful materials. Look for chlorine-free paper and avoid PVC vinyl, which can contain lead. Both chlorine and lead can harm the environment. You should also try to reduce your waste. Pack your lunch in reusable containers instead of paper and plastic bags. You can make a big difference if you try.

1. What is the writer's position? What is the writer's reasoning for this?

____

____

____

____

2. What evidence supports the writer's argument? Give examples of the support the writer provides for this argument.

____

____

____

____

Academic Vocabulary

Write about your **position** on saving water. Is it a good idea? Would it help the environment? What are some ways to save water?

____

____

____

____

Focus on Vocabulary

Name ______________________________

Use Context Clues: Specialized Vocabulary and Language

Read the passages. Follow these steps to figure out the meaning of each underlined word or phrase.

1. Think about the topic of the text.
2. Reread the sentence and look for clues in the other words.
3. Read the sentences before and after to find more clues.
4. Check your word in a dictionary. Check the denotation against the meaning you determined from the context clues.

A. Follow the directions above. Write the meaning of each underlined word or phrase.

> Ethanol is a fuel made from sugars found in grains, such as corn. Ethanol is considered a renewable resource. Some people feel it is better for the environment than gasoline. Ethanol is nontoxic, so it is safe to handle. If it spills, it breaks down naturally because it is biodegradable. If more people turn their backs on gasoline and use ethanol, we could have a cleaner, safer environment.

nontoxic ______________________________

biodegradable ______________________________

turn their backs on ______________________________

B. Follow the directions above. Write the meaning of each underlined word or explain its connotation.

> Do you know what a carbon footprint is? It's not like the footprints you see on the beach. Scientists use carbon footprints to measure how much pollution an individual person contributes to the environment. Many factors are used to figure out someone's carbon footprint. People who ride their bikes to work instead of driving have smaller carbon footprints. You can reduce your own carbon footprint by using recycled products and walking when you can.

footprint ______________________________

factors ______________________________

contributes ______________________________

Academic Vocabulary

Sometimes you may **associate** a certain smell with a memory. Write about a smell and the memory you **associate** with it. ______________________________

____

Name ______________________

Critical Viewing Guide

Take Notes

A. View the images. Take notes on at least three things that you learned.

Analyze the Images

B. Review your notes to help answer these questions.

1. Write two sentences to explain what was in the images.

2. What was the most interesting thing you learned?

3. How do glaciers and ice caps **benefit** everyone? Explain how taking care of the environment will **benefit** all people.

Learn Key Vocabulary

Name ______________________________

Handle With Care: Key Vocabulary

▲ Litter is an **issue** in many communities. The problem can be solved if people remember to put **waste** where it belongs.

A. Study each word. Circle a number to rate how well you know it. Then complete the chart.

Rating Scale	1	2	3
	I have never seen this word before.	I am not sure of the word's meaning.	I know this word and can teach the word's meaning to someone else.

Key Words	Check Understanding	Deepen Understanding
❶ **damage** (**dam**-ij) *verb* **Rating:** 1 2 3	☐ to cause harm ☐ to give help	List three things that might be damaged by a storm: ______ ______ ______ ______
❷ **issue** (**ish**-ü) *noun* **Rating:** 1 2 3	☐ a problem ☐ a solution	List three issues in your community: ______ ______ ______ ______ ______
❸ **prevent** (pri-**vent**) *verb* **Rating:** 1 2 3	☐ to watch something ☐ to stop something	List three things that we should try to prevent: ______ ______ ______ ______ ______
❹ **protect** (prō-**tekt**) *verb* **Rating:** 1 2 3	☐ to give something away ☐ to keep something safe	List three things we should protect: ______ ______ ______ ______ ______

Name ______________________________

Recycling is one way to **protect** the environment. ▶

Key Words	Check Understanding	Deepen Understanding
5 recycle (rē-sī-kul) *verb* Rating: 1 2 3	☐ use up ☐ use again	List three things you can recycle: ______
6 resource (rē-sors) *noun* Rating: 1 2 3	☐ something you can use ☐ something you don't want	List three examples of Earth's resources: ______
7 source (sors) *noun* Rating: 1 2 3	☐ where something comes from ☐ where something goes	List three sources of water: ______
8 waste (wāst) *noun* Rating: 1 2 3	☐ something you throw away ☐ something you keep	List three examples of waste: ______

B. Use at least two of the Key Vocabulary words. Write about an issue that is important to you.

____

____

____

Prepare to Read

Name ______________________________

Analyze Argument and Reasons

A. As you read, "Handle with Care," look for the kinds of appeals made by the author. Complete the Three-Column Chart.

Kind of Appeal	Example	My Evaluation
appeal to emotion and logic	Human activities such as plowing fields, mining, and building highways can destroy the land.	

Name ______________________________

Handle with Care

Key Vocabulary

damage	recycle
issue	resources
prevent	source
protect	waste

A. Read the paragraph.
Write a Key Vocabulary word in each blank.
Reread the paragraph to make sure the words make sense.

We have only one Earth. To protect Earth, we must conserve our valuable natural ____________ . This is an important ____________ for each of us. If we don't ____________ the environment and ____________ things like pollution and global warming, we might do permanent ____________ to Earth. Humans are the greatest ____________ of trouble. We all need to reduce the ____________ we produce, reuse the products we make, and ____________ as much as we can.

B. Write complete sentences to answer these questions about "Handle with Care."

1. How could you set up a center to **recycle** paper, cans, and bottles at your school?

____

____

____

____

____

____

2. How can laws help **prevent** pollution and **protect** the environment?

____

____

____

____

____

____

____

____

Name ______________________________

Understand Denotation and Connotation

Follow the steps below to figure out the meaning of each word.

1. Look up the denotations, or dictionary definitions, of the underlined words. Write the definition.
2. Use the context to identify the words' connotations and write them down if different.
3. Write whether the underlined words have a positive or negative connotation.

1. Cars that run on gasoline can spew toxic fumes into the air.

spew ______________________________

Positive or Negative? ______________________________

2. Some people oppose drilling for oil, because they believe it is detrimental to the environment.

detrimental ______________________________

Positive or Negative? ______________________________

3. Scientists have figured out how to harness wind to produce energy.

harness ______________________________

Positive or Negative? ______________________________

4. Southern California, with its plentiful sunshine, is a prime location for using solar power.

prime ______________________________

Positive or Negative? ______________________________

5. Pollutants that are dumped into a lake may produce contaminated drinking water.

contaminated ______________________________

Positive or Negative? ______________________________

6. It is possible to help the environment just by walking to school instead of taking the bus.

possible ______________________________

Positive or Negative? ______________________________

7. If you turn off lights as you leave a room, you will conserve electricity.

conserve ______________________________

Positive or Negative? ______________________________

Name ______________________________

Academic Vocabulary	
appeal	logical
associate	position
benefit	

Handle with Care: Academic Vocabulary Review

A. Write the Academic Vocabulary words next to their definitions.

Definition	Word
1. to connect or relate two things	
2. believable; reasonable	
3. to gain good from	
4. what you think about an issue	
5. a strong request	

B. Complete the sentences.

1. If I could make an **appeal** to the school librarian, I would ______________________________
____.

2. A tradition I **associate** with the holidays is ______________________________
____.

3. One **benefit** of exercise is ______________________________
____.

4. My **position** on an important issue that affects my school is ______________________________
____.

5. If you are doing a project on global warming, it is **logical** to ______________________________
____.

Name ______________________________

Critical Viewing Guide

Take Notes

A. View the video. Take notes on at least three things that you learned.

____

____

____

____

____

____

____

____

Analyze the Video

B. Review your notes to help answer these questions.

1. Write two sentences to explain what was in the video.

____

____

____

2. What was the most interesting thing you learned?

____

____

____

3. What are some things you can do to **benefit** the environment? Use the word *benefit* in your answer.

____

____

____

____

Learn Key Vocabulary

Name ____________________________

▲ A big chunk of the **glacier** breaks off as the ice **melts**.

Melting Away: Key Vocabulary

A. Study each word. Circle a number to rate how well you know it. Then complete the chart.

Rating Scale	1	2	3
	I have never seen this word before.	I am not sure of the word's meaning.	I know this word and can teach the word's meaning to someone else.

Key Words	Check Understanding	Deepen Understanding
❶ **area** (air-ē-u) *noun* **Rating:** 1 2 3	An **area** is part of a year. **Yes** **No**	An area in my community is ____________________.
❷ **atmosphere** (at-mu-sfir) *noun* **Rating:** 1 2 3	Our **atmosphere** is made of ice. **Yes** **No**	Our atmosphere is in danger because ____________________.
❸ **feature** (fē-chur) *noun* **Rating:** 1 2 3	A **feature** is something that stands out. **Yes** **No**	My best feature is my ____________________.
❹ **glacier** (glā-shur) *noun* **Rating:** 1 2 3	A **glacier** is made of air. **Yes** **No**	You might see a glacier ____________________.

Name ______________________

Did You Know?
Reefs are endangered. The Earth has lost 10% of its **reefs** because of global warming.

Key Words	Check Understanding	Deepen Understanding
❺ **melt** (melt) *verb* **Rating: 1 2 3**	A solid becomes a liquid when it **melts**. **Yes** **No**	Ice cream melts when ______________________.
❻ **reef** (rēf) *noun* **Rating: 1 2 3**	**Reefs** are in the mountains. **Yes** **No**	Some things you might see on a reef are ______________________.
❼ **soil** (soi-ul) *noun* **Rating: 1 2 3**	**Soil** covers the roots of trees and plants. **Yes** **No**	Some things you can see in soil are ______________________.
❽ **temperature** (tem-pur-u-chur) *noun* **Rating: 1 2 3**	You measure **temperature** to find the length of something. **Yes** **No**	I like when the outside temperature is ______________ because ______________________.

B. Use at least two of the Key Vocabulary words. Write about your favorite season.

____

____

____

Prepare to Read

Name ______________________________

Analyze Argument and Evidence

As you read "Melting Away," identify claims made by the author. Use the **Evidence Chart** to record and evaluate the **evidence** for each claim.

Claim: The once mighty Grinnell Glacier could vanish completely.

Text Evidence	My Evaluation
It is much smaller than it was in 1938.	This fact can be checked and is supported by photos from a reliable source.

Claim: ______________________________

Text Evidence	My Evaluation

Claim: ______________________________

Text Evidence	My Evaluation

Name ______________________________

Melting Away

Key Vocabulary	
area	melt
atmosphere	reefs
feature	soil
glaciers	temperature

A. Read the paragraph.
Write a Key Vocabulary word in each blank.
Reread the paragraph to make sure the words make sense.

Every ____________ of Earth is affected by global warming. As Earth's ____________ rises, heat becomes trapped in the ____________. This causes ____________ to ____________, uncovering rocks and ____________. Delicate coral ____________ are affected, too. As ocean waters become warmer, the coral's bright colors, a distinctive ____________ of the reefs, begin to fade to white.

B. Write complete sentences to answer these questions about "Melting Away."

1. Why is it important to prevent global warming?

____

____

____

____

____

____

2. How could you organize a tree-planting project in your community?

____

____

____

____

____

____

____

____

Vocabulary Study

Name ______________________________

Understand Technical Language

Follow the steps below to figure out the meaning of the technical language.

1. Look for clues to the meaning of the underlined technical language.
2. If you still do not have enough information, check a dictionary.
3. Write the meaning of the underlined technical language.

1. The epicenter of the earthquake was near San Francisco, where the damage was the worst.

   epicenter ______________________________

2. In very windy places, scientists use wind turbines to turn wind into energy.

   wind turbines ______________________________

3. The directions say to use lightbulbs that are no more than 75 watts.

   watts ______________________________

4. Ethanol is created by using sugar to make fuel.

   ethanol ______________________________

5. A tornado that measures EF1 on the Enhanced Fujita scale will probably cause only minor damage.

   Enhanced Fujita scale ______________________________

6. Earth is made up of large plates that are constantly moving. When these plates rub up against each other, an earthquake occurs.

   plates ______________________________

7. The defendant pleaded not guilty to the charges against him.

   charges ______________________________

8. Oil must be refined in order to make gasoline.

   refined ______________________________

9. The nurse slid the boy's leg under an x-ray machine to see if the bone was broken.

   x-ray machine ______________________________

Name ______________________________

Key Vocabulary

appeal	logical
associate	position
benefit	process
evidence	unique

Melting Away: Academic Vocabulary Review

A. Use your own words to tell what each Academic Vocabulary word means.

Word	My Definition
1. **associate**	
2. **benefit**	
3. **evidence**	
4. **logical**	
5. **position**	
6. **appeal**	
7. **unique**	

B. Rewrite each sentence. Replace the underlined words with an Academic Vocabulary word.

1. We made a strong request for the rules to be changed.

____

2. I relate the smell of salty air with the sea.

____

3. My viewpoint on recycling is based on plenty of facts.

____

4. It was reasonable for us to be tired after the long, busy week.

____

5. Her ideas about ways to reduce global warming are unusual.

____

Name ________________________________

Critical Viewing Guide

Take Notes

A. View the video. Take notes on at least three things that you learned.

____

____

____

____

____

____

____

____

Analyze the Video

B. Review your notes to help answer these questions.

1. Write two sentences to explain what was in the video.

____

____

____

2. What was the most interesting thing you learned?

____

____

____

3. Myths and stories sometimes tell people how their actions can **benefit** or harm Earth. Why do these myths **benefit** a culture?

____

____

____

____

Name ______________________________

The Legend of the Yakwawiak: Key Vocabulary

A. Study each word. Circle a number to rate how well you know it. Then complete the chart.

Rating Scale	1	2	3
	I have never seen this word before.	I am not sure of the word's meaning.	I know this word and can teach the word's meaning to someone else.

▲ Many legends are about a **battle** between a **human** and a **monster**.

Key Words	Check Understanding	Deepen Understanding
❶ **battle** (**bat**-ul) *noun* **Rating: 1 2 3**	A **battle** is an animal. **Yes** **No**	Write a sentence using *battle* and another Key Vocabulary word. ______
❷ **council** (**kown**-sul) *noun* **Rating: 1 2 3**	A **council** is an individual. **Yes** **No**	Write a sentence using *council* and another Key Vocabulary word. ______
❸ **creature** (**krē**-chur) *noun* **Rating: 1 2 3**	You can see **creatures** at the zoo. **Yes** **No**	Write a sentence using *creature* and another Key Vocabulary word. ______
❹ **destroy** (di-**stroi**) *verb* **Rating: 1 2 3**	When you **destroy** something, you fix it. **Yes** **No**	Write a sentence using *destroy* and another Key Vocabulary word. ______

Name ______________________________

Did You Know?

One of the most **powerful** women in the world is Keyla Ortiz of Peru. She won the Strong Woman Contest in 2007.

Key Words	Check Understanding	Deepen Understanding
5 gather (**gath**-ur) *verb* **Rating: 1 2 3**	When you **gather** something, you spread it out. **Yes No**	Write a sentence using *gather* and another Key Vocabulary word. ______
6 human (**hyū**-man) *adjective, noun* **Rating: 1 2 3**	People are **human**. **Yes No**	Write a sentence using *human* and another Key Vocabulary word. ______
7 monster (**mahn**-stur) *noun* **Rating: 1 2 3**	**Monsters** are gentle creatures. **Yes No**	Write a sentence using *monster* and another Key Vocabulary word. ______
8 powerful (**pau**-ur-ful) *adjective* **Rating: 1 2 3**	A **powerful** person has strength. **Yes No**	Write a sentence using *powerful* and another Key Vocabulary word. ______

B. Use at least two of the Key Vocabulary words. Write about a monster movie you have seen or heard about.

____

____

____

Prepare to Read

Name ___________________________

Analyze Theme

Read the theme at the top of the chart. As you read "The Legend of the Yakwawiak," summarize the main events of the story in the first column. Then tell how the author uses each of those events to develop the story's theme. Complete the Theme Development Chart as you read the selection.

Theme: All beings on earth should live together in harmony.

What Happens	How This Develops the Theme
The Yakwawiak hurl down trees, muddy springs, and trample everything; people and animals hide in caves to escape.	Shows how the Yakwawiak's destructive behavior hurts others

Selection Review

Name ______________________________

The Legend of the Yakwawiak

Key Vocabulary

battle	**gathered**
council	**humans**
creatures	**monsters**
destroyed	**powerful**

A. Read the paragraph.
Write a Key Vocabulary word in each blank.
Reread the paragraph to make sure the words make sense.

The Yakwawiak were among the largest ____________ that roamed Earth. They did not respect other living things. With the help of the Creator, ____________ and all of the other beings ____________ for a meeting. At the ____________, everyone agreed that the scary ____________ must be ____________. A huge war, or ____________, took place. Many animals that were just as ____________ as the Yakwawiak were killed. Many brave fighters also lost their lives while making the world a safer place.

B. Write complete sentences to answer these questions about "The Legend of the Yakwawiak."

1. Describe the **monsters** in "The Legend of the Yakwawiak."

____

____

____

____

____

____

2. How do you think the surviving Yakwawiak will act now that it is alone?

____

____

____

____

____

____

____

Vocabulary Study

Name ______________________

Understand Figurative Language

Follow the steps below to figure out the figurative language.

1. Use context clues to figure out the meaning of each example of figurative language.
2. Write the meaning of each underlined phrase.

1. We ran as if our feet were on fire.

____

2. The full moon loomed over the horizon.

____

3. Her heart felt as if it were shattered glass.

____

4. Her silken hair glowed in the moonlight.

____

5. Memories from my past flooded my mind.

____

6. The baby cried as if there were no tomorrow.

____

7. The music was booming through my body.

____

8. The boy lunged across the lawn to catch the frisbee.

______________________.

9. When my mother sings, it brings me back to my childhood.

______________________.

Name ______________________________

Academic Vocabulary	
associate	position
benefit	symbol
definition	

The Legend of the Yakwawiak
Academic Vocabulary Review

A. Draw a line to match each Academic Vocabulary word with its meaning.

Word	Definition
1. **associate**	thoughts or beliefs about an issue
2. **benefit**	to improve from something
3. **definition**	to relate ideas
4. **position**	an object that represents something else
5. **symbol**	the meaning of a word

B. Circle the word that best fits into each sentence.

1. Lions are a (**symbol** / **definition**) of bravery in some cultures.
2. Students (**associate** / **benefit**) from the efforts of a dedicated teacher.
3. Homophones are words that sound the same but have different (**positions** / **definitions**).
4. I have not chosen a (**position** / **symbol**) on whether it is right to censor the media.
5. Most people (**associate** / **benefit**) a ringing sound with the telephone.

C. Answer the question in complete sentences.

How can a person **benefit** from learning about new cultures?

____

____

____

____

from GRAND CANYON SPEECH by Theodore Roosevelt

Arizona, May 6, 1903

1 In the Grand Canyon, Arizona has a natural wonder which, so far as I know, is **in kind absolutely unparalleled** throughout the rest of the world. I want to ask you to do one thing in connection with it in your own interest and in the interest of the country—to keep this great wonder of nature as it now is.

2 I was delighted to learn of the wisdom of the Santa Fe railroad people in deciding not to build their hotel on the brink of the canyon. I hope you will not have a building of any kind, not a summer cottage, a hotel, or anything else, to **mar the wonderful grandeur, the sublimity,** the great loneliness and beauty of the canyon. Leave it as it is. You cannot improve on it. The ages have been at work on it, and man can only mar it.

3 What you can do is to keep it for your children, your children's children, and for all who come after you, as one of the great sights which every American if he can travel at all should see. We have gotten past the stage, my fellow citizens, when we are to be **pardoned** if we treat any part of our country as something to be skinned for two or three years for the use of the present generation, whether it is the forest, the water, the scenery.

4 Whatever it is, handle it so that your children's children will get the benefit of it. If you deal with irrigation, apply it under circumstances that will make it of benefit, not to the speculator who hopes to get profit out of it for two or three years, but handle it so that it will be of use to the home-maker, to the man who comes to live here, and to have his children stay after him. Keep the forests in the same way.

5 Preserve the forests by use; preserve them for the ranchman and the stockman, for the people of the Territory, for the people of the region **round about.** Preserve them for that use, but use them so that they will not be squandered, that they will not be wasted, so that they will be of benefit to the Arizona of 1953 as well as the Arizona of 1903.

Historical Background
Before they became states, many regions of the Western U.S. were Territories. Land was given away or sold for very little.

In Other Words
in kind absolutely unparalleled unique
mar the wonderful grandeur, the sublimity mess up the wonderful, awesomeness
pardoned forgiven
round about around there

"...keep this
great wonder of
NATURE
as it is now..."

Name ______________________________

Read for Understanding

A. What kind of text is this? How do you know?

____

____

B. Write a sentence that tells the topic of the selection.

____

Reread and Summarize

C. On **Practice Book** pages 264–265, circle the 3–5 most important words in each section. Make notes about why you chose each word. Why is the word important?

1. Section 1: (paragraphs 1–2)

____

____

2. Section 2: (paragraphs 3–4)

____

____

3. Section 3: (paragraph 5)

____

____

D. Use your topic sentence from above and your notes to write a summary of the selection.

____

____

____

Name ____________________

Reread and Analyze

E. Analyze how the author uses convincing reasons and evidence to support his position an argument.

1. Reread paragraphs 1–2 on **Practice Book** page 264. What is Theodore Roosevelt's position on the Grand Canyon? What does Roosevelt say to support his position? Underline words and phrases to support your answers. Use evidence from the text to support your answer.

2. Underline another reason on **Practice Book** pages 264–265 that Theodore Roosevelt presents for his position on the Grand Canyon. Explain what it shows about his position on this issue.

F. Analyze how the author chooses compelling words to persuade others to support his position on an issue.

1. Reread paragraph 2 on **Practice Book** page 264. What words does the writer use to appeal to others and persuade others to his position? Underline the words and phrases that support your answer. Use evidence from the text to support your answer.

2. In the **Practice Book**, underline other words and phrases the author uses to persuade others to support his position on this issue.

Name ______________________________

Discuss and Write

G. Synthesize your ideas about how the author presents an argument.

1. With the class, discuss how the writer uses reasons to support his position. List the facts, opinions, or personal experience you discuss.

____

____

____

2. Choose one of arguments that you listed. Write a paragraph about how the writer supported his position. Use the questions below to organize your thoughts.
   - What is the author's position?
   - What reasons and evidence support this position? Give 2 examples.
   - What compelling words and phrases support this position? Give 2 examples.

____

____

____

____

Connect with GUIDING QUESTION

H. Discuss the Guiding Question: How can changing our ways benefit the Earth?

1. Why do you think the writer felt that he needed to write this speech?

____

____

2. Who does this speech address? How do you know?

____

____

3. In what ways is the argument in this speech as important today as it was in 1903?

____

____

Unit 8 Review

Name ______________________________

Academic Vocabulary		
appeal	definition	position
associate	evidence	symbol
benefit	logical	unique

Academic Vocabulary Review

A. Use four Academic Vocabulary words to complete the paragraph.

There is ______________, or proof, that learning vocabulary is not always an easy process. Many words have more than one ______________. You must choose the most ______________ meaning, or the meaning that makes the most sense. It will ______________ you most to understand the context of the word.

B. Read each statement. Circle **Yes** or **No** to answer.

1. When you make an **appeal**, you ask for something. **Yes** **No**
2. Opinions are the most reliable type of **evidence**. **Yes** **No**
3. A **logical** choice is the one that makes no sense. **Yes** **No**
4. It is best to avoid things that **benefit** you. **Yes** **No**
5. Two **unique** paintings will look different from each other. **Yes** **No**

C. Answer the questions in complete sentences.

1. What is **unique** about your culture?

____

____

____

2. What is your **position** on recycling? Explain.

____

____

3. What is one **symbol** that you **associate** with the United States?

____

____

____

Name ____________________

Key Vocabulary Review

A. Read each sentence. Circle the Key Vocabulary word that best fits into each sentence.

1. All people are (**human** / **powerful**).
2. When you (**prevent** / **damage**) something, you cause it harm.
3. A big (**issue** / **resource**) is global warming.
4. Wind is a (**source** / **temperature**) of energy.
5. Look up at the sky if you want to see the (**atmosphere** / **soil**).
6. (**Glaciers** / **Reefs**) can make mountains.
7. If you don't eat your ice cream quickly on a warm day, it can (**damage** / **melt**).
8. Plants need (**soil** / **temperature**) to grow.

B. Use your own words to write what each Key Vocabulary word means. Then write a synonym for each word.

Word	My Definition	Synonym
1. **battle**		
2. **destroy**		
3. **feature**		
4. **gather**		
5. **powerful**		
6. **prevent**		
7. **protect**		
8. **waste**		

Name ______________________________

Unit 8 Key Vocabulary

area	creature	gather	melt	protect	soil
atmosphere	damage	glacier	monster	recycle	source
battle	destroy	human	powerful	reef	temperature
council	feature	issue	prevent	resource	waste

C. Answer the questions in complete sentences.

1. If you could create a **monster**, what would it look like and what would it do?

____

____

2. Imagine you've been asked to create a **recycling** campaign. Write about your campaign.

____

____

3. What do you think is Earth's most important **resource**? Explain.

____

____

4. Describe your favorite **area** in your community.

____

____

5. Imagine you have been asked to help save an endangered **reef**. What will you do to **protect** it?

____

____

6. What do you think is the ideal outdoor **temperature**? Why?

____

____

7. Whom do you think would be important to include on a **council** to address school **issues**?

____

____

8. Describe a **creature** that you find interesting.

____

____

Grammar Practice

Name ______________________

1 Are All Sentences the Same?

No. They Have Different Purposes.

Four Kinds of Sentences

1. Make a **statement** to tell something. End with a period.
   I am upset about my friend Bernie.
2. Ask a **question** to find out something. End with a question mark.
   Would you like to talk about it?
3. Use an **exclamation** to express a strong feeling. End with an exclamation point.
   Yes, I need help!
4. Give a **command** to tell someone what to do. End with a period.
   Stop worrying. Tell me about it. Don't leave anything out.

Start every sentence with a capital letter.

Try It

A. Read each sentence. Decide what kind of sentence it is. Write statement, question, exclamation, or command on the line.

1. What did Bernie do? question
2. He cheated on the math test. ______________
3. Don't tell anyone. ______________
4. I can't believe it! ______________

B. Change each sentence to the kind in parentheses. Use correct punctuation.

5. Bernie looked at another student's paper. **(question)** Did Bernie look at another student's paper?
6. Did you tell Mrs. Lynch about it? **(command)** ______________

Write It

C. Answer the questions about a difficult choice you have made. Use at least two different kinds of sentences in your responses. Use correct punctuation.

7. What kind of choice did you make? I had to choose ______________________________

______________________________.

8. Why was it difficult to make your choice? ______________________________

____

9. Did anyone help you make that choice? ______________________________

____

D. (10–14) Write at least five sentences that tell more about your choice. Vary the kinds of sentences in your response.

____

____

____

____

____

Edit It

E. (15–20) Edit the journal entry. Fix the six mistakes in punctuation. The first is done for you.

December 10

Our school does not do enough recycling

The cafeteria uses foam cups Why don't they use paper cups and plates I want to help the environment I'm just so frustrated Should I complain to the principal

Proofreader's Marks

Add a period:

I am happy with my choices.

Add an exclamation point:

What a tough decision!

Add a question mark:

How did you make your choice?

See all Proofreader's Marks on page xi.

Name ______________________________

2 How Many Ways Can You Ask a Question?

There Are Many Ways.

- If you want a "yes" or "no" answer, start a question with words such as **Is**, **Are**, or **Can**.

  Are you reading this book? **(yes)**

- If you want specific information, start with question words such as **Who**, **What**, **When**, **Where**, **Why**, and **How**.

Question Word	Asks About	Question	Answer
Who?	A person	Who wrote that book?	A famous author wrote it.
What?	A thing	What type of book is it?	It is a mystery novel.
When?	A time	When did you start reading it?	I started it yesterday.
Where?	A place	Where does it take place?	It takes place in a haunted mansion.

Try It

A. Write the correct question word to complete each question.

1. ______________ do you like this author?
Why/Where

2. ______________ other books did she write?
How/What

3. ______________ did she write her first book?
When/Who

4. ______________ else would like this author?
Who/Where

5. ______________ is your favorite place to read?
Where/When

Write It

B. Write a question for each kind of specific information about a friend's reading habits.

6. Ask about a time: ________________ do you like to ______________________
____?

7. Ask about a place: ____
____

8. Ask about a person: ____
____

9. Ask about a reason: ____
____

Edit It

C. (10–13) Edit the journal entry. Fix the four mistakes.

Saturday, April 3

Why do I love Saturdays? I go to the library that day. "Where book would you like today?" the librarian asks me. "I want something scary!" I reply. "When you sure?" she asks. "Yes, I am!" I say every week. "Who can you read so many horror stories?" she asks. I tell her I don't scare easily! Why wants to read with me?

Proofreader's Marks

Change text:

~~Who~~ Why do you like mystery stories?

See all Proofreader's Marks on page xi.

Name ______________________________

3 What Do You Need for a Sentence?

A Subject and a Predicate

A complete sentence has two parts: the **subject** and the **predicate**.

subject **predicate**

Kim plays baseball.

To find the parts, in most sentences, ask yourself:

1. Whom or what is the sentence about? Your answer is the **subject**.
2. What does the subject do? Your answer is the **predicate**.

Sentence	Whom or What?	What Does the Subject Do?
I joined the team.	I	joined the team
The coach gives me advice.	The coach	gives me advice

Try It

A. Match each subject with a predicate to make a complete sentence.

1. Our team	is one of the best teams around.
2. Mr. Harrison	try to beat us.
3. All of his players	coaches our team well.
4. He	asks us to do our best.
5. Other teams	work hard during practice.
6. The crowds	win a lot of games!
7. We	cheer when we play.
8. Strong effort	is necessary on our team.

B. Choose a subject and a predicate from each column to make four sentences. The first one is done for you. Write the sentences on the lines. Use the words only once.

Subject	Predicate
One player	goes to every practice now.
Coach Harrison	gave Harry one more chance.
The team	agreed with that decision.
Harry	missed practice often.

9. One player missed practice often.

10. ____________________

11. ____________________

12. ____________________

Write It

C. Imagine that your best friend is on a rival baseball team. When your team plays against his team, what do you do? Make sure you use a subject and predicate in each sentence.

13. Do you hope he makes mistakes so your team can win? I hope he ____________________.

14. Is it hard to play against your friend? Why or why not? ____________________

15. How do you think your friend feels about the rivalry? ____________________

D. (16–20) Write at least five sentences that tell more about how you would handle the situation. Use subjects and predicates correctly.

____

Name ______________________________

4 What's a Plural Noun?

A Word That Names More Than One Thing

One	More Than One
A **singular noun** names one thing.	A **plural noun** names more than one thing.

Use these spelling rules to form plural nouns.

1. To make most nouns plural, just add **-s**.
2. If the noun ends in **s**, **z**, **sh**, **ch**, or **x**, add **-es**.

One	More Than One
choice	**choices**
fox	**foxes**
dress	**dresses**
beach	**beaches**
flash	**flashes**

Try It

A. **(1–4) Read these nouns: classes, box, plans, inch. Which nouns are singular and which are plural? Put each noun in the correct column. Then add its other form. The first one is done for you.**

Singular Nouns (one)	Plural Nouns (more than one)
class	classes

B. **Write the plural form of the singular noun in parentheses.**

5. Good ______________ can't always be made alone. **(decision)**

6. Some ______________ are swayed by their peers. **(student)**

7. It's important to remember your parents' ______________. **(wish)**

Write It

C. Answer the questions about how you make decisions. Use singular and plural nouns in your response.

8. Whom do you listen to most when you are making a decision?

I listen to ______________________________.

9. Do you feel pressure to be like your friends? ______________________________

10. Do people you see on television or in movies sway you?

____

____

D. (11–14) Write at least four sentences that tell more about who or what affects your choices. Use at least two singular nouns and two plural nouns in your response.

____

____

____

Edit It

E. (15–20) Edit the journal entry. Fix the six mistakes.

I have some choices to make at school this year. There are so many clubes I could join! A lot of my friendss are joining the drama club. They will have to go to three practice a week. Some of my friends are skipping lunchs to go to club meetings. My parents remind me that classess have to come before clubs. I will respect their wishs.

Proofreader's Marks

Change text: Think about your ~~choies~~ choices.

See all Proofreader's Marks on page xi.

Name ______________________

5 Can You Just Add *-s* or *-es* to Make a Noun Plural?

Not Always

One	More Than One
A **singular noun** names one thing.	A **plural noun** names more than one thing.

Use these spelling rules to form plural nouns.

1. If the noun ends in **y** after a consonant, change the **y** to i and add **-es**.
2. If the noun ends in **y** after a vowel, just add -s.
3. Some nouns have special plural forms.

One	More Than One
story	**stories**
boy	**boys**
woman	**women**
person	**people**
child	**children**

Try It

A. (1–4) Read these nouns: **mummies**, **fly**, **toys**, **woman**. Which nouns are singular and which are plural? Put each in the correct column. Then add its other form.

Singular Nouns (one)	Plural Nouns (more than one)

B. Write the plural form of the singular noun in parentheses.

5. Lots of fun ______________ happen after school. **(activity)**
6. The girls and ______________ at my school have a lot to choose from. **(boy)**
7. With so many choices, ______________ are never bored. **(child)**

Write It

C. **Answer the questions about what you do after school. Use the correct form of plural nouns.**

8. What is your favorite thing to do after school? After school, I like to ________________
____.

9. What do some of your friends do after school? They ________________
____.

10. What are some other ways students spend their time after school?
____
____

D. **(11–14) Now, write at least four sentences about what you like to do after school. Use at least two singular nouns and two plural nouns in your response.**

____
____
____

Edit It

E. **(15–20) Edit the journal entry. Fix the six mistakes with nouns.**

September 15
Tomorrow I sign up for some after-school activity. A class for babysitters meets on all four Thursday this month. I will learn to take care of young child. Then I can help some family on my block. I could spend my time in other way. But I like to help person.

Proofreader's Marks

Change text:
Babies
Babys need lots of care.

See all Proofreader's Marks on page xi.

Name ____________________

6 What Is a Sentence About?

The Subject

The **complete subject** can be one word or several words. Zoom in on the most important word. Is it a noun? A **noun** is the name of a person, place, thing, or idea.

1. My **neighborhood** had trouble with telephone service last night.
2. A **storm** damaged the telephone lines.
3. The **wind** knocked down some trees.
4. My **friend** tried to call me.
5. **Liz** didn't know the phone didn't work.
6. "The **problem** was the phone," I explained to her.

Nouns in the Subject	
Person	friend Liz
Place	neighborhood
Thing	storm wind
Idea	problem

Try It

A. Add a noun to complete the subject of the sentence.

1–2. My best friend lives next door. His ______ is Sidney.

3. Our funniest ______ is the day we met.

4. His ______ moved to our neighborhood last year.

5. My ______ decided to bake them cookies.

B. Complete each sentence with a subject. Use the type of noun in parentheses.

6. ______ offered to bring them the cookies. **(person)**

7. The ______ slipped out of my hand. **(thing)**

8. Their ______ was covered with cookies. **(place)**

9. The ______ made us laugh so hard our stomachs hurt! **(idea)**

Write It

C. Answer the questions about a good friend. Make sure each sentence has a subject.

10. Is your friend an old or a new friend? ______________________________

11. How did you meet? ______________________________

12. What do you like best about your friend? ______________________________

____

13. What do you think your friend likes about you? ______________________________

____

14. Does your friend ever help you? How? ______________________________

____

D. (15–19) Write at least five sentences to tell about things you and your friend enjoy doing together.

____

____

____

____

____

Edit It

E. (20–25) Edit the article to include subjects. Fix the six mistakes.

My Best Friend

A best plays a big part in a kid's life. Is my best friend. Have a great time together. Some have team friends and school friends. Am glad I have one best friend. My tells stories about her childhood best friend. They are still best friends after thirty years!

Proofreader's Marks

Add text:

Best ^ are fun. (insert: friends)

See all Proofreader's Marks on page xi.

Name ______________________________

7 What's the Most Important Word in the Predicate?

The Verb

- The **complete predicate** in a sentence often tells what the subject does. The **verb** shows the action.

  We **talk** about the school election.

  We **vote** for our favorite candidate.

- Sometimes the predicate tells what the subject has. It uses these **verbs**:

  I **have** a friend named Janice.

  She **has** a good chance of winning.

- Other times, the predicate tells what the subject is or is like. The **verb** is a form of **be**.

  The school election **is** next week.

  We **are** great supporters of Janice.

  I **am** on the election committee.

Try It

A. Complete each sentence with a verb.

1. Our school ___needs___ a president.

2. Every year we ______________ for a new president.

3. I think Janice ______________ a fine candidate.

4. Tim ______________ everyone about Janice.

5. Janice ______________ many friends at school.

6. Her friends ______________ very loyal.

7. They ______________ a lot of respect for her.

8. Even Ben ______________ her for her honesty.

B. Choose words from each column to build five sentences about school elections. You can use words more than once.

Janice We Tom and Ben	is are need want	her to win. a good candidate. volunteers. a good school president.

9. ______________________________

10. ______________________________

11. ______________________________

12. ______________________________

13. ______________________________

Write It

C. Answer the questions about school elections. Use verbs correctly.

14. Do your classmates get involved in school elections? ______________________________

____

15. What makes someone a good school president? ______________________________

____

D. (16–20) Write at least five sentences to tell why you would be a good school president. Use verbs correctly.

____

____

____

____

____

Name ____________________

8 What Is a Fragment?

It's an Incomplete Sentence.

A **fragment** is a group of words that begins with a capital letter and ends with a period. It looks like a sentence, but it is not complete. A subject or a verb may be missing.

Fragments	Sentences
1. Moves to a new town.	Tina moves to a new town.
2. She the school.	She likes the school.
3. The girls in the park.	The girls meet in the park.
4. Makes new friends.	She makes new friends.

Try It

A. Write whether each group of words is a fragment or a sentence. If it is a fragment, add a subject or a verb. Write the complete sentence.

1. Jason to a new school. fragment; Jason goes to a new school.

2. Students at the new school study hard. ____________________

3. Decides to study harder this year. ____________________

B. (4–8) Each group of words in the paragraph is a fragment. Add a subject or a verb to complete each sentence.

Most kids __________ sports at my new school. All students __________ to play on a team. My old __________ was different. Most __________ there did not play sports. I __________ glad to be here because I love sports!

Write It

C. Answer the questions about your school. Use complete sentences.

9. What do you like best about your school? My favorite ______________________

____.

10. Do you and your classmates share many of the same interests? ______________

____

11. Do you think a new student would feel welcome at your school? Why or why not? ______

____

D. (12–14) Write at least three sentences that would give a new student a good idea of what your school is like. Read your sentences aloud. Fix any fragments you hear.

____

____

____

____

____

Edit It

E. (15–20) Edit the letter. Fix the six fragments. Add a subject or a verb.

Dear Samantha,

You are on my mind today. I miss you at school. This school is different from our school back in Oklahoma. The here are very full and noisy. I to fit in. It not always easy. A is helping me. Her is Clarisse. She encourages me to join the chorus. I to sing. I guess it is good to try new things!

Your friend,

Marion

Proofreader's Marks

Add text:

They ^make^ friends easily.

See all Proofreader's Marks on page xi.

Name ______________________________

9 What's One Way to Fix a Fragment?

Combine Neighboring Sentences.

Writers may create a fragment by starting a new sentence when they shouldn't. These fragments are easy to fix. Just combine the fragment with the sentence before it.

sentence / fragment

1. Irina used to set the table. While her father cooked dinner.
   Irina used to set the table while her father cooked dinner.

sentence / fragment

2. Now Irina cooks dinner. Because her father is busy.
   Now Irina cooks dinner because her father is busy.

Try It

A. Find each fragment. Combine it with the other sentence and write the new sentence.

1. Irina's sister is a good role model. Because she is so intelligent. ______________________________

2. Irina was much younger. When she wanted to be a nurse like her sister. ______________________________

3. Now she has other ideas. Because she now knows about more careers. ______________________________

4. She learned about new careers. When she attended Career Day at school. ______________________________

5. She is interested in law. Or finance. ______________________________

6. Her father is a lawyer. And a businessman. ______________________________

B. Rewrite each sentence by adding a fragment from the box. Punctuate your sentences correctly.

Because her interests have changed.	And speaks Spanish.
Even though she is younger.	Because his brother is one.

7. John wants to be an electrician. John wants to be an electrician because his brother is one.

8. Gretchen is influenced by her sister. ______________________

9. Kate's mother is from Ecuador. ______________________

10. Tina doesn't know what to do. ______________________

Write It

C. Complete each sentence with your own ideas and beliefs about how you and your interests have changed over time. Use complete sentences.

11. I used to enjoy ______________________.

12. I was interested in that because ______________________.

13. Now I prefer to ______________________.

14. My interest changed because ______________________.

15. Another way I have changed is ______________________.

D. (16–20) Write at least five sentences that tell more about how you and your interests have changed. Then read your sentences aloud. Fix any fragments.

Name ______________________________

10 Write Complete Sentences

Remember: You need a **subject** and a **predicate** to make a complete sentence. Often, the most important word in the subject is a **noun**. Every predicate needs a **verb**.

Subject	Predicate
My brother	is a volunteer firefighter.
Our family	helps other families in need.
My sister	raises money for charities.
This town	has many services for older people.

Try It

A. Add a subject or a predicate to complete each sentence.

1. Sometimes ________________ need a helping hand.

2. ________________ reads to young children once a week.

3. ________________ encourages me to help others.

4. I ________________ she is right.

5. I ________________ I will volunteer, too.

6. The library ________________ a good place to volunteer.

B. Circle the noun in the subject and underline the verb in the predicate in each sentence.

7. My parents set a good example for me.

8. Their choices are usually logical.

9. I follow their example.

10. My family talks about a choice I made.

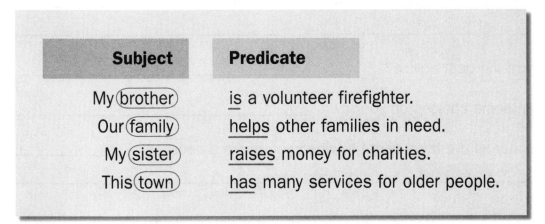

Write It

C. Answer the questions about how you make decisions. Use complete sentences.

11. How do family members help you make decisions? Sometimes ________________ help ____.

12. Who gives you the best advice? ____

13. Do you make some choices on your own? ____

14. Do you consider all the facts carefully when you make a decision? ________________ ____

D. (15–18) Write at least four sentences about how you make good decisions. Make sure each sentence includes both a subject and a predicate.

____

____

____

____

____

Grammar at Work

E. (19–25) Edit the list. Fix the <u>seven</u> mistakes to make complete sentences.

Rules to Live By

1. I always use good judgment.
2. I decisions logically.
3. First, think carefully about the facts.
4. Second, I about the consequences.
5. I to trustworthy people. Then give me their advice.
6. I to their words.
7. Finally, I my desision.

Proofreader's Marks

Add text:

I always ^think carefully.

See all Proofreader's Marks on page xi.

Name ______________________________

11 Fix Sentence Fragments

Remember: You can fix a fragment by adding a subject or predicate that includes a verb. Or, you can combine the fragment with another sentence.

Fragment:	Tells Ella about the race.
Sentence:	Bonnie tells Ella about the race.
Fragment:	Ella every day after school.
Sentence:	Ella runs every day after school.
Fragment:	Ella is not sure. If she wants to enter the race.
Sentence:	Ella is not sure if she wants to enter the race.

Try It

A. Fix the fragments and write complete sentences.

1. Is a big influence on Juan. ______________________________
2. Juan. ______________________________
3. Juan listens carefully to Kevin. Because he has good ideas. ______________________________
4. Thinks things over, but he makes his own decisions. ______________________________

B. Each group of words is a fragment. Add a subject or a verb or combine the fragment with the other sentence. Write the complete sentence.

5. Had to make a choice. ______________________________
6. David me advice. ______________________________
7. Had a similar experience. ______________________________
8. His comments were helpful. Because he has a lot of experience. ______________________________

Write It

C. Answer the questions about a decision you made. Make sure your sentences are complete. Include a subject and a predicate with a verb.

9. What was a decision you made? I decided to ______________________________

____.

10. Did anyone give you advice? ______________________________

____

11. Did you do what they suggested? Why or why not? ______________________________

____

D. (12–15) Write at least four sentences that tell more about your decision. What other influences did you consider when you made your decision? Then read your sentences aloud. Fix any fragments.

____

____

____

____

____

Grammar at Work

E. (16–20) Edit the advice letter. Fix the five fragments.

Dear Chris,

I am glad you asked for my advice about your friend. Have a difficult decision to make. Think you should tell your friend the truth. A good friendship involves honesty. And kindness. That just my opinion. You have to decide. What seems right to you.

Your cousin,

Andy

Proofreader's Marks

Delete:
I know what to do. now.

Do not capitalize:
They Told me.

Add text:
It ^is my idea.

See all Proofreader's Marks on page xi.

Name ______________________________

12 Is the Subject of a Sentence Always a Noun?

No, It Can Be a Pronoun.

- Use **I** when you talk about yourself.
  I love to paint. **I** want to learn more about it.
- Use **you** when you talk to another person.
  You learned to play the drums at a very young age.
- Use **he** when you talk about one man or one boy.
  My father is a comic book artist. **He** began drawing in high school.
- Use **she** when you talk about one woman or one girl.
  My aunt likes to write. **She** writes poems for a magazine.
- Use **it** when you talk about one place, thing, or idea.
  My brother wrote a song. **It** has a great rhythm.

Subject Pronouns
Singular
I
you
he, she, it

Try It

A. Complete each sentence. Use a subject pronoun from the chart.

1. We can express our creativity in many ways. ______________ makes the world interesting and exciting.
2. Phillip is a wonderful writer. ______________ wrote an excellent story.
3. The story is about a lost airplane. ______________ has a happy ending.
4. I know many songs. ______________ sing almost every day.
5. Mayalinn painted a picture of a sailboat. ______________ used bright colors.
6. I told the artist, "______________ are very talented."
7. My mother has a good imagination. ______________ paints beautiful murals.

B. (8–14) **Complete each sentence with a subject pronoun from the box.**

She	**He**	**It**	**I**	**You**

My older sister Julia is a dancer. ______________ began to dance at five years old. My father saw that she had talent. ______________ signed Julia up for dance lessons. After high school, Julia went to a special school for dancers. There, ______________ danced in shows. A man from a theater company saw one of the shows. ______________ asked my sister to join his theater. She accepted. Now Julia travels with many dancers across the country. Her job is tiring. ______________ requires a lot of hard work, but Julia loves it. I see several of her shows each year. ______________ am proud of my sister. ______________ would enjoy her dancing, too.

Write It

C. **Answer the questions about creative talents. Use complete sentences and subject pronouns.**

15. What special skill or talent do you have? ______________ am talented at ______________

____.

16. Who helped you realize you had this skill or talent? ______________ helped me. ______________ told me that ____.

17. What steps can you take to develop your skill or talent? ______________________________

____

____

D. (18–20) **Write at least three sentences about a person you know with a special skill or talent. Use subject pronouns in your sentences.**

____

____

____

____

____

____

Name ____________________

13 Can a Pronoun Show "More Than One"?

Yes, It Can.

- Use **we** to talk about yourself and another person.
  My friends and I wrote a play.
  We will act it out on Friday.
- Use **you** to talk to one or more persons.
  You like our school plays, don't you?
  You should all be there on Friday.
- Use **they** to talk about more than one person or thing.
  Many other students helped us.
  They wanted to help tell the story.

Subject Pronouns	
Singular	**Plural**
I	we
you	you
he, she, it	they

Try It

A. Read the first sentence. Complete the second sentence with the correct subject pronoun.

1. My friends and I love acting. ______________ wrote a play.
2. The main character is a boy named Miguel. ______________ is from El Salvador.
3. Miguel and his family leave El Salvador. ______________ move to Boston.
4. Miguel and his brothers play music. ______________ start a band.
5. Other kids hear the band. ______________ recognize Miguel's talent.
6. My friends and I worked hard on the play. ______________ had fun, too.
7. We perform it tonight. ______________ will be a hit!
8. I am glad you are here. ______________ will enjoy the play.

B. **Draw a line from the first sentence to the one that could come next. Be sure the subject nouns and pronouns match.**

9. My younger sister is very creative.	They said the cartoons were great.
10. The art teacher asked my sister to draw for the school newspaper.	We think she will enjoy the camp.
11. Students saw her cartoons in the paper.	He asked her to draw cartoons to go with articles.
12. My parents thought my sister could find other artistic activities.	They helped her find other ways to use her art talent in the community.
13. The directors of a local day care center wanted an artist to paint murals.	She took an art class and made beautiful drawings.
14. My mom and I think my sister should go to an art camp this summer.	They asked my sister to paint a picture in each room.

Write It

C. **Answer the questions about a creative project you would like to do. Use subject pronouns where needed.**

15. What creative project would you like to do? ________________ would like to ____.

16. What person would you like to work with? ______________ would like to work with ____.

17. What would you do on the project? I would ____________________________________.

18. What would the other person do on the project? ______________ would ______________ ____.

19. How would having a partner make a difference to the project? ______________________ ____

D. **(20–25) Write at least six sentences that tell more about what each person would do for the project. Use subject pronouns.**

____

____

____

____

Name ______________________________

14 How Do You Avoid Confusion with Pronouns?

Match the Pronoun to the Noun.

If you're not sure which **pronoun** to use, first find the **noun** it goes with. Then ask yourself:

- Is the noun a man, a woman, or a thing?
  Use **he** for a man, **she** for a woman, and **it** for a thing.
- Is the noun singular or plural? If plural, use **we**, **you**, or **they**.

If a pronoun does not refer correctly to a noun, change the pronoun.

Incorrect: My **friends** play in a band.
He knows different instruments.

Correct: My **friends** play in a band.
They know different instruments.

The pronouns in these sentences are correct. Do you know why?

1. **Will** plays the drums. **He** is also the lead singer.
2. **Julian and Blake** play the guitar. **They** are great!

Try It

A. Complete the sentence with a pronoun that matches the underlined noun.

1. My friends practice every weekend. ______________ play in Will's basement.
2. Will's mom is understanding about the noise. ______________ thinks Will is talented.
3. My classmates and I planned a talent show. ______________ asked the band to perform.

B. (4–7) Complete the sentences with correct pronouns.

Our class takes a field trip to a museum. ______________ see lots of art. Thanh and Marie see a landscape painting. ______________ like the bold colors. My favorite is a portrait. ______________ looks like my dad! My class and I enjoy the museum. ______________ learn so much about art.

Write It

C. Answer the questions about an art show or a performance you saw. Use pronouns correctly.

8. What type of show or performance did you see? ____________ saw ________________.

9. Who went with you? ____________________ and ____________________ went with me.

10. When did you go? ____

11. What did you see or hear there? ____________________________________

12. How did you feel about the show or performance? Did everyone with you agree? ______

____

13. Would you recommend this show or performance to others? Why or why not? _________

____

D. (14–16) Write at least three sentences that tell more about this show or performance.

____

____

____

____

Edit It

E. (17–20) Edit the letter. Fix the four mistakes by inserting the correct pronouns.

Dear Chelsey,

I want to invite you to a music festival on Sunday. Would she like to go with me? A few of our other friends are going, too. would meet them there. Musicians from Honduras are playing. He are bringing special instruments. If we get hungry, don't worry. She can buy lunch at a food stand there. I hope you can go!

Your friend,

Chris

Proofreader's Marks

Change text:

You
~~It~~ should go.

Add text:

she
Maria said ^ would go.

See all Proofreader's Marks on page xi.

Name ______________________________

15 How Do You Know What Verb to Use?

Match It to the Subject.

- Use **I** with **am**.

  I am in the school gym.

- Use **he**, **she**, or **it** with **is**.

  It is filled with students.

  Our guest **speaker is** the mascot for a basketball team.

  He is here to talk about exercise and to do some tricks.

- Use **we**, **you**, or **they** with **are**.

  The **students are** excited. **They are** amazed by his tricks.

  We are basketball fans. **Are you**?

Forms of *Be*
I **am**
he, she, or it **is**
we, you, or they **are**

Try It

A. Complete each sentence. Use am, is, or are.

1. The speaker ______________ named Lucky.
2. He ______________ dressed up like an elf.
3. "I ______________ here to discuss healthy living," he tells us. "Kids should get lots of exercise and eat healthy foods."
4. We ______________ amazed when Lucky performs his tricks.
5. They ______________ a combination of slam dunks and gymnastics.
6. "You ______________ such a great audience," says Lucky.

B. (7–13) Complete the sentences with the correct form of be.

I ______________ on a basketball team. We ______________ the best team in our league. Our coaches ______________ great. They ______________ high school juniors. Sam ______________ the head coach. He ______________ a player on his school team. ______________ you sure you can't come to my game today?

Write It

C. **Answer the questions about a sport or activity you do. Use am, is, or are.**

14. What sport or activity are you involved in? I ________________ involved in ________________.

15. What are your favorite things about this activity? My favorite things ________________ ________________.

16. Who is the leader of this activity? ________________

17. What other people are involved? ________________ ________________

D. **(18–20) Write at least three sentences that tell more about your involvement in this sport or activity. Use the correct forms of be.**

____

____

____

Edit It

E. **(21–25) Edit the journal entry. Fix the five mistakes with the forms of be.**

February 7

I love to play soccer, and I is pretty good at it. I is not the best player, but I am always the kid who tries the hardest. My family is very supportive. My parents be at most of my games, and my older sister are often there, too. My dad is extremely loud when he cheers! We is amazed that we can always hear his voice on the field.

Proofreader's Marks

Change text:

We ~~is~~ are teammates.

See all Proofreader's Marks on page xi.

Name ______________________

16 How Do You Know What Verb to Use?

Match It to the Subject.

Use the form of the verb **have** that matches the subject.

- I **have** a poem in the school magazine.
- He **has** a drawing.
- Our school **has** an art club.
- We **have** talented students at our school.
- You **have** a story in the magazine.
- They **have** an art club meeting tomorrow afternoon.

Forms of *Have*
I **have**
he, she, or it **has**
we, you, or they **have**

Try It

A. Complete each sentence with have or has.

1. Our school ______________ a magazine.

2. The magazine ______________ a poetry section.

3. I ______________ a poem I might submit.

4. Do you ______________ a piece of writing or art to submit?

5. Lucinda ______________ a story in this issue of the magazine.

B. (6-12) Complete the sentences with have or has.

My English teacher ______________ an activity called Writer's Workshop. We ______________ partners, and we edit each other's writing. I ______________ Ben as my partner. He ______________ helpful things to say. Today we ______________ a weird assignment called "Stolen Line Poem." We write a poem that includes a line from another poem. It ______________ a "stolen line" in it. I ______________ no idea what line to use!

Write It

C. **Answer the questions about creative activities. Use have or has.**

13. What experience do you have with creative writing? I ________________ experience ________________.

14. Do students at your school have ways to publish or display their writing? Explain. Students at my school ________________ ________________.

15. What other ways do students have to be creative at your school? Students at my school ________________ ________________.

D. **(16–19) Write at least four sentences that tell more about your experience with creative writing. Use the correct forms of have.**

____

____

____

____

____

Edit It

E. **(20–25) Edit the reflection. Fix the six mistakes with have and has.**

Reflection on My Poem (Draft #1)

I has a few thoughts about my poem. I think I did a good job, but the poem have some lines that could be better. The first two lines has a strong, vivid image. But the other lines have too many dull words and boring expressions. Lots of poems has a simple, conversational style, but maybe mine is too simple. Ben several good suggestions for revisions. I has some more work to do!

Proofreader's Marks
Add text: Ben ^has a suggestion.
Change text: Ben ~~have~~ ^has a suggestion.
See all Proofreader's Marks on page xi.

Name ______________________________

17 How Do You Know What Verb to Use?

Match It to the Subject.

- Use the form of **do** that matches the subject. You can use **do** as a **main verb** or as a **helping verb**.

  I **do** my best at the tryout.

  Jared **does** his best, too.

  We **do hope** we get parts in the musical.

  At the tryout, Jared and Lucy **do** a scene.

  The tryout **does make** me nervous.

Forms of *Do*
I **do**
he, she, or it **does**
we, you, or they **do**

- The short form of **does not** is **doesn't**. The short form of **do not** is **don't**.

  1. He **does not** sing well.
  He **doesn't** sing well.

  2. We **do not** want to miss the tryout.
  We **don't** want to miss the tryout.

Try It

A. Write the correct form of the verb to complete each sentence.

1. Our middle school ______________ (do/does) a musical every year.

2. ______________ (Do/Does) you like musicals?

3. Our musical this year ______________ (do/does) seem to have a lot of good parts.

4. I ______________ (do/does) a lot of singing, so I decided to try out.

5. Students ______________ (do/does) have to be prepared for the tryout.

6. We ______________ (don't/doesn't) have to know the whole musical, but we should know one song.

7. This show ______________ (doesn't/don't) have a lot of famous songs.

8. I ______________ (don't/doesn't) know which song to practice.

B. Choose words from each column to write five statements. You may use words more than once.

One thing I Thierry and I always But this year I This time, I Thierry	does do don't doesn't	every year is help with the school play. the costumes and props. want to sew or build things. hope to get a small acting part. want to act in the play, too.

9. ______________________________

10. ______________________________

11. ______________________________

12. ______________________________

13. ______________________________

Write It

C. Answer the questions about performing. Use **do**, **don't**, **does**, or **doesn't** as needed in your responses.

14. Do you like to perform for an audience? Why or why not? ______________,
I ______________ *because* ______________.

15. Do you like to see plays and musicals? Why or why not? ______________,
I ______________ *because* ______________.

16. Many people help put on a play other than the actors. How do these other people help?
They ______________________________.

D. (17–20) Write at least four sentences about what you like or don't like about performing for an audience. Use forms of **do** and **do not** in your responses.

____

____

____

____

____

Name ______________________________

18 What Adds Action to a Sentence?

An Action Verb

- An **action verb** tells what the subject does. Some action verbs tell about an action that you cannot see.

  My mom **listens** to folk music.

  She **sings** along with every song.

- Make sure the action verb agrees with its subject. Add -s if the subject tells about one place, one thing, or one other person. Do not add -s if the subject is **you**.

  I listen mostly to hip-hop music.

  My **dad listens** to jazz.

  My older **brother sings** in a rock band.

  My **friends sing** in our school chorus.

Try It

A. Complete each sentence with an action verb.

1. I ______________ all kinds of music at home.
2. My brother ______________ his rock music loudly.
3. Sometimes my parents ______________ him to turn it down.
4. My dad ______________ the saxophone.
5. He ______________ every day.

B. Complete each sentence with the correct form of the verb in parentheses.

6. Hip-hop songs ______________ dreams and struggles. **(describe)**
7. Country songs often ______________ about love. **(tell)**
8. Liliana ______________ the lyrics of all her favorite songs. **(memorize)**
9. I ______________ new songs very easily. **(learn)**

Write It

C. Answer the questions about music. Check that your verbs match their subjects.

10. What types of music do you and your friends listen to? My friends and I ______________________________.

11. What types of music does your family listen to? My family ______________________________.

12. How do you choose songs or CDs for your music collection? I ______________________________.

13. When do you listen to music? ______________________________

14. What role does music play in your life? Music ______________________________.

15. What music activities does your school offer? Do you participate? My school ______________________________.

I ______________________________.

D. (16–20) Write five sentences about your family's favorite types of music. Use action verbs correctly in your sentences.

____

____

____

____

____

____

Name ______________________

19 How Do You Know What Action Verb to Use?

Match It to the Subject.

- **Action verbs** tell when a subject does something, like **ride**, **look**, or **drive**. If the sentence is about one other person, place, or thing, add -s to the action verb.

1. My sisters **ride** the bus.	**2.** Our cousin **rides** the bus, too.
3. We **look** out the window.	**4.** A driver **looks** at us.
5. My parents **drive** the car.	**6.** Dad **drives** us to school.

- If there is more than one action verb in a sentence, all verbs must agree with the subject:

  My friend **rides**, **parks**, and **locks** his bike.

Try It

A. Complete each sentence about money. Write the correct verb.

1. My parents ____give____ me money for lunch at school. (give / gives)
2. I ______________ to earn my own spending money. (decide/decides)
3. My older sisters ______________ after school. (work / works)
4. I ______________ many reasons for spending money. (find / finds)
5. My mom ______________ me to save for an emergency or vacation. (ask/asks)
6. I ______________ to babysit for neighbors. (want/wants)
7. Mom ______________ me that I am too young to babysit. (tell/tells)
8. My sisters ______________ that I take a babysitting class. (suggest/suggests)
9. In the class, you ______________ what to do in an emergency. (learn/learns)

B. Choose words from each column to write six sentences. You may use words more than once.

My mom My sisters I	take tells learn ask takes get	me to the class. a certificate at the end. me she is proud of me. what I learned. the babysitting class. simple first aid.

10. ______________________________

11. ______________________________

12. ______________________________

13. ______________________________

14. ______________________________

15. ______________________________

Write It

C. You need money for a special event. Answer the questions. Check that your verbs match their subjects.

16. How can you save money? I ______________________________

______________________________.

17. How can you earn money? I ______________________________

______________________________.

D. (18–20) Write three sentences about your experiences saving or earning money.

____

____

____

____

Name ________________________________

20 What Kinds of Verbs Are *Can, Could, May,* and *Might*?

They Are Helping Verbs.

- An action verb can have two parts: a **helping verb** and a **main verb.** The main verb shows the action.

  I **play** drums. I **can play** drums.

- Some helping verbs change the meaning of the action verb.

  1. Use **can** or **could** to tell about an ability.

  Yesenia **can play** the guitar well. She **could teach** guitar lessons.

  2. Use **may**, **might**, or **could** to tell about a possibility.

  Raoul **may learn** to play the keyboards. He **might take** lessons. He **could begin** today.

- **Can**, **could**, **may**, and **might** stay the same with all subjects. Do not add -s.

  Oleg **plays** the saxophone. He **can play** very well. He **might play** a song for us.

Try It

A. Complete each sentence with can, could, may, or might.

1. Anna plays the guitar. She said she ______________ teach me, too.

2. I ______________ learn the guitar quickly. My fingers are very long.

3. Anna ______________ teach me to play one song tomorrow after school.

4. I ______________ try to play a different instrument if I don't like guitar.

B. (5–8) Read each sentence. Write whether it shows an ability or possibility. Then complete the sentences with the correct helping verb.

My neighbor Pavel plays drums. He **(might / can)** ____________________ win a contest next week. I **(might / can)** ____________________ hear him practicing all the time. He **(may / can)** ____________________ teach me a few rhythms if he has time. Maybe I **(could / can)** ____________________ learn to play drums, too.

Write It

C. **Answer the questions about a talent or skill that you have, using can, could, may, and might.**

9. Describe a talent or skill that you are proud of. I ________________________________

____.

10. How might you develop this talent or skill? In the future, I ____________________

____.

11. What could you do to share this talent or skill with other people? ______________

____

12. What other talents or skills might you explore in the next few years? ___________

____

D. **(13–16) Write at least four sentences about a creative talent you encouraged someone else to explore. Use can, could, may, and might.**

____

____

____

____

Edit It

E. **(17–20) Edit the letter. Fix the four mistakes with helping verbs.**

Dear Selma,

Thank you for giving me the idea to take voice lessons! I didn't think I could sing. I am surprised at the notes my voice may hit. Now I miht take more lessons. If so, I sing may in the school musical at the end of the year. One suggestion may make such a difference!

Sincerely,

Nicole

Proofreader's Marks

Change text:

You ~~might~~ can sing a wide range of notes.

Transpose words:

We play might in a band.

See all Proofreader's Marks on page xi.

Name ______________________________

21 Use Subject Pronouns

Remember: The subject of a sentence can be a pronoun. A **subject pronoun** can be singular or plural.

- Use **I** when you talk about yourself.
- Use **you** to talk to one or more persons.
- Use **we** to talk about another person and yourself.
- Use **he**, **she**, **it**, and **they** to talk about other people or things.

How do you know which pronoun to use? Look at the noun it goes with.

1. If the noun is a man or boy, use **he**. If it is a woman or girl, use **she**.
2. If the noun is a place or thing, use **it**. If the noun is plural, use **they**.

Try It

A. Complete each sentence. Write the correct subject pronoun.

1. Franco did a science project. ____________ worked on it for months. (**He / They**)

2. Sophie gave good advice. ____________ said the project should be creative. (**He / She**)

3. Many students entered the science fair. ____________ all worked hard. (**They / It**)

4. Franco did an experiment. ____________ thought it was creative. (**She / He**)

B. (5–8) Read the interview. Complete each sentence with the correct pronoun.

Q. How did you make your project the most creative at the science fair?

A. First, I chose an interesting subject. Then, my friend Sophie gave me advice. ____________ said my project should stand out. The other students and I discussed ideas. ____________ thought of many ways to make our projects creative. I decided to make my project about global warming. The judges spent a long time at my display. ____________ said that my project was the most original. The science fair was great. ____________ was more fun than I expected!

Write It

C. Answer the questions about a creative project you completed. Use subject pronouns.

9. What was the project you made? ______________ made ______________________.

10. Who saw your project? Did anyone help you with it? ______________________

____

11. What did you learn from your project? I learned ______________________

____.

D. (12–14) Write three sentences that tell more about your creative project. Use subject pronouns in your sentences.

____

____

____

____

Grammar at Work

E. (15–20) Edit the journal entry. Fix the <u>four</u> pronoun mistakes. Fix the <u>two</u> fragments by adding a verb.

My friends and I painted a mural at our school. They painted it in the hall near the gym. Mr. Hill helped us come up with ideas. She is our art teacher. Mr. Hill's idea was to focus on creative activities at our school. Emily wanted to include sports teams, too. She a sketch of her plan. The mural turned out great! They was also fun to paint. Our classmates and teachers loved it. They so proud of us! He want us to do another mural next year.

Proofreader's Marks

Change text:
She
~~It~~ won the award.

See all Proofreader's Marks on page xi.

Name ____________________

22 Use the Verbs *Be*, *Have*, and *Do*

Remember: The verbs **be, have,** and **do** each have more than one form. Use the form that goes with the subject.

Forms of *Be*	Forms of *Have*	Forms of *Do*
I **am**	I **have**	I **do**
he, she, or it **is**	he, she, or it **has**	he, she, or it **does**
we, you, or they **are**	we, you, or they **have**	we, you, or they **do**

Try It

A. Complete the sentences with the correct form of the verb in parentheses.

1. My English teacher ______________ really excited about creative writing. **(be)**
2. She ______________ lots of poetry books. **(have)**
3. Every year her students ______________ a magazine. **(do)**
4. The magazine ______________ writing and artwork. **(have)**
5. We ______________ a lot of work on this magazine. **(do)**

B. (6–11) Read the interview. Write the correct verb to complete each sentence.

Q. What do you and your classmates do on the magazine?

A. My classmates and I ______________ (do / does) so much work on the magazine.

Some students ______________ (is / are) responsible for posters.

We ______________ (is / are) all in charge of what gets published.

We ______________ (have / has) lively discussions about the work. Sometimes we ______________ (do / does) disagree. But we always ______________ (have / has) a great time.

Write It

C. Answer the questions about your experience with creative writing. Use forms of be, have, and do.

12. What are your feelings about stories, poems, or other forms of creative writing? Why do you have these feelings? ______________________________

____

13. Do you enjoy creative writing? Why or why not? I ______________________________ *because* ______________________________.

14. Who is your favorite poet or writer? What is your favorite work? ______________________________

____

D. (15–18) Write four more sentences that describe your experience with poetry. Use the correct forms of be, have, and do.

____

____

____

____

Grammar at Work

E. (19–25) Fix the five mistakes with be, have, and do. Fix the two fragments by adding a subject.

My school have a newspaper. I is on the staff. I do sports writing. Write articles on our school teams and athletes. I has an interview this month with a girl on the track team. Also do some of the layout for the paper. Staff members has meetings after school twice a week. We does a lot of work. But it is fun!

Proofreader's Marks

Add text:

My article ^is done.

Change text:

We ~~has~~ ^have a newspaper.

See all Proofreader's Marks on page xi.

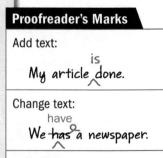

Name ______________________________

23 Make Subjects and Verbs Agree

Remember: The verb you use depends on your subject. These subjects and verbs go together:

Forms of *Be*	Action Verbs
I **am** interested.	I **join** the club.
You **are** interested.	You **join** the club, too.
He, she, or it **is** interested.	He, she, or it **joins** the club.
We, you, or they **are** interested.	We, you, or they **join** the club.
Students **are** interested.	Students **join** the club.
My friends and I **are** interested.	My friends and I **join** the club.

Try It

A. Complete each sentence about school clubs. Write the verb that goes with the subject.

1. My school ______________________ several clubs.
offer / offers

2. They ______________________ after school.
meet / meets

3. My friend Marina ______________________ in the computer club.
is / are

4. She ______________________ a lot in her club.
learn / learns

B. Write the correct form of the verb in parentheses.

5. Jonah ______________ interested in math. **(be)**

6. He and Gabe ______________ a hard math class. **(take)**

7. They ______________ on the math team. **(compete)**

8. The math team ______________ a lot of competitions. **(win)**

Write It

C. Answer the questions about your interests. Make sure your subjects and verbs agree.

9. What are your favorite subjects at school? My favorite subjects ____________________

____.

10. What clubs or activities does your school offer? ____________________

____

11. Are you involved in any of these clubs or activities? If so, describe what you do.

____

____

D. (12–14) Write three sentences to tell more about your involvement with school clubs or activities. Make sure each verb agrees with its subject.

____

____

____

Grammar at Work

E. (15–20) Edit the letter. Fix the <u>four</u> mistakes with verbs. Then combine the <u>two</u> fragments with other sentences.

Dear Grandpa,

How are you? I am fine. This year I is in the computer club at my school. We designs Web pages. And create computer games. We even builds simple robots and program them! My friend Kylie and I might learn digital filmmaking next year. The club advisor explain things very clearly. You and I are both interested in computers. Even though we use them for different things.

Love,

Marina

Proofreader's Marks

Change text:

She ~~are~~ is successful.

See all Proofreader's Marks on page xi.

Name ______________________________

24 What Are Adjectives?

They Are Describing Words.

- You can describe people, places, or things with **adjectives**. They answer the question: What is it like?
- Use adjectives to describe:
  1. how something looks: **strange, bumpy, scary, huge**
  2. how something sounds: **loud, squeaky, buzzing**
  3. how something feels, tastes, or smells: **rough, cold, salty**
  4. a person's mood: **tired, happy, sad, angry**
- Place a comma between adjectives that come before a noun only if you can reverse their order. If you cannot reverse their order, do not add a comma.

  Billowing, dark clouds sped across the **stormy** sky.

  Loud warning sirens woke the **sleepy** residents.

Try It

A. Add excitement to the story about the storm. Use adjectives from the box. Use two adjectives in at least two sentences.

howling	scary	terrible	loud	sudden

1. The ______________ storm was unexpected.
2. I heard a very ______________ noise, and the lights went out.
3. The ______________ silence disturbed me.
4. Then the ______________ wind began to screech outside my windows.

B. Now, think of your own adjectives. Write them to complete the sentences.

5. Usually, I don't mind storms, but this ______________ storm was scaring me.
6. I heard every ______________ sound.
7. Was a ______________ stranger in the house with me?

Write It

C. Answer the questions about a time when something surprising happened when you were home alone. Use at least one adjective in each answer.

8. What happened? I ____
____.

9. Were you scared? Why? ____
____

10. What did you do? ____
____

D. (11–14) Write at least four sentences about a time the power went out unexpectedly during a storm. Use one or two adjectives in each sentence.

____
____
____
____
____

Edit It

E. (15–20) Improve the journal entry. Add five adjectives. Add one missing comma.

September 30

Tonight, a scary thing happened to me. I was home all alone when we had a storm. My house lost power. I heard noises all evening long. The only light I had was the light from my flashlight. My dogs hid under my old creaky bed. I sat alone in the house until my parents came home.

Proofreader's Marks

Add text: There was a ^ wind. (howling)

See all Proofreader's Marks on page xi.

Name ______________________________

25 How Do You Use a Predicate Adjective?

After a Form of the Verb *Be*

- Most of the time, **adjectives** come before **nouns**.
  A **scary event** happened to me yesterday.
- If the verb is a form of **be**, you can put the adjective after the verb. The forms of **be** are **am**, **is**, **are**, **was**, and **were**.
  The **event** was **scary**. At first, **I** was **worried**.
- If you use two predicate adjectives, join them with **and**, **but**, or **or**.
  Yesterday, I was **shocked and nervous**. Today, I am **afraid but excited**.
  Are you **jumpy or calm** when you perform?

Try It

A. Use adjectives from the box to complete the sentences.

great	scared	ready	sick	surprised	happy

1. Yesterday, I was ____________ to get a call from the play's director.
2. She told me that the lead actor was ____________.
3. She asked me, "Are you ____________ to stand in for him?"
4. I was ____________ but ____________.
5. This chance was ____________ for me.

B. Now, think of your own adjectives. Write them to complete the sentences.

6. I am ____________ and ____________ on opening night.
7. I am not ____________, though.
8. I am ____________ and ____________ with my lines.
9. It is ____________ to get up on stage.
10. But in the end, acting is ____________.

Write It

C. Tell about a time when you were nervous about speaking or performing in front of a group. Use predicate adjectives.

11. I was ____________ and ____________ when ______________________

____.

12. The experience was ____________ because ______________________

____.

13. Now I am ____________ that it happened because ______________________

____.

D. (14–16) Write three sentences. Describe something that could happen during a school performance or sport event. Use predicate adjectives.

____

____

____

____

____

Edit It

E. (17–20) Edit the concert review for the school newspaper. Add four predicate adjectives.

Last night, our school choir sang for a large crowd of people. The performance was excellent. All of the singers were. The solo singer had only one day to practice his part. I think he did a terrific job. His performance was. I am that I attended the event. I think our choir is.

Proofreader's Marks

Add text:

I was happy to sing in the choir.

See all Proofreader's Marks on page xi.

Name ________________________________

26 When Do You Use an Indefinite Adjective?

When You Can't Be Specific

- If you are not sure of the exact number or amount of something, use an **indefinite adjective**.

  The ocean has **many** sharks. **Several** kinds of sharks swim in warm water. **Some** areas have **a lot of** sharks, and **some** areas have **a few** sharks.

- Do you know which adjective to use?

These adjectives go before a noun you can count, such as **sharks**:		These adjectives go before a noun you can't count, such as **water**:	
many sharks	**a lot of** sharks	**much** water	**a lot of** water
a few sharks	**several** sharks	**a little** water	**not much** water
some sharks	**no** sharks	**some** water	**no** water

Try It

A. Complete each sentence with an indefinite adjective from the chart. More than one answer is possible.

1. I have ______________ fear when I swim in the ocean.

2. That's because I have seen ______________ movies about sharks.

3. In ______________ movies, people get hurt.

4. I also have ______________ fear when I swim in lakes.

5. That's because I have seen ______________ movies about lake monsters.

B. (6–12) Write adjectives from the chart to complete the paragraph. More than one answer is possible.

Yesterday, I swam ______________ laps in the ocean. I was proud of myself because I faced ______________ fears. Suddenly, I felt ______________ fear when I saw ______________ shark fins! My worst fears came true! I felt ______________ panic. Then I noticed that ______________ fins were moving. The "fins" were ______________ rocks sticking up in the water.

Write It

C. Describe an ocean or a lake. Use indefinite adjectives from the chart.

13. I see ____

____.

14. I hear ____

____.

15. I enjoy ____

____.

16. I fear ____

____.

D. (17–20) Write at least four sentences about an experience you have had while you were swimming. Use indefinite adjectives.

____

____

____

____

____

Edit It

E. (21–25) Edit the report about sharks. Fix the five incorrect indefinite adjectives. There is more than one correct answer.

There are many kinds of sharks. A little sharks are dangerous. The great white shark is dangerous. Much sharks are harmless. The whale shark is harmless but huge. Much sharks have sharp teeth and eat fish. A little sharks, like the megamouth, eat plankton. Much knowledge goes a long way in understanding sharks!

Proofreader's Marks

Change text:

Many
~~Much~~ sharks live in the ocean.

See all Proofreader's Marks on page xi.

Name ______________________________

27 Can You Use an Adjective to Make a Comparison?

Yes, But You Have to Change the Adjective.

- Use a **comparative adjective** to compare two people, places, or things.

  My basketball team is **strong**, but the other team is **stronger**.
  That team is **more athletic** than ours.

- There are two ways to turn an adjective into a comparative adjective:

1. If the adjective is short, add **-er**. If it ends in **y**, change the **y** to **i** before you add **-er**.	**long** **longer**	**old** **older**	**scary** **scarier**
2. If the adjective is long, use **more** before the adjective.	**unexpected** **more unexpected**		**frightening** **more frightening**

- If an adjective is medium length, use the form that is easier to say:

  friendly — **friendlier** or **more friendly**
  nervous — **more nervous**

Try It

A. Complete each sentence about another basketball team. Write the comparative form of the adjective.

1. Our players are **tall**, but the other players are ______________________.
2. We are **successful**, but they are ______________________.
3. Our guards are **fast**, but their guards are ______________________.
4. Our hopes are **high**, but theirs are ______________________.
5. Usually I am **excited** before the game, but this time I am ______________________.
6. My coach is **fearful** that we will lose, but I am ______________________.

Try It

B. **Complete each sentence. Write the correct form of the adjective in parentheses.**

7. The buzzer is very ____________________ at the beginning of the game. **(loud)**

8. Their center is ____________________ than ours, and he taps the jump ball to his player. **(quick)**

9. Their second shot is ____________________ than their first shot. **(close)**

10. We score a ____________________ two points. **(fast)**

11. Our defense is ____________________ than it should be, and we foul them on the shot. **(careless)**

12. We are up two to one, and we feel ____________________ now than we did before the game. **(happy)**

Write It

C. **Compare two competing athletes or teams. Use at least one comparative adjective in each sentence.**

13. ________________ is ________________, but ________________ is ________________.

14. Right now, ________________ is ________________ than ________________.

15. In the end, ________________ will be ________________ than ________________.

16. I am ________________ than I was ________________.

D. **(17–20) Write at least four sentences to compare your favorite sports team to another. Use comparative adjectives in your sentences.**

____

____

____

____

____

Name ______________________

28 Can an Adjective Compare More Than Two Things?

Yes, But You Have to Use a Different Form.

- A **superlative adjective** compares three or more people, places, or things. You can turn an adjective into a superlative adjective:

1. Add **-est** to a short adjective.	This is the **toughest** team we've ever played.
2. Use **most** before a long adjective.	It is the **most difficult** game ever.

- Adjectives have different forms. Use the form that fits your purpose.

To Describe 1 Thing	dark	interesting
To Compare 2 Things	darker	more interesting
To Compare 3 or More Things	darkest	most interesting

- Never use **more** and **-er** together. Never use **most** and **-est** together.

  It is the ~~most~~ longest game ever.

Try It

A. Write the correct adjective to complete each sentence about how the team's fear becomes a reality.

1. This game is turning into the ______________ game my team has ever played.
more challenging / most challenging

2. By halftime, their lead is even ______________ than it was after the first quarter.
greater / greatest

3. I feel the ______________ feelings in the world.
hopelessest / most hopeless

4. At halftime, our coach is ______________, though.
wonderful / wonderfuler

5. He thinks that this is the ______________ team we've ever played.
strongest / most strongest

B. **Edit the sentences. Fix the adjectives.**

6. Well, my most horriblest fears came true.

7. We had our more terrible loss ever.

8. I am happiest after the game than I was before it, though.

9. I played my most hardest game ever.

10–11. I learned that sometimes the difficult losses teach us the importantest lessons.

12. I feel unhappier that we lost but pleased that we only lost by 10 points. It could have been worse.

Proofreader's Marks

Change text:
They had the ~~strong~~ strongest players in the league.

Add text:
They were more powerful than we were.

Delete:
One of their players was the ~~most~~ tallest sophomore in the state.

See all Proofreader's Marks on page xi.

Write It

C. **Write three new facts about the game. Use superlative adjectives in each sentence.**

13. I felt the ______________ when ________________________________.

14. The ______________ player on the other team was ____.

15. The ______________ moment in the game was when ____.

D. **(16–20) Write an article for the school newspaper. Use at least five sentences that describe the game. Include a comparative or superlative adjective in each sentence.**

____

____

____

____

____

____

Name ___________________________

29 Which Adjectives Are Irregular?

Good, *Bad*, *Many*, *Much*, and *Little*

- These adjectives have special forms.

Adjective	good	bad	many	few	much	little
Comparative Form	better	worse	more	fewer	more	less
Superlative Form	best	worst	most	fewest	most	least

I have a **little** air in my tires.
Fred has **more** air in his tires than I do.
Walter's tires have the **most** air of all.

Try It

A. Write the correct adjective to complete each sentence.

1. I had a ______________________ feeling about riding down the deserted road.
bad / worst

2. Walter had a ______________________ feeling than I did.
worse / worst

3. Why did Fred think this was a ______________________ idea?
good / best

4. The old road was ______________________ than a horse trail.
worse / bad

5. There were ______________________ sharp rocks than dirt.
more / most

B. Now write adjectives from the chart above to complete the sentences.

6. My _______________ fears suddenly came true.

7. The bike path has _______________ prickly weeds.

8. It was a _______________ thing I had my cell phone.

9. My mom arrived with a new tire and a talk about using _______________ judgment.

Write It

C. Complete the sentences about when one of your fears came true. Use adjectives from the chart.

10. My _____________ fear came true when _____________________________

____.

11. That experience was _____________ than I thought because _______________

____.

12. Now I have the _____________ memories of all because _______________

____.

D. (13–16) Write at least four sentences about fears you hope will not come true. Use adjectives from the chart on page G57.

____

____

____

____

Edit It

E. (17–20) Edit the journal entry. Fix the four incorrect adjectives.

January 15

Yesterday was the worse day of my life. I made a worst decision. I rode my bike down a bumpy, deserted road. It turned out to be a bad decision than I thought. The better thing of all was that Mom didn't get mad at me. She said that she'd done some silly things when she was a kid, too.

Proofreader's Marks

Change text:

I had ~~most~~ more problems last night than I expected.

See all Proofreader's Marks on page xi.

Name ______________________________

30 Why Do You Need Adverbs?

To Tell *How*, *When*, or *Where*

- Use an **adverb** to describe a verb. Adverbs often end in -ly.

  The moon shines **brightly**. (how)
  My dad and I are camping **tonight**. (when)
  We look **up** at the sky. (where)

- Use an **adverb** to make an adjective or another adverb stronger.

  The woods are **extremely** quiet.
  adjective

  Our campfire burns **very** slowly.
  adverb

- Adverbs add details and bring life to your writing.

  We are **really** content, and we talk **quietly**.
  Suddenly, we hear a loud shriek.

Try It

A. Write an adverb to make each sentence about the camping trip more interesting.

1. My dad and I ________________ freeze.
2. We look all ________________.
3. Our hearts start beating ________________.
4. We feel ________________ frightened.
5. Was the sound a wild animal roaming ________________?

B. (6–12) Add details with adverbs.

My imagination is ________________ active under normal circumstances. Now it is ________________ working overtime. I look ________________, ________________, and all around, but I see nothing. My dad and I get up ________________ and run into the tent. Then, everything gets ________________ quiet. We wait ________________.

Write It

C. What happens next? Complete the sentences about a frightening experience. Use an adverb in each sentence.

13. Just then, we hear ______________________________.

14. The loud shriek ______________________________.

15. My dad and I ______________________________.

16. In the end, we ______________________________.

D. (17–20) Now, use your imagination. Write at least four sentences about a place that might fill you with fear. Use at least one adverb in each sentence.

____

____

____

____

____

Edit It

E. (21–25) Add details to the conversation. Add five adverbs.

Dad: Our campfire is burning brightly, so it will keep animals away.

Jake: The wind is howling, so we cannot hear what might be out there.

Dad: Don't let your imagination run wild. We will wait.

Jake: Was that loud shriek an animal or a person?

Dad: I looked and didn't see anything. It's probably the wind. Let's sit.

Proofreader's Marks

Add text:

frightfully
The ^ loud noises scared Sandra.

See all Proofreader's Marks on page xi.

Name ______________________________

31 Can You Use an Adverb to Make a Comparison?

Yes, But You Need to Change the Adverb.

- Adverbs have different forms. Use the form that fits your purpose.

To Describe 1 Action	fast	soundly	well	badly
To Compare 2 Actions	faster	more soundly	better	worse
To Compare 3 or More Actions	fastest	most soundly	best	worst

- How many things are being compared in these sentences?

  Last week, I slept the **most soundly** that I've ever slept on a camping trip.

  I'll enjoy this camping trip **better** than I enjoyed the last camping trip.

Try It

A. Write the correct adverb to describe the action in each sentence.

1. Dad heard something shriek ______________________ than usual.
   more fiercely / most fiercely
2. My imagination worked the ______________________ ever.
   more furiously / most furiously
3. We laughed ______________________ when we discovered a lost cat.
   loudly / more loudly

B. Write the correct form of the adverb in parentheses to complete each sentence.

4. Then, it started to rain ______________ than I've ever seen. **(fiercely)**
5. It rained the ______________ of all at night. **(hard)**
6. We heard thunder roaring ______________ through the woods. **(loudly)**
7. Then, we saw lightning flashing the ______________ ever. **(brightly)**
8. I waited ______________ than before for the storm to end. **(desperately)**

Write It

C. Describe a rainstorm that would make your imagination work overtime. Use adverbs that compare.

9. The wind blows ______________________________.

10. The rain falls ______________________________.

11. Thunder roars ______________________________.

12. Lightning flashes ______________________________.

D. (13–16) Now imagine that you and your family are in a tent in the woods at night. Write at least four sentences to tell what would make your imagination work overtime. Use adverbs that compare.

____

____

____

____

Edit It

E. (17–20) Edit the journal entry. Fix the four incorrect adverbs.

June 10

I think my camping days are over! Last week, Dad and I waited anxiously for morning because an animal was shrieking most loudly than before. Last night, we waited even anxiously for the rainstorm to end. The wind was blowing furiously. The thunder roared more deafeningly than ever. The lightning scared me the worse of all. I think I'll sleep happily in my own bed than in a tent!

Proofreader's Marks

Change text:
It rained ~~hard~~ harder this week than last week.

Delete:
It rained ~~more~~ harder this week than last week.

Add text:
It rained ^harder this week than last week.

See all Proofreader's Marks on page xi.

Name ___________________________

32 What Happens When You Add *Not* to a Sentence?

You Make the Sentence Negative.

- The word **not** is an adverb. Add **not** to a sentence to make it negative. If the verb is an **action verb**, change the sentence like this:
  Jeff **enters** the house. Jeff **does not enter** the house.
- If the verb is a form of **be**, just place **not** after the verb:
  He **is** alone. He **is not** alone.
- When you shorten a verb plus **not**, replace the **o** in **not** with an apostrophe (**'**).

1. Jeff **does not** enter the house.	**2.** He **is not** alone.
Jeff **doesn't** enter the house.	He **isn't** alone.

Try It

A. Rewrite each sentence. Add not to make it negative.

1. Jeff likes being in the big, old house. ___________________________
2. He feels safe. ___________________________
3. The house is very quiet. ___________________________
4. Jeff concentrates on reading his book. ___________________________
5. The strange noises are comforting to him. ___________________________
6. He wants to stay there overnight. ___________________________
7. Jeff stops his imagination from getting the best of him. ___________________________

B. **Answer each question. Use not to write a negative sentence.**

8. Is the moon shining brightly?

____

9. Are other people in the house?

____

10. Is the house haunted?

____

11. Do the strange sounds stop?

____

12. Does Jeff run out of the scary house?

____

13. Do people always imagine the worst when they are home alone?

____

Write It

C. **Complete each sentence about a house you live in or have visited. Use not to make the sentences negative.**

14. The house ____.

15. I ____.

16. At night, the noises ____

____.

D. **(17–20) Write at least four negative sentences to tell about a time when your imagination ran wild and filled you with fear.**

____

____

____

____

____

Name ______________________________

33 Use Adjectives Correctly

Remember: You can use adjectives to describe or compare people, places, or things.

Adjective	sick	uncomfortable	good	many/much	few/little
Comparative	sicker	more uncomfortable	better	more	fewer/less
Superlative	sickest	most uncomfortable	best	most	fewest/least

I am **sick** today, but I was **sicker** yesterday. Monday was the **most uncomfortable** day of all. I am **more comfortable** today.

Try It

A. Write the correct adjective to complete each sentence.

1. My team has ______________________ games this year than last year.
   fewer / fewest

2–3. So when I came down with the ______________________ sore throat in the world, I
   worse / worst
   was the ______________________ ever.
   more worried / most worried

4. I wanted to ignore it, but Mom thought it would be a ______________________ idea to go to the doctor.
   better / best

5. I was ______________________ the doctor would say I couldn't play on Saturday.
   afraid / more afraid

6. Then my ______________________ fear would come true, and I would miss the game.
   more horrible / most horrible

B. Write the correct form of the adjective in parentheses.

7. It was the ________________ wait ever at the doctor's office. **(long)**

8. I was even ________________ than before I arrived. **(nervous)**

9. Then I heard the ________________ news of all. I had strep throat. **(scary)**

10. I wish the doctor had some ________________ news than that for me. **(good)**

Write It

C. Complete each sentence about being sick. What did you miss while you were sick? Use comparative and superlative adjectives.

11. When I was sick, I felt ______________________________.

12. That was bad, but it was even ____________ when ______________________________

______________________________.

13. I missed ______________________________.

14. When I got ____________, I ______________________________.

D. (15–18) Different things frighten different people. Write at least four sentences about what frightens you. Use comparative and superlative adjectives.

____

____

____

____

Grammar at Work

E. (19–25) Fix <u>four</u> mistakes with adjectives. Then fix <u>three</u> errors in agreement with **be**, **have**, or **do**.

September 15

Today, I has the sorest throat ever. It is the painfullest experience in the world to swallow. I am happier to miss a day of school, but I are worried about missing the game. In fact, I am most worried than happy. Then, the doctor calls with the good news ever. I has strep throat, but it isn't that bad. I will be better for the game. What can be better than that?

Proofreader's Marks

Change text:

I am ~~healthy~~ healthier now than I was before.

See all Proofreader's Marks on page xi.

Name ______________________________

34 Use Adverbs Correctly

Remember: You can use adverbs to describe and compare actions. An adverb can also make another adverb or adjective stronger.

Describe	Compare	Make Stronger
I went **hesitantly** to the scary movie.	The music boomed **more frightfully** than before.	It was a **really** scary movie.
I watched **fearfully**.	I screamed the **most loudly** ever.	I was **very** scared.

Try It

A. Write adverbs to add details to the sentences.

1. I ________________ like scary movies.
2. This movie was ________________ scary, though.
3. The music boomed the most ________________ ever.
4. The special effects were ________________ scary.
5. Once, I jumped right ________________ of my seat.

B. Complete each sentence. Write the correct form of the adverb in parentheses.

6. This movie was made from the ________________ scary book of all time. **(amazingly)**
7. The movie scared me ________________ than the book did. **(badly)**
8. It seemed to be ________________ suspenseful than the book. **(thoroughly)**
9. I was so ________________ scared that I had to close my eyes. **(extremely)**
10. Don't see this movie unless you want to see the ________________ scary movie in the world! **(powerfully)**

Write It

C. Answer the questions about a scary movie you have seen. Use the correct forms of adverbs in your answers.

11. What was the most terribly scary movie you have ever seen? ______________________

____

12. Why was the movie so very scary? ______________________

____

13. Which scene was the most thoroughly scary of all? What did you do when you watched that scene? ______________________

____

____

D. (14–16) Write at least three sentences about a scary movie that set off your imagination. Use adverbs to describe what you did and how you felt after the movie.

____

____

____

____

____

Grammar at Work

E. (17–20) Fix the <u>three</u> mistakes with adverbs. Fix <u>one</u> error in subject pronoun/verb agreement.

I has the most unbelievably active imagination in the world. When I am home alone, all the normal house noises sound to me like prowlers. If I'm camping, every sound is a wild animal growling most fiercely than the one before. When I'm writing a story, though, my imagination works most best. I write better quickly when I am scared. I imagine many scary things to write about!

Proofreader's Marks

Change text:

I listen ~~most~~ more carefully when I'm home alone than when my family is home.

Delete:

I listen ~~more~~ better when I'm home alone than when my family is home.

See all Proofreader's Marks on page xi.

Name ______________________________

35 How Do I Show Possession?

One Way Is to Use a Possessive Noun.

- Use a **possessive noun** to show that someone owns, or possesses, something.

  The **school's** magazine drive starts today.

  Rosa's parents ordered three magazines.

- A possessive noun can name one owner. Add **'s** to a singular noun to make it a possessive noun that names one owner.

Singular Noun	Possessive Noun
the magazine drive of the **school**	the **school's** magazine drive
the parents of **Rosa**	**Rosa's** parents
the order of one **student**	one **student's** order

Try It

A. Write the underlined words so they include a possessive noun.

1. The class of Mr. Chen has a big order. ______________________________
2. The order of the class is for fifty magazines. ______________________________
3. The family of Julio is getting ten magazines. ______________________________
4. Some magazines are for the office of the dentist. ______________________________

B. Rewrite each sentence to include a possessive noun.

5. The favorite magazine of one dentist is about sports.

   ____

6. The cover of the magazine shows a soccer player.

   ____

7. The face of the player is red and sweaty.

   ____

Write It

C. Answer each question. Use a possessive noun in your answer.

8. Will your school's magazine drive be a success? Why? ______________________

____

9. Whose class do you think will sell the most magazines? ______________________

____

10. Which student will have the biggest order? ______________________

____

11. What magazines will your family's order include? ______________________

____

D. (12–14) Imagine your school is trying to raise money. What might your school do? Write three sentences that have singular possessive nouns.

____

____

____

Edit It

E. (15–20) Edit the journal entry. Fix the six mistakes with possessive nouns.

October 6

I helped at my schools magazine drive today. One boy order was huge. The biggest order, though, came from Mrs. Mitchell' class. One girl had an order from a doctors office. That girl order was for 20 magazines! Another boy had an order from a dentist' office. That order was big, too. I guess the patients read a lot of magazines.

Proofreader's Marks

Add text:

I like Mom's magazine.

Add an apostrophe:

I like Dad's magazine, too.

See all Proofreader's Marks on page xi.

Name ______________________________

36 How Do I Show Possession?

One Way Is to Use a Possessive Noun.

- A **possessive noun** can name more than one owner. Use a possessive noun to show that people own, or possess, something.

  The **students'** field trip will be fun.

  The **children's** teachers are taking them to the city.

- Add only an apostrophe (') if a plural noun ends in -s.

Plural Noun	Possessive Noun
the field trip of the students	the students' field trip

- Add 's if a plural noun does not end in -s.

Plural Noun	Possessive Noun
the teachers of the **children**	the **children's** teachers

Try It

A. Write the underlined words so they include a possessive noun.

1. The classes of the teachers are going to see a play. ______________________
2. The buses of the eighth graders are over here. ______________________
3. Some chaperones are parents of students. ______________________
4. The children of the parents are already on the buses. ______________________

B. Rewrite each sentence to include a possessive noun.

5. The lines of the characters are really funny.

   ____

6. Do you hear the laughter of the people?

   ____

7. The audience likes the parts of the clowns the best.

   ____

Write It

C. Complete the sentences about a field trip to see a play.

8. The teachers' ______________________________.
9. The girls' ______________________________.
10. The children's ______________________________.
11. The characters' ______________________________.

D. (12–14) Imagine you can go on a field trip. Where would you go? What would you see? Write three sentences that have plural possessive nouns.

____

____

____

____

____

Edit It

E. (15–20) Edit the list about a field trip to the zoo. Fix the six mistakes with possessive nouns.

1. At the zoo, I see three giraffes long necks.
2. I see two peacocks beautiful feathers.
3. The many feathers colors amaze me!
4. The wind blows all the boy's hats off their heads.
5. Two teachers' classes see the seals.
6. Three seals balls balance on their noses.
7. The peoples' applause is loud.

Proofreader's Marks

Add text:
The girl'^s trip was fun.

Add an apostrophe:
The childrens class went, too.

Transpose:
The mens children laughed.

See all Proofreader's Marks on page xi.

Name ______________________________

37 How Do I Show Possession?

One Way Is to Use a Possessive Noun.

- Use a **possessive noun** to show that someone owns, or possesses, something. Add **'s** if the possessive noun names one owner.

  Kathy's teacher asks the class to read newspaper articles.

  One **friend's** article is about sports.

  Ted's newspaper has interesting articles in it.

- A possessive noun can name more than one owner. Follow these rules:

  1. Add only an apostrophe if the plural noun ends in **-s**.

  The **students'** newspaper articles are interesting.

  2. Add **'s** if the plural noun does not end in **-s**.

  One article is about **women's** sports.

Try It

A. Change the underlined words to a possessive noun. Write the possessive noun after each sentence.

1. The story of the athlete was wonderful. ______________________

2. The interview by the reporter was excellent. ______________________

3. The interest of readers was high. ______________________

4. I like to read articles by sportswriters. ______________________

B. Rewrite each sentence to include a possessive noun.

5. The newspaper of my school is popular.

____

6. Most articles by students teach me something new.

____

7. Sometimes the articles give the views of people outside the school.

____

Write It

C. Answer the questions about reading the newspaper. Use a possessive noun correctly in each sentence.

8. What newspaper stories have you read about men's sports? ______________________________

____

9. What is your family's favorite part of the newspaper? ______________________________

____

10. Do you think teachers' assignments to read newspapers are good ones? Why or why not? ______________________________

D. (11–14) Write four more sentences about reading newspapers. Use possessive nouns in your response.

____

____

____

____

Edit It

E. (15–20) Edit the letter. Fix the six mistakes with possessive nouns.

Dear Tanya,

Yesterday, Terry and her parents' visited us. Terrys' father is a newspaper reporter. He wrote an article about mens' soccer. My parents and I read the story. Moms reaction to the story was great. She really liked it. Dad's reaction was not so great. He did not agree with the articles' ideas about soccer. That led to a discussion. I enjoyed taking part in the adults discussion!

Love,

Rachel

Proofreader's Marks

Delete:	My family's views' are similar.
Add an apostrophe:	The girls mom listened.
Transpose:	We read the mans' article.

See all Proofreader's Marks on page xi.

Name ______________________________

38 What's a Possessive Adjective?

It's an Ownership Word.

- Use a **possessive adjective** to tell who has or owns something. Put the possessive adjective before the **noun**.

  I like Tim. He is **my cousin**.

  Tim is an artist. I like **his artwork**.

  Many people do artwork for **their jobs**.

- Match the possessive adjective to the **noun** or **pronoun** that it goes with.

  Tim told me about **his** friends at work.
  noun

  They are artists. **Their** artwork is great.
  pronoun

Subject Pronoun	Possessive Adjective
I	my
you	your
he	his
she	her
it	its
we	our
they	their

Try It

A. Complete each sentence about jobs. Use the correct form.

1. ____________________ uncle Arnold is a firefighter.
   Me / My

2. I visited ____________________ firehouse because I want to be a firefighter, too.
   he / his

3. Other firefighters also brought ____________________ families to work.
   they / their

4. The firefighters said, "We really like ____________________ job."
   we / our

B. (5–8) Complete each sentence from the writer's point of view. Use possessive adjectives from the chart above.

I want to be a doctor, just like ______________ father. I know that ______________ city will need more doctors in the future. I asked my father about ______________ education. I wondered if medical schools teach ______________ students different things today.

Write It

C. Answer these questions about careers. Use possessive adjectives.

9. Whom do you talk to about his or her job? I talk with ____________________
about ____________________.

10. What kind of job does that person have? ____________________
____

11. Is this person's job one you would like to have? Why or why not? ____________________
____

D. (12–15) Write four more sentences about other people and their jobs. Use a possessive adjective in each sentence.

____
____
____
____

Edit It

E. (16–20) Edit the journal entry. Fix the five mistakes with possessive adjectives.

December 3
I visited Cousin Vito at he job. Then I told me classmates all about it. Vito has an awesome job! He is an oceanographer. I told the students that Vito works underwater. They jaws dropped. Laura raised she hand. She asked if I had gone underwater, too. I had not. I had visited Vito at he lab.

Proofreader's Marks

Change text:
That is ~~he~~ his career.

See all Proofreader's Marks on page xi.

Name ______________________________

39 What Are the Possessive Pronouns?

Mine*, *Yours*, *His*, *Hers*, *Ours*, and *Theirs

Possessive Adjectives	my	your	his	her	our	their
Possessive Pronouns	mine	yours	his	hers	ours	theirs

Possessive adjectives are used before a noun.

Possessive pronouns stand alone.

This is **our computer lab**.	This computer lab is **ours**.
That computer is **my computer**.	That computer is **mine**.
Joe points to **his desk**.	That desk is **his**.
Ms. Green teaches **her class**.	This class is **hers**.
Which seat is **your seat**?	Which seat is **yours**?

Try It

A. Rewrite each sentence. Change the underlined words to the correct possessive pronoun.

1. My computer isn't working, so Sara lets me use her computer. ______________________________

____

2. Sara's computer is nicer than my computer. ______________________________

____

3. I use the computer for my work, and then Zack uses it for his work. ______________________________

____

4. Ms. Green turns off her computer and asks us to turn off our computers. ______________________________

____

B. **Complete each sentence with a possessive pronoun.**

5. My friends and I play our game on the computer. This game is ________________.

6. My car in the game is blue. That blue car on the screen is ________________.

7. Stephen's car is in the lead right now. The first car is ________________.

8. My brothers are waiting to play their game. That game is ________________.

9. Where is your game? Which game is ________________?

10. Now Mom wants to use her computer for work. This computer is ________________.

Write It

C. **Answer the questions about computers and other technology. Use possessive pronouns.**

11. Is the computer you work on yours, or does it belong to someone else? ________________

____

12. Do your friends depend more on their computers or their books to do homework? ________

____

13. Do you have a calculator or other tools that you use to do your homework? ________

____

14. Would you like to have a video camera that is all yours? Why? ________________

____

15. How could students use their computers to help them write a report? ________________

____

D. **(16–20) Write five questions about computers or computer games. Use a possessive pronoun in each question.**

____

____

____

____

____

____

Name ______________________________

40 What Are Reflexive and Intensive Pronouns?

They Are Pronouns with Special Purposes.

- Use a reflexive pronoun to talk about the same person or thing twice in a sentence.

  You know **yourself** and your study habits.

- Use an intensive pronoun to provide emphasis or make something stronger.

  I myself have to study with music on.

- Avoid these common mistakes with reflexive and intensive pronouns.

  1. Hashid told ~~hisself~~ himself that he would ace the test.

  2. The twins ~~theirselves~~ themselves were nervous about it.

Reflexive and Intensive Pronouns	
Singular	**Plural**
myself	ourselves
yourself	yourselves
himself,	themselves
herself, itself	

Try It

A. Complete each sentence about joining a study group. Write the correct reflexive or intensive pronoun.

1. We must all prepare ______________________ for the big exam.
ourselves / ourself

2. Karen and Kim prepare ______________________ by studying together.
theirselves / themselves

3. I ______________________ do better when I study alone.
meself / myself

B. Draw a line from each noun or pronoun to the correct reflexive pronoun.

4. We surprised	"You can be proud of yourselves."
5. The teacher said,	ourselves by getting top grades.
6. Kim said, "I	myself have more confidence now."
7. Other students were mad	at themselves for not joining our group.

Write It

C. Complete these sentences about how people study. Use a reflexive or intensive pronoun in each sentence.

8. If I study alone, I ____________________.

9. My friends __________ prepare by ____________________.

10. When you study by ____________________.

D. (11–14) Write four sentences that tell how a study group can help you and other students. Use reflexive and intensive pronouns correctly.

____

____

____

____

____

Edit It

E. (15–20) Edit the letter. Fix the six mistakes with pronouns.

Dear Parents,

Next week, students will take a final math exam. Students must prepare themselves for the test. Students can study by theirselves, but study groups can help. You are welcome to set up study groups by ourselves. I will also make me available for private tutoring. Last year, one student gave himselves extra help by joining two study groups. I meself get help in my Chinese study groups. We can consider ourselfs lucky because our students are so hardworking.

Sincerely,

Ms. Juarez

Proofreader's Marks

Change text:

I will study by ~~yourself~~ myself.

See all Proofreader's Marks on page xi.

Name ____________________

41 When Do You Use an Indefinite Pronoun?

When You Can't Be Specific

- When you are not talking about a specific person or thing, you can use an **indefinite pronoun**.

  Everybody helps out. **Someone** reads to the first graders.

- Some indefinite pronouns are always singular, so they need a **singular verb** that ends in **-s**.

  Everything seems to be ready. **Everyone wants** to read.

Singular Indefinite Pronouns			
another	each	everything	nothing
anybody	either	neither	somebody
anyone	everybody	nobody	someone
anything	everyone	no one	something

Try It

A. Complete each sentence. Use the correct form of the verb.

1. Everybody ____________________ our reading club.
   join/joins

2. No one ____________________ left out.
   is/are

3. Everyone ____________________ a turn reading to younger kids.
   take/takes

4. Somebody ____________________ a book to read.
   choose/chooses

B. (5–9) Complete each sentence. Use indefinite pronouns from the chart above.

______________ asks me to read. ______________ wants to hear the the same story. ______________ chooses a different book! What will I do? ______________ makes everybody happy. ______________occurs to me. I can choose the book to read.

Write It

C. Answer the questions about reading. Use indefinite pronouns in your answers. Make sure that the verbs agree with the pronouns.

10. Why would someone want to read to younger kids? ______________________

____

11. Does everybody like to read? ______________________

D. (12–15) Write four sentences about what people like to read and why. Use indefinite pronouns in your sentences.

____

____

____

____

____

Edit It

E. (16–20) Edit the journal entry. Fix the five mistakes in agreement with indefinite pronouns.

October 17

Everyone are busy at our school reading club. Someone passes out magazines. Everybody love to read magazines. Sue reads an article to the first graders. Everything seem interesting to them. Some kids discuss a book. Jen and Al like it. No one else enjoy it. Nothing are as much fun for me as my reading club.

Proofreader's Marks

Change text:

Everyone ~~learn~~ learns to read.

See all Proofreader's Marks on page xi.

Name ______________________________

42 Which Indefinite Pronouns Are Plural?

Both*, *Few*, *Many*, and *Several

- Use an **indefinite pronoun** when you are not talking about a specific person or thing.

  Several of the science classes study water.

  Many of the students do experiments.

- Some **indefinite pronouns** are always plural, so they need a **plural verb**.

  A **few** of the students **write** reports.

  Both **are** good ways to learn.

Plural Indefinite Pronouns	
both	many
few	several

Try It

A. Complete each sentence. Use the correct form of the verb.

1. Many of the students ______________ (read/reads) about water pollution.
2. A few ______________ (learn/learns) about the water supply.
3. Both ______________ (is/are) serious problems.
4. Several of our scientists ______________ (think/thinks) a lot of our water is polluted.
5. A few of my friends ______________ (want/wants) to start a club at school.
6. Many ______________ (discuss/discusses) a name for the club.

B. **Complete each sentence with an indefinite pronoun from the box.**

both	few	many	several

7. ______________ of our teacher advisors like the name Green Group.

8. ______________ of the students do, too.

9. A ______________ prefer the name Water Wonders.

10. ______________ suggest that we vote on a name.

11. ______________ of us vote for Green Group, and it wins.

Write It

C. **Imagine that you are a member of Green Group. Describe it by completing each sentence. Make sure the verb agrees with the indefinite pronoun.**

12. Many of the members ____
____.

13. Several of the issues ____
____.

14. A few of our activities ____
____.

15. Both of our advisors ____
____.

D. **(16–20) Are you concerned about water pollution? Write five sentences about what you could do to learn more or to help out. Use an indefinite pronoun in each sentence. Make sure the verb agrees with the pronoun.**

____

____

____

____

____

Name ______________________________

43 Which Indefinite Pronouns Are Tricky?

The Ones That Can Be Singular or Plural

- The **indefinite pronouns** in the chart can be either singular or plural.
- The **prepositional phrase** after the pronoun shows whether the sentence talks about one thing or more than one thing. Use the correct **verb**.

Singular or Plural Indefinite Pronouns	
all	none
any	some
most	

Singular: **Some** of my town **is** rural.

Plural: **Some** of the houses **are** far apart.

Singular: **Most** of my family **works** downtown.

Plural: **Most** of the people **take** public transportation.

Singular: **All** of the public transportation **travels** to the city.

Plural: **All** of the buses **stop** in my town.

Try It

A. Complete each sentence about commuting to work. Use the correct form of the verb.

1. None of our neighbors ______________ (walk/walks) to work.
2. Most of the work places ______________ (is/are) too far away.
3. Some of the neighborhood ______________ (use/uses) public transportation.
4. All of the public transportation ______________ (consist/consists) of buses.
5. Any of the buses ______________ (take/takes) commuters to the city.
6. Some of our community ______________ (carpool/carpools) to work.

B. **Complete each sentence about commuting with the correct form of a verb.**

7. Some of my friends' parents ______________ their bikes to work.

8. Most of the bike riders ______________ on bike paths.

9. All of the exercise ______________ the parents healthy.

10. None of that transportation ______________ pollution.

Write It

C. **Complete each sentence about different kinds of transportation that people use. Make sure the verb agrees with the indefinite pronoun.**

11. Some of my friends ____

____.

12. None of the transportation ________________________________

____.

13. All of the transportation __________________________________

____.

14. To get to school, most of the school ________________________

____.

15. Any of the vehicles ______________________________________

____.

D. **(16–20) What kinds of transportation are best for commuting? Write five sentences, using an indefinite pronoun in each one. Make sure the verb agrees with the pronoun.**

____

____

____

____

____

____

Name ____________________

44 Show Possession

Remember: Use possessive words to show that someone owns something. A possessive adjective comes before a noun. A possessive pronoun stands alone.

Possessive Adjectives	my	your	his	her	its	our	your	their
Possessive Pronouns	mine	yours	his	hers		ours	yours	theirs

Try It

A. Complete each sentence. Write the correct possessive word.

1. ____________________ cat Molly has yellow fur. (**My/Mine**)
2. Does ____________________ have yellow fur, too? (**your/yours**)
3. Every day, we give Molly ____________________ vitamins. (**her/hers**)
4. We take Molly to ____________________ veterinarian for checkups. (**our/ours**)
5. It is the same veterinarian as ____________________. (**your/yours**)

B. Write possessive words from the chart to complete the sentences.

6. "You take really good care of ______________ cat," the vet told us.
7. "Molly is lucky to be ______________ ," she said.
8. "We try ______________ best," Mom said.
9. We are glad that Molly is ______________.

Write It

C. Underline the possessive pronoun in each question. Then answer the question. Use the correct possessive adjective in your answer.

10. Think about friends or neighbors that have more than one pet. Which pets are theirs?

____

11. Think about a girl you know who has a dog. What kind of dog is hers? ____________

____

12. If you could have any pet at all, which pet would be yours? ____________

____

D. (13–15) Write three sentences about pets. Use three different possessive words in your sentences.

____

____

____

Grammar at Work

E. (16–20) Fix the four errors with possessive words. Fix one error in comparing with adjectives.

Mine Cat Molly

Molly is 12 years old, but she still acts like a kitten. When Mom takes out hers knitting, Molly attacks the yarn. Molly thinks the yarn is a toy, and she thinks the toy is her. Whenever we sit down, Molly jumps right up on ours laps and purrs. I always pet her soft fur. Molly is most cuddly now than when she was a kitten. I think Molly is the best cat in the world.

Proofreader's Marks

Change text:

Is that cat ~~your~~ yours?

See all Proofreader's Marks on page xi.

Name ______________________________

45 Use Indefinite Pronouns and Verbs

Remember: Use an indefinite pronoun when you are not talking about a specific person or thing. Match the verb to the pronoun.

- Use a singular verb with a singular pronoun:

another	**each**	**everything**	**nothing**
anybody	**either**	**neither**	**somebody**
anyone	**everybody**	**nobody**	**someone**
anything	**everyone**	**no one**	**something**

- Use a plural verb with a plural pronoun:

both	**few**	**many**	**several**

- Choose the correct verb for a pronoun that can be singular or plural:

all	**any**	**most**	**none**	**some**

Try It

A. Write the correct form of the verb to complete each sentence.

1. All of my friends ______________________ in the play.
am/are

2. Everyone ______________________ the lines.
learn/learns

3. A few ______________________ the lines already.
know/knows

4. Most of the cast ______________________ in the play.
sing/sings

B. Write an indefinite pronoun to complete each sentence.

5. _______________ wants to see our play.

6. _______________ of the auditorium is full.

7. Only a _______________ of the seats are empty.

8. _______________ of the people clap when the play starts.

Write It

C. Complete each sentence about the play. Make sure to use the correct form of a verb with each indefinite pronoun.

9. Everyone ______________ because ______________________________.

10. After the play, most of the audience ______________________________.

11. Several of the actors ______________________________.

12. No one ______________________________.

D. (13–15) Would you like to be in a play? Write three sentences to tell why. Use an indefinite pronoun in each sentence. Make sure to use the correct form of the verb.

____

____

____

____

Grammar at Work

E. (16–20) Fix the four errors with verbs to make them match the indefinite pronouns. Fix one error in comparing with adverbs.

Dear Aunt Lil,

The play is tonight. Everyone are very excited. All of my family want to see me in my first play. Several of my friends helps me get ready. None of them are in the play. A few works in the crew, though. This play is extremely funny. Many of the lines make people laugh the more uproariously ever.

Love,

Kelsey

Proofreader's Marks

Change text: Everybody ~~love~~ loves the play.

See all Proofreader's Marks on page xi.

Name ____________________________________

46 How Do You Know When the Action Happens?

Look at the Verb.

An **action verb** tells what the subject does. The tense of a verb tells when the action happens.

Present Tense
sing
sing**s**

Use the **present tense** to talk about actions that happen now or that happen on a regular basis.

My family **sings** in a chorus together.

We **practice** at the community center once a week.

Try It

A. Complete each sentence with the correct form of the verb in parentheses.

1. My father ________________ my family to chorus practice. **(drive)**

2. We ________________ music together. **(enjoy)**

3. Sometimes, my brother ________________ the guitar while the chorus sings. **(play)**

4. My brother and I ________________ to perform for large audiences. **(like)**

5. Our chorus ________________ several times each month. **(perform)**

B. (6–11) Complete each sentence with a verb from the box.

believes	feel	play	learn	takes	values

My family ________________ that everyone should develop musical skills. My brother ________________ guitar lessons. I ________________ to play the drums. My sister and father ________________ the piano. We all ________________ that music is an important part of life. Our family ________________ music.

Write It

C. Answer the questions about musical talents, using present tense verbs.

12. What musical skills do you or your family learn through lessons and practice?
Through lessons and practice, ______________________________.

13. How do music studies help you? Music studies help me because ______________________________
______________________________.

14. In what other ways do you learn about music? ______________________________
____

15. Would you tell a friend to play an instrument or learn to sing? ______________________________
____

16. Whose musical skills do you admire? ______________________________

17. How do you think musical talent and study affect this person? ______________________________
____

D. (18–20) Write three sentences about your musical studies or skills using the present tense.

____
____
____

Edit It

E. (21–25) Edit the music review. Fix the five mistakes with present tense verb form.

Music Review

The band called "We Are Family" performs well. They shines on stage together. Ricardo play keyboard. His sister Marta sings and play guitar. Their uncle Daniel plays drums and sings, too. The family members writes and play their own music. They travel from city to city across the country. Audiences all over loves their shows.

Proofreader's Marks

Delete:
Greg and Suri raps well.

Add text:
He play the violin. (s)

See all Proofreader's Marks on page xi.

Name ____________________

47 Which Action Verbs End in *-s*?

The Ones That Go with *He*, *She*, or *It*

- An **action verb** tells what someone or something does.
- Add -s to the action verb if the subject tells about one place, one thing, or one other person.

  Tina listens to music when she exercises. The music gives her energy.

  Aunt Dee plays the radio in the car. She keeps the volume low to be safe.
- If the verb ends in **sh**, **ch**, **ss**, **s**, **z**, or **x**, add -es.

  Sharese **relaxes** when she listens to songs with a slow rhythm.

  My family **teaches** me about music.
- Do not add -s to the action verb if the subject is **I**, **you**, **we**, **they**, or a plural noun.

  I **watch** my family. You could **learn** from them.

  The musicians **experiment** with different styles. They **get** feedback from the audience.

Try It

A. Complete each sentence about music. Write the correct form of the verb.

1. Music ____________________ people.
   affect / affects
2. It ____________________ people in many ways.
   help / helps
3. People in my family ____________________ to music in different ways.
   react / reacts
4. My sister ____________________ music videos to understand the songs more clearly.
   watch / watches
5. When my brother wakes up to his favorite song, he eagerly ____________________ out of bed.
   spring / springs
6. My aunt ____________________ her high school friends when she hears certain songs.
   miss / misses

B. Complete each sentence with the correct form of the verb in parentheses.

7. I see how music ______________ other people. **(affect)**

8. My baby cousin ______________ asleep to quiet music. **(fall)**

9. When I cannot sleep, I ______________ to slow music. **(listen)**

10. My brother ______________ the music when he does his homework. **(stop)**

11. My sister ______________ to play her favorite radio program after school. She says it puts her in a better mood. **(rush)**

Write It

C. Answer the questions about how people react to music. Use action verbs.

12. How do your friends like upbeat music? My friends ______________________________

______________________________.

13. How do they like quiet music? They ______________________________

______________________________.

14. How do you react to music in different situations? ______________________________

____

15. In what situations does music seem more or less helpful? ______________________________

____

D. (16–20) Write five more sentences about how people react to your favorite style of music. Use action verbs correctly in your sentences.

____

____

____

____

____

____

Name ______________________________

48 How Do You Show That an Action Is in Process?

Use *Am*, *Is*, or *Are* Plus the *-ing* Form of the Verb.

- The **present progressive** form of the verb ends in -ing.
- Use **am, is,** or **are** plus a **main verb** with -ing to show that an action is in the process of happening.
  The **helping verb** must agree with the subject.
  I **am writing** a new poem.
  The poem **is taking** a long time to write.
  My friends **are asking** to read it.
  They **are waiting** patiently to read the new poem.

Try It

A. Write the correct form of the present progressive to complete each sentence.

1. My friends and I ______________________ a band.
   is forming / are forming
2. I ______________________ drums.
   am playing / are playing
3. Jorge and Delilah ______________________ the vocals.
   is singing / are singing
4. We ______________________ after school today.
   is practicing / are practicing
5. The band ______________________ many kinds of music.
   is performing / are performing

B. Draw lines to connect the words in the first column with those in the second column. Create sentences that make sense.

6. My classmates and I	am taking photographs of places in our city and school.
7. We	are forming a photography club.
8. I	is teaching us about our view of the community.
9. DeShaun	are planning to have an exhibit next month.
10. This project	is taking photographs of his friends and family.

Write It

C. Answer the questions about a creative project that is teaching you about yourself or others. Use the present progressive form in your responses.

11. What creative project are you working on now? I am ______________________________
____.

12. Who is helping you with the project? ______________________ me on my project.

13. What activities are you or others doing as part of the project? ______________
____

14. What are you learning about your own skills and talents? ______________
____

15. What is the project teaching you about working with others? ______________
____

D. (16–19) Write four sentences about a current project and what you are learning from it. Use the present progressive form in your responses.

____
____
____
____

Edit It

E. (20–25) Edit the radio broadcast. Fix the six mistakes with the present progressive form.

Liam is describing the scene here at Fairview High for our radio listeners:

"A young man are standing on a ladder in the cafeteria. A female student is put tape around the windows. A group of students is carry boxes. What are they do? They painting a mural! We is waiting anxiously to see it when it's done."

Proofreader's Marks

Add text:	We are paint^ing the gym.
Change text:	~~We is~~ We are working hard.

See all Proofreader's Marks on page xi.

Name ______________________________

49 Can You Just Add *-ed* to Form a Verb in the Past?

Not Always

Most verbs end with **-ed** to show the past tense. Sometimes you have to change the spelling of the verb before you add **-ed**.

1. If a verb ends in silent **e**, drop the **e**. Then add **-ed**.

My grandmother liv**ed** in a small village when she was younger. **(live)**

The people in the village relat**ed** this story for many years. **(relate)**

2. Some one-syllable verbs end in one vowel and one consonant. Double the consonant before you add **-ed**.

There were men who robb**ed** villages. **(rob)**

The story tells how a girl stopp**ed** the robbers. **(stop)**

Try It

A. Complete each sentence with the past tense of the verb in parentheses.

1. One day, at home alone, the girl ______________ some strangers. **(notice)**

2. She ______________ they were robbers. **(believe)**

3. The girl ______________ how to stop them. **(plan)**

4. She ______________ a white cloth. **(grab)**

5. Then she ______________ outside. **(race)**

6. The robbers ______________ people to catch them. **(dare)**

B. (7–11) Complete each sentence with a past tense verb.

At dusk, the girl ______________ behind the house. She ______________ on the walls. She ______________ the white cloth like it was a ghost. She ______________ the robbers so much that they left the village. The villagers ______________ the girl Clever One.

Write It

C. Answer the questions using the past tense.

12. What did the robbers do when they thought they saw a ghost? They ____.

13. What did the girl do after the robbers left? She ____.

D. (14–17) Think about a story you know about a hero or legend. Write four sentences telling the main events in the story. Use the past tense.

____

____

____

____

____

Edit It

E. (18–25) Edit the journal entry. Fix the eight mistakes with verbs.

January 14

Last week, it snowed so much that we works inside. We use up all our food, so Father decides to go to town. Ice covers the roads. The horse slips on the ice, so Father walks many miles to the store. Then he drags a box of food back to us through the snow. Finally, he open the door.

Proofreader's Marks

Change text:

We ~~close~~ ^closed the door after Father.

See all Proofreader's Marks on page xi.

Name ______________________________

50 Can You Just Add *-ed* to Form a Verb in the Past?

Not Always

Most verbs end with **-ed** to show the past tense. Follow these rules to add **-ed** to words that end with **y**:

1. If a verb ends in a vowel + **y**, do not double the consonant. Add only **-ed**.

Last summer, my family stay**ed** in a cabin in the woods. **(stay)**

My sister and I play**ed** next to a lake. **(play)**

2. If a verb ends in a consonant + **y**, change the **y** to **i**. Then add **-ed**.

try + -ed = tried — We tr**ied** to catch fireflies. **(try)**

carry + -ed = carried — We carr**ied** jars into the woods. **(carry)**

Try It

A. Write the past tense of the verb in parentheses.

1. For our vacation, Mom ________________ maps. **(study)**

2. We ________________ to get ready. **(hurry)**

3. "Do you remember the cabin we ________________ in last year?" my sister asked. **(stay)**

4. That year, we ________________ inside because of poison ivy. **(play)**

B. (5–7) Complete the conversation between two sisters. Use the past tense of the verbs in the box.

try	cry	bury

Teresa: I touched poison ivy when I ________________ the secret box.

Gina: You really ________________ about the rash!

Teresa: I itched even *after* I ________________ that pink lotion!

Write It

C. Answer the questions about a family trip. Use past tense verbs.

8. What family vacation do you remember well? I ______________________________

______________________________.

9. Where did you stay? My family ______________________________

______________________________.

D. (10–14) Now, write five sentences about a family trip. Use the past tense of two verbs that end in y.

____

____

____

____

____

Edit It

E. (15–20) Edit the journal entry. Fix the six mistakes with verbs.

My brother's friend Shirley camped with us. Shirley annoyied me at first. She cryed about the dirt. She sprays bug spray everywhere. She almost destroy our tent. Still, we all play cards with her. Mom even fry fish for her dinner.

Proofreader's Marks

Change text:

Last year, I ~~worries~~ worried about Shirley.

See all Proofreader's Marks on page xi.

Name ______________________________

51 When Do You Use *Was* and *Were*?

When You Tell About the Past

The verb **be** has special forms to tell about the present and the past.

Past Tense	Present Tense
I **was**	I **am**
you **were**	you **are**
he, she, or it **was**	he, she, or it **is**
we **were**	we **are**
they **were**	they **are**

Present: Our school's soccer team **is** not very good.

Past: Last year, it **was** the worst team in the league.

Present: Our athletes **are** always surprised when they do well.

Past: They **were** really surprised when Felipe scored the winning goal.

Try It

A. Rewrite each sentence using the past tense of the verb.

1. It is our first game of the season. ______________________________

____

2. We are behind. ______________________________

3. There are only two minutes left. ______________________________

4. Felipe is in the middle of the field. ______________________________

____

5. His teammates are excited. ______________________________

B. **(6–13) Complete each sentence with the correct past tense form.**

Felipe ______________ small but quick. Two guys from the other team ______________ in his way. Felipe kicked the ball and jumped between them. It looked like he ______________ in the air! When he landed, Felipe ______________ near the goal. All the fans ______________ excited when Felipe scored. At the kick-off, Felipe ______________ the first to get the ball. We ______________ happy when Felipe scored yet again. It ______________ unbelievable!

Write It

C. **Answer the questions. Use was and were in your answers.**

14. What was your response to Felipe's part in the soccer game? ______________________________

____

15. What do you think the fans said to Felipe after the game? ______________________________

____

16. What do you think Felipe said about the game? ______________________________

____

D. **(17–20) Think about someone or something that amazed you. Write four sentences about what happened. Use was and were.**

____

____

____

____

____

____

Name ______________________________

52 How Do You Show That an Action Already Happened?

Change the Verb.

Add -ed to most verbs to show that an action already happened.
Use special past tense forms for **irregular verbs.**

Present	Past	Example in the Past
come	came	The fire alarm **came** as no surprise.
bring	brought	The alarm **brought** my dad to his feet.
know	knew	Dad and the other firefighters **knew** what to do.
do, does	did	They **did** everything they had to.
get	got	They **got** dressed.
find	found	They **found** their gear.
go, goes	went	Then they **went** to the fire truck.
stand	stood	Dad **stood** in the back of the truck.
see	saw	Then they **saw** the house on fire.
have, has	had	They **had** everything they needed to fight it.

Try It

A. Rewrite each sentence, changing the verb to the past tense.

1. The firefighters know what to do. ______________________________
____

2. They find their helmets. ______________________________

3. They get out the hoses. ______________________________

4. Some of the firefighters stand with the hoses outside the house. ______________________________
____

5. Then they see a man. ______________________________

B. **Complete each sentence with the past tense of the verb in parentheses.**

6. Dad ______________ a mask to help him breathe. **(get)**

7. Then he ______________ into the house. **(go)**

8. He ______________ he had to hurry. **(know)**

9. He ______________ a man inside. **(find)**

10. Dad ______________ the man out. **(bring)**

Write It

C. **Answer the questions. Use some irregular verbs in the past tense.**

11. How did Dad find the man in the house? He ______________________________

____.

12. What did the firefighters do that was brave? They ______________________________

____.

D. **(13–16) Think about a brave person in your community. Write four sentences about what this person did that was brave. Use the past tense of some irregular verbs.**

____

____

____

____

____

Edit It

E. **(17–20) Edit the news report. Fix the four mistakes.**

Yesterday, there was an accident. A truck goes off the road. They find the driver asleep at the wheel. Paramedics come and treated the driver. Then they bringed him to the hospital.

Proofreader's Marks

Change text:

They ~~come~~ came in time to help.

See all Proofreader's Marks on page xi.

Name ___________________________

53 How Do You Show That an Action Was in Process?

Use *Was* or *Were* Plus the *-ing* Form of the Verb.

- When you want to show that an action was happening over a period of time in the past, use the past progressive form of the verb.
- To form the past progressive, use the helping verb **was** or **were** plus a **main verb** that ends in **-ing**. Make sure that the **helping verb** agrees with the subject.

  Fall **was lasting** into December.

  All the kids **were wondering** if winter would ever come.

  We **were begging** for a snow day.

Try It

A. Complete each sentence. Use the past progressive form of the verb in parentheses.

1. My brothers and I ______________ for our first snowfall. **(wait)**
2. I ______________ the sky. **(watch)**
3. The clouds ______________ fuller and darker. **(get)**
4. I ______________ they were snow clouds. **(hope)**
5. Suddenly, snow ______________ everywhere! **(fall)**

B. Use verbs in the past progressive form to complete each sentence.

6. Within seconds, we ______________ our friends.
7. They ______________ us at the same time.
8. One friend on my street ______________ snowballs already.
9. Within a half hour, everyone ______________ in the snow.

Write It

C. Write about the weather. Use the past progressive forms of verbs.

10. Tell about a time when something unusual was happening in the weather. ____________

____

11. What were you doing at the time? ____________

____

12. What were you thinking about? ____________

____

D. **(13–15) Tell about a time when you were waiting for something exciting to happen. Use the past progressive form of verbs.**

____

____

____

____

Edit It

E. **(16–20) Edit the paragraph. Fix the five mistakes in use of the past progressive.**

Last year, we was having the driest winter ever! It was March, and we were still waiting for our first snow day. I were sitting in the kitchen, gobbling down my oatmeal. Dad were yelling for me to hurry. And then I saw them. Fat snowflakes was falling outside the window. We turned on the radio. Yay! They were just announcing that school being called off for the day!

Proofreader's Marks

Add text:
was
I ^ listening to the radio.

Change text:
were
We ~~was~~ hoping for a snow day.

See all Proofreader's Marks on page xi.

54 How Do You Tell About the Future?

Use *Will* Before the Verb.

The **future tense** of a verb shows that an action will happen later.

Earlier Now Later

Past ⟵——○————————○————————●——⟶ Future

Future Tense
will complete

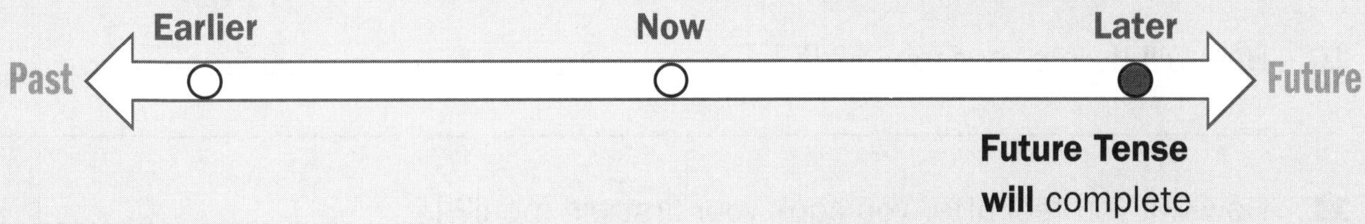

- To form the future tense, use **will** before the main verb.
 We **will complete** safety training at school.

- You can also use **am**, **is**, or **are** plus **going to** before the main verb.
 We **are going to complete** safety training at school.

Try It

A. Complete each sentence. Use the future tense of the verb in parentheses.
More than one answer is possible.

1. In school, we _____ how to cook safely. **(learn)**

2. Our teacher _____ a video about food safety. **(show)**

3. Then she _____ how to make soup. **(explain)**

4. We _____ the stovetop. **(use)**

5. We _____ a test to show what we learned. **(take)**

B. Complete each sentence. Use the future tense of a verb from the box. More than one answer is possible.

help cook know

6. Learning to cook _____ us later.

7. We _____ some great meals.

8. We _____ how to cook safely.

Write It

C. Answer the questions. Use future tense verbs in your sentences.

9. How will learning to cook help you? It ______________________________
______________________________.

10. How will it help your family? It ______________________________
______________________________.

11. How will you feel after you cook your first big meal? I ______________________________
______________________________.

D. (12–16) **Imagine you will cook a big meal for your family. What will you cook? Write five sentences about what you will cook. Use future tense verbs in your sentences.**

____
____
____
____
____
____

Edit It

E. (17–20) **Edit the class description. Use the future tense with will. Fix the four mistakes.**

Baking 101

This course will teach how to bake cakes. Also, students learn about cookies. At the end of the course, students show their skills. The instructor present material in different ways. Students have a test on the last day.

Proofreader's Marks

Change text:

It ~~help~~ ^will help me at work.

See all Proofreader's Marks on page xi.

Name ______________________

55 Use Verb Tenses

Remember: You have to change the verb to show the past tense.

Add **-ed** to most verbs. You may need to make a spelling change before you add **-ed**.

Present Tense	Past Tense
work, works	worked
want, wants	wanted
drag, drags	dragged
live, lives	lived

Use special forms for the past tense of **be** and **have**.

Forms of *Be*

Present Tense	Past Tense
am, is, are	was, were

Forms of *Have*

Present Tense	Past Tense
have, has	had

Try It

A. Complete each sentence, using the correct form of the verb.

1. Last year, I ______________ (**have / had**) an assignment to write about someone who helped people.

2. I ______________ (**decide / decided**) to research César Chávez.

3. I ______________ (**learn / learned**) that César Chávez and his family ______________ (**are / were**) farm workers.

4. César Chávez ______________ (**help / helped**) the farm workers ask for changes.

B. Complete each sentence with the past tense of the verb in parentheses.

5. Chávez ______________ a better life for farm workers. **(want)**

6. Many farm workers ______________ the effort. **(join)**

7. Some grape growers ______________ to listen to the workers. **(refuse)**

Write It

C. Answer the questions. Use the past tense.

8. Why did Chávez ask people not to buy grapes? He ______________________________

____

____.

9. What do you think happened because people didn't buy grapes? I think ______________

____

____.

D. (10–14) What do you think about César Chávez? Write five sentences to explain your opinion. Use the past tense in some of your sentences.

____

____

____

____

____

Grammar at Work

E. (15–20) Fix the five mistakes with verbs. Fix one mistake with a possessive word.

As a boy, César Chávez and his family moves around California. They live where there was work for them. Most of the time, theirs work was very hard. Sometimes, César has a sore back at the end of the day. But he earn a little money for his family. Later, César Chávez helps many more farm workers.

Proofreader's Marks

Change text: worked

César Chávez ~~work~~ hard.

See all Proofreader's Marks on page xi.

Name ______________________________

56 Use Verb Tenses

Remember: Change the verb to show when an action happens.

- The verb tense tells if an action happens in the **present**, **past**, or **future**.
- Show an action happening over time with the progressive form.
- There are two ways to show the future tense.

Present Tense	Aunt Dell **is** in Costa Rica.
Present Progressive	She is **helping** people.
Past Tense	She **went** there last fall.
Past Progressive	She **was responding** to a need.
Future Tense	She **will stay** there for a month. She **is going to work** hard.

Try It

A. Complete each sentence. Use the correct tense of the verb in parentheses.

1. Last year, a big storm ______________ homes in Costa Rica. **(past progressive form of *damage*)**
2. The Costa Ricans ______________ people to help them rebuild. **(past tense of *need*)**
3. Yesterday, my aunt ______________ on her way home. **(past tense of *be*)**
4. She ______________ a poster about Costa Rica. **(past tense of *see*)**
5. It said that people in Costa Rica ______________ help. **(past progressive form of *need*)**
6. "I ______________ to Costa Rica," she said. **(future tense of *go*)**
7. My aunt ______________ for Costa Rica next month. **(future tense of *leave*)**
8. She ______________ already. **(present progressive form of *pack*)**

Write It

B. Answer the questions. Use different tenses to make your meaning clear.

9. Why does Aunt Dell want to go to Costa Rica? ______________________________

____

10. What are you going to do to help others this year? ______________________________

____

C. (11–14) Think about someone who helped people from far away. Write four sentences about what this person did and will do in the future. Use different tenses to make your ideas clear.

____

____

____

____

____

Grammar at Work

D. (15–22) Fix the <u>six</u> mistakes with verbs. Fix the <u>two</u> mistakes in agreement with indefinite pronouns.

Dear Anna,

Yesterday is a great day for me. I complete my first house! In Costa Rica, I am always work with others. Everybody have a job. Many of the volunteers is so handy. Last night, the volunteers and I was feeling very proud. Tomorrow, we worked on a new house. I send pictures soon!

Love,
Aunt Dell

Proofreader's Marks

Change text:

Aunt Dell ~~help~~ helped build houses.

See all Proofreader's Marks on page xi.

Name ______________________________

57 How Do Nouns Work in a Sentence?

They Can Be the Subject or the Object.

- Nouns can be the **subject** of a sentence.

  Dogs are good pets.
  subject

- Nouns can also be the **object** of an action verb. To find the object, turn the verb into a question like: "Fear what?"
  Your answer is the object.

  Some people fear **dogs**.
  verb object

- Many English sentences follow this pattern: **subject → verb → object.**

  Some dogs cause problems.
  subject verb object

  But my dog saved a life!
  subject verb object

Try It

A. Read each sentence. Write whether the underlined noun is a subject or an object.

1. My family owns a German shepherd. ______________
2. Lucky is huge! ______________
3. Some people fear Lucky. ______________
4. But Dad trained Lucky well. ______________
5. Lucky loves children. ______________
6. Last week, a child fell into the river. ______________
7. Lucky and I heard the splash. ______________
8. Lucky pulled the child to safety. ______________
9. The child's parents thanked Lucky. ______________
10. My family gave Lucky treats. ______________

Write It

B. Choose an object from the box to complete each sentence.

buildings	jobs	movie	mountains
victims	rain	noses	people

11. Some search-and-rescue dogs find lost ______________.

12. They search ______________.

13. They find ______________ after plane accidents.

14. Search-and-rescue dogs have strong ______________.

15. They are not bothered by snow and ______________ .

16. I watched a ______________ about search-and-rescue dogs.

17. The dogs search the ______________ for lost hikers.

18. They seem to like their ______________!

C. Answer the questions. Be sure your sentences contain a subject and an object.

19. How do search-and-rescue dogs help people? ______________________________

____

20. What else can search-and-rescue dogs do? ______________________________

____

D. (21–25) Your friend wants to train search-and-rescue dogs. Write five sentences about what you think of the idea. Use subjects and objects in your sentences.

____

____

____

____

____

____

Name ________________________________

58 Why Are There So Many Pronouns?

Some Work as Subjects, and Some Work as Objects.

- Use a **subject pronoun** as the subject of a sentence.

  My **uncle** is an emergency room doctor. **He** (subject) saves lives every day.

  His **hospital** treats 400 patients every day. **It** (subject) is a busy place.

- Use an **object pronoun** as the object of the verb.

  Yesterday a bad storm occurred. Many people feared **it** (object).

  A boy got hurt. His parents rushed **him** (object) to the hospital.

- The pronouns **you** and **it** stay the same as subjects and objects.

Pronouns

Subject	Object
I	me
you	you
he	him
she	her
it	it

Try It

A. Complete each pair of sentences with a pronoun. Circle the noun from the first sentence that the pronoun refers to.

1. Nathan fell down during the storm. ______________ hurt his leg.

2. My uncle examined the leg. ______________ was broken.

3. My uncle calmed Nathan. He told ______________ not to worry.

4. Nathan was brave. His parents praised ______________.

B. (5–9) Complete the sentences with subject and object pronouns.

The mayor wrote a letter about my uncle. The letter praised ______________. My mother framed ______________. ______________ gave the framed letter to Uncle Lee yesterday. ______________ thanked ______________ with a hug.

Write It

C. Answer the questions. Use subject and object pronouns.

10. How does Uncle Lee help people? He ______________________________

______________________________.

11. Why is his job important? It ______________________________

______________________________.

D. (12–15) Think about a real or made-up doctor. Write four sentences about this person. Use subject and object pronouns.

____

____

____

____

____

____

Edit It

E. (16–20) Edit the letter. Fix the five mistakes with pronouns.

Dear Dr. Hill,

I want to thank he. You fixed my leg. I can use him well now. Yesterday, me even walked a mile! My parents say thank you, too. You helped they feel calm. Them will never forget all of your help.

Sincerely yours,

Nathan

Proofreader's Marks

Change text:

She
~~Her~~ wanted to thank you.

See all Proofreader's Marks on page xi.

Name ___________________________

59 Which Pronouns Refer to More Than One Person?

We, You, They, and Us, You, Them

With so many pronouns, how do you know which one to use in a sentence?

- Use a **subject pronoun** as the subject.

  My **friends and I** like school dances. **We** (subject) enjoy the music.

  The teachers hold a meeting. **They** (subject) want to end the dances.

- Use an **object pronoun** as the object of the verb.

  But **dances** are important. Students like **them** (object).

  We (subject) talk to the teachers. The teachers listen to **us** (object).

Pronouns	
Subject	**Object**
we	us
you	you
they	them

Try It

A. Complete each pair of sentences with a pronoun. Circle the word or words each pronoun refers to.

1. The teachers explain the problem. ________________ say the dances are expensive.
They / Them

2. The dances matter to the other students and me. They give ________________ a place to see friends.
us / we

3. "You and I will raise money for the dances," said my friend. "________________ will wash people's cars."
Us / We

4. We made signs for the carwash. Then we posted ________________ around town.
they / them

5. My friends and I collected supplies. A store gave ________________ soap.
we / us

B. **(6–10) Complete the sentences, using subject and object pronouns.**

My friend and I stood on a corner with a sign. A lot of people saw _______________. _______________ drove into the carwash. Some people got out of their cars. Other people sat in _______________. The other students and I washed the cars. _______________ made them shine. The people paid _______________ five dollars per car.

Write It

C. **Answer the questions. Use subject and object pronouns in your sentences.**

11. What do you think the students did with the money they earned? I think _______________

____

____.

12. What do you think the teachers might say to the students? _______________

____

____

D. **(13–15) Think of something about your school that you would like to change. Write three sentences about ways to change it. Use subject and object pronouns.**

____

____

____

____

____

Name ______________________________

60 What Kinds of Things Do Prepositions Show?

Location, Direction, and Time

Prepositions That Show Location: in, on top of, on, at, over, under, above, below, next to, beside, in front of, in back of, behind

- Use a preposition of **location** to tell where something is.

  Hector's mom keeps her old books **under** her bed.
  She keeps them **in** a big box.

Prepositions That Show Direction: into, throughout, up, down, through, across, to

- Use a preposition of **direction** to tell where something is going.

  Hector's sister Sonrisa reaches **into** the box for some books.
  She and Hector walk **through** the house, looking for more books to read.

Prepositions That Show Time: after, until, before, during

- Use a preposition of **time** to tell when something happens.

  Sonrisa finds a book **before** dinner. Hector finds his book **after** dinner.

Try It

A. Complete each sentence about reading a book. Add a preposition.

1. Hector reads the book ______________ the bus.
2. He sees that his mother wrote her name ______________ the book.
3. Donna sits ______________ Hector.
4. He holds the book ______________ her so she can see it, too.

B. Complete each sentence about reading a book. Choose the correct preposition.

5. The book is about a boy in California ____________________ the 1960s.
   during / on
6. Donna tells Hector that she wants to go ____________________ California.
   at / to
7. Hector says he wants to live ____________________ the ocean someday.
   beside / in

Write It

C. Answer the questions about reading. Use prepositions.

8. At what time of day do you usually read? ______________________

9. Where do you read? ______________________

10. What do you do with books after you read them? ______________________

11. Where do you get most of your books? ______________________

12. Do your friends or family suggest books to you after they read them? ______________________

____

D. (13–17) Write five sentences that tell about the books you most like to read. Use prepositions.

____

____

____

____

____

Edit It

E. (18–25) Edit the letter. Fix the eight mistakes with prepositions.

Dear Uncle Bernie,

Thank you for the great book. I loved reading it. I also like science fiction stories about life in other planets. I gave the book over my friend Tim until school. He took it at his house. Don't worry, he will return it during next Friday. I can't wait before your next visit! Will that be above Saturday? I can return the book under your visit.

Your nephew,

Aaron

Proofreader's Marks

Change text: I read ~~before~~ after dinner.

See all Proofreader's Marks on page xi.

Name ______________________________

61 How Do You Recognize a Prepositional Phrase?

Look for the Preposition.

- A **prepositional phrase** is a group of words that begins with a preposition and ends with a noun or pronoun. Use prepositional phrases to add information to your sentences.

  Felix sat **near the window**.
  (near = preposition; window = noun)

  Victor walked **through the library** **to Felix**.
  (through = preposition; library = noun; Felix = noun)

- The **noun** at the end of a prepositional phrase is called the **object of the preposition**.

Try It

A. Add a prepositional phrase to tell more.

1. Victor found the book. He found the book ______________.
2. He read the story. He read the story ______________.
3. Alex liked the book's setting. He liked the book's setting ______________.
4. His sister liked the picture. She liked the picture ______________.
5. Alex showed the book. He showed the book ______________.

B. (6–11) Write a prepositional phrase to complete each sentence. You may use the same preposition more than once.

Victor finds a new novel ____________________. The story takes place ____________________. He shows it to Paco. Paco looks quickly ____________________. He hands it back ____________________. He says that his family plans a visit ____________________. He wants to read a book about Spain. Victor puts the book back ____________________.

Write It

C. Answer the questions below about your school library. Use prepositional phrases.

12. Where is the library in your school? ______________________________

13. Are there many books on the shelves? ______________________________

14. Where do you like to sit in the library? ______________________________

15. Do you sit near your friends? ______________________________

16. When do you go to the library? ______________________________

D. (17–20) Write four sentences that describe your school library. Use prepositional phrases.

____

____

____

____

____

Edit It

E. (21–25) Edit the letter. Fix the five mistakes with prepositional phrases.

Dear Lillie,

Yesterday, I found some old postcards in the garage. The message under one card reads "Dear Mother, last night we pitched our tents over Yosemite Valley. One tree is 250 feet tall!" Lillie, this card is so exciting! I want to go at Yosemite Valley soon. Yosemite Valley is located over California. It will be fun to camp for that tree.

Love,

Pat

Proofreader's Marks

Change text:

We stood ~~over~~ inside the house.

See all Proofreader's Marks on page xi.

Name ______________________________

62 Can I Use a Pronoun After a Preposition?

Yes, Use an Object Pronoun.

- Use an **object pronoun** after a **preposition**.

  This is a good book **for me**.

  Dad discusses the topic **with me**.

Object Pronouns

Singular	Plural
me	us
you	you
him, her, it	them

Try It

A. (1–5) Read this paragraph about a test at school. Add object pronouns.

Dad brought home a book about rescue workers for ______________. The book will help me with tomorrow's test. I read carefully through ______________. Then Dad discussed the book with ______________. The test was in the morning. I felt prepared for ______________. Dad wished me luck. He said, "This will be a good day for ______________!"

B. Complete each sentence. Choose the correct object pronoun.

6. Ava and I arrived early. The teacher gave the test to ______________. (**we / us**)

7. I raised my hand, and he called on ______________. (**me / you**)

8. "Do you have advice for ______________?" I asked. (**him / us**)

9. "This test will be easy for both of ______________," he answered. (**her / you**)

10. The teacher sat behind ______________ as I took the test. (**me / you**)

Write It

C. Answer the questions about rescue workers. Use object pronouns.

11. Why do people become rescue workers? ______________________________

12. Where could you become a rescue worker? ______________________________

D. (13–15) Write three sentences about how reading books can help you. Use object pronouns.

____

____

____

____

Edit It

E. (16–20) Edit the journal entry. Fix the five mistakes with object pronouns.

March 14

Today was a good day for me. But it wasn't such a good day for Nathaniel and Rakia. Things went wrong for they all day. Our teachers taught about rescue work. Unfortunately, Rakia did not listen to they. She didn't pass the test. I felt sorry for she. Nathaniel read the book he got from I, but he was late for the test. The teacher looked at his watch. He saw that Nathaniel was ten minutes late. The teacher would not give the test to he.

Proofreader's Marks

Change text: My interview is ~~in~~ on Tuesday.

See all Proofreader's Marks on page xi.

Name ____________________

63 What's an "Antecedent"?

It's the Word a Pronoun Refers To.

- A **pronoun** usually refers back to a noun. This noun is called the **antecedent**.

  Mr. Howard teaches me to play guitar. **He** is a good teacher.
  antecedent — pronoun

- A pronoun must **agree** with its antecedent. This means that the pronoun has to go with the noun it refers to.

  My **guitar** is new. **It** sounds beautiful.

  My **family** loves to hear me practice. **They** enjoy music.

Try It

A. Identify the antecedent for the underlined pronoun. Add a sentence using the pronoun.

1. Mr. Harrison tells me to practice. He says that practice helps me learn. ____________________

____

2. My brother and I play music together. We both love to play. ____________________

____

3. Music is my favorite activity. It is important to me. ____________________

____

4. My cousins also play music. They play piano and violin. ____________________

____

B. Add a sentence to each item to continue the idea of the first sentence. Use the correct pronoun for each underlined antecedent.

5. My mother likes Mr. Harrison. ____________________

6. My teacher has many students. ____________________

7. My brother and I want to teach music someday, too. ____________________

Write It

C. Answer the questions about learning a skill. Include pronouns and the correct antecedents.

8. What skill would you like to learn? I would like to ______________________.

9. Where might you learn this skill? ______________________

10. How might you use this skill? ______________________

D. (11–14) Write four sentences about someone who has the skill that interests you. Use pronouns and antecedents correctly.

____

____

____

____

____

Edit It

E. (15–20) Edit the journal entry. Fix the six mistakes with pronouns.

November 14

Aunt Roberta painted a picture today. It is a fine artist. My aunt has a gallery. He is a big space in a fancy building. Many people buy my aunt's paintings. She admire my aunt very much. Aunt Roberta's latest painting is very large. They is more than four feet wide! I would like a career as a painter. They won't always be easy, but I really love to paint. My cousin Arnie is also an artist. It promises to teach me to paint.

Proofreader's Marks

Change text:

Arnie paints. ~~They~~ He is an artist.

See all Proofreader's Marks on page xi.

Name ____________________

64 How Do You Know Which Pronoun to Use?

Figure Out the Noun That It Refers To.

- Use a **subject pronoun** in the subject of a sentence. Use an **object pronoun** after the verb or after a preposition.

  Jeff talks to **Karen**. **He** tells **her** about a family trip.

  Jeff's family went to **Colorado**. **They** loved **it**.

- All **pronouns** must agree with the **noun** they refer to. This noun is called the antecedent.
  1. If the noun names a male, use **he** or **him**.
  2. If the noun names a female, use **she** or **her**.
  3. If a noun names one thing, use **it** or **it**.
  4. If a noun names "more than one," use **they** or **them**.

Try It

A. Complete each sentence. Write the correct pronouns.

1. Jeff hiked up the mountain. ____________ was a long hike.
   It / He
2. Jeff hiked ahead of his sister. ____________ hiked slowly.
   She / It
3. Jeff heard Lisa scream. He looked back at ____________.
   her / him
4. Lisa lay in a heap. One leg was twisted under ____________.
   her / them
5. Jeff and another hiker ran down the mountain. ____________ needed to reach Lisa quickly!
   It / They

B. **(6–9) Complete each sentence. Use the correct subject and object pronouns.**

Jeff sat next to Lisa on the trail. ______________ cried a little. Jeff felt afraid. But help was on the way to ______________. Soon, three rangers arrived. Jeff explained the accident to ______________. ______________ examined Lisa's leg. The rangers carried Lisa down the mountain.

Write It

C. **Answer the questions about the accident. Use subject and object pronouns correctly.**

10. How did Jeff help his sister? ______________________________

11. What do you think happened after Jeff and Lisa came down the mountain? ______________

____

D. **(12–14) Write three sentences about a time you helped a hurt person. Use subject and object pronouns correctly.**

____

____

____

Edit It

E. **(15–20) Edit the letter. Fix the six mistakes with pronouns.**

Dear Aunt Monica,

Last week, Lisa broke a leg. She broke him on our trip to Colorado. Me was with Lisa when the accident happened. I was really worried about him. But the doctors set Lisa's leg perfectly. My parents were so grateful to they. They also were grateful to I for helping Lisa. I hope to hear from we soon.

Love,

Jeff

Proofreader's Marks

Change text:
~~Him~~ He is a doctor.

See all Proofreader's Marks on page xi.

Name ____

65 Do You Ever Talk About Yourself?

Then Learn to Use the Words *I* and *Me*.

Subject Pronoun: I

- Use the pronoun **I** in the **subject** of a sentence.

  I like Angelo's Grocery.

- In a compound subject, name yourself last.

  Correct: **Tess and I** go there after school.

  She and I like to buy a snack.

  Incorrect: Me and Tess like Mr. Angelo.

Object Pronoun: me

- Use the pronoun **me** as the **object**.

  Mr. and Mrs. Angelo are friendly to **me**.

- In a compound object, name yourself last.

  Correct: Mrs. Angelo smiles at **Tess and me.**

  Mr. Angelo says hello to **her and me.**

  Incorrect: Mr. Angelo gave samples to Tess and I.

  He asked me and her if they were good.

Try It

A. Complete each sentence with I or me.

1. "_____________________ have a problem," said Mr. Angelo.
I/me

2. Tess and _____________________ learned that a big grocery might open next door.
I/me

3. "That store will put _____________________ out of business," said Mr. Angelo.
I/me

4. My friend and _____________________ want to help Mr. Angelo.
I/me

B. (5–8) Complete the sentences with I or me.

I wrote ten reasons why people should shop at Angelo's Grocery. Tess helped _______________ make copies of the list. Tess and _______________ posted the list around town. Some people asked Tess and _______________ questions. Tess and _______________ answered them.

Write It

C. **Answer the questions. Use I and me.**

9. What would you do if Angelo's Grocery were near your home? If Angelo's Grocery were in my neighborhood, ______________________________.

10. What kinds of shops are important to you and your friends? ______________________________

D. **(11–14) Now write four sentences about why a particular shop is important to you. Explain what you can do to support it. Use I and me in your sentences.**

____

Edit It

E. **(15–20) Edit the letter. Fix the six mistakes with pronouns.**

Dear Mayor Roberts:

My friends and I think you should not let a big grocery store come to our neighborhood. Angelo told my friends and I that he would go out of business. Me like shopping at Angelo's Grocery. My family and me will not shop anywhere else. Please listen to we. My friends and me hope you can help us. Me think we have to support our local shops.

Sincerely,

Greg Yee

Proofreader's Marks

Change text:

My friends and ~~me~~ I wanted to help.

See all Proofreader's Marks on page xi.

Name ______________________________

66 Use Subject and Object Pronouns

Remember: Use a subject pronoun as the subject of a sentence. Use an object pronoun as the object of the verb.

Subject Pronouns	I	you	he	she	it	we	you	they
Object Pronouns	me	you	him	her	it	us	you	them

My friends and **I** have many heroes. **We** read about **them**. Helen Keller is one of our heroes. Do you know about **her**? **She** inspired many people. César Chávez is another hero. **He** helped farm workers.

Try It

A. Rewrite each sentence, replacing the underlined words with the correct pronoun.

1. Susan B. Anthony is a hero of mine. ______________________________
____
2. Susan B. Anthony wanted women to be able to vote. ______________________________
____
3. Women did not have the same rights as men. ______________________________
____
4. Some men did not agree with Susan B. Anthony. ______________________________
____
5. My dad says that Susan B. Anthony is his hero, too. ______________________________
____

B. (6–10) Complete the sentences with subject or object pronouns.

My friends and ______________ read about Mohandas Gandhi. ______________ think Gandhi was a great man. ______________ helped people in India fight against British rule. Although ______________ suffered a lot, Gandhi encouraged ______________ to be peaceful.

Write It

C. Answer the questions. Use subject and object pronouns.

11. Who is a hero to you? I think ____________________
____
____________________.

12. How can an ordinary person be a hero? ____________________
____
____

D. (13–15) Think about one of your heroes. Write three sentences about what this person has done that inspires you. Use subject and object pronouns.

____
____
____
____
____
____

Grammar at Work

E. (16–20) Edit the paragraph. Fix the four mistakes with subject and object pronouns. Fix one problem with verb tense.

Nelson Mandela is one of my heroes. He was born in a small village in South Africa. Him fought against bad laws and changed they. The government sent he to jail. But Mandela continued to inspire people. Them worked with Mandela to change the laws. Mandela become South Africa's first black president in 1994.

Proofreader's Marks

Change text:

Mandela gave ~~we~~ us hope.

See all Proofreader's Marks on page xi .

Name ______________________________

67 Use Pronouns in Prepositional Phrases

Remember: You can use prepositions to add details to your sentences. If you need a pronoun in a prepositional phrase, use an object pronoun.

Sentences with Prepositional Phrases

- I have books **about science, countries, and famous people.**
- Books have special importance **to me.**
- Many of the books are **for my sister and me.**
- Our grandparents gave most of the books **to us.**

Object Pronouns

Singular	Plural
me	us
you	you
him, her, it	them

Try It

A. Add a noun or an object pronoun to complete each prepositional phrase.

1. I have one book about ______________.
2. My grandfather is a scientist, and he gave the book to ______________.
3. The book about dancers is for ______________ and ______________.
4. My grandparents gave it to ______________ when we were little.
5. We used to create silly dances for ______________.
6. That book brings back fond memories for ______________ all.

B. Complete each sentence. Use the correct pronouns.

7. My grandparents always give nice gifts to ______________ and ______________.
8. For ______________, the books were the most special gifts.
9. When I was little, my grandmother made a cookbook for both of ______________.
10. We used a recipe from it to bake a birthday cake for ______________.

Write It

C. Answer the questions about books. Use prepositional phrases with object pronouns.

11. In what ways are books important to you? ______________________________

12. What kinds of books are special to you? ______________________________

13. Where did you get those books? ______________________________

14. Do the books bring back good memories for you? Explain. ______________________________

15. What other kinds of books might interest you? ______________________________

D. (16–20) Write five sentences about books that are important to you. Use prepositional phrases with object pronouns.

____

____

____

____

____

____

Grammar at Work

E. (21–25) Edit the paragraph. Fix the four mistakes with pronouns in prepositional phrases. Fix one problem with verb tense.

My friend Emanuel says that books are important to him. I agree! To we, the library is fun. The nonfiction section has the best books for me and Emanuel. I like the books on nature and animals. For me, these books are the best. Emanuel likes books about space travel. To he, space is exciting. I said, "Emanuel, here is a book about animals in space. This book would be great for you and I." I borrow it.

Proofreader's Marks

Change text:

Books are interesting to you and I. me

See all Proofreader's Marks on page xi.

Name ______________________________

68 What's a Compound Subject?

It's a Subject with Two or More Nouns.

When a subject has two or more nouns joined by **and** or **or**, it is called a **compound subject**.

1. **Adults and children** help our community.
2. **Henry and Fiona** plan a fundraiser.
3. A **book sale or** a **cake sale** makes money.
4. The **parents or** the **school** needs to help.
5. The **school or** the **parents** need to help.

How do you know what verb to use with a compound subject?

- If you see **and**, use a plural verb like **help** or **plan.**
- If you see **or**, look at the last noun in the subject. Is it singular? Then use a singular verb. Is it plural? Then use a plural verb.

Try It

A. Complete each sentence, using the correct form of the verb.

1. My classmates and our community ______________ (**work / works**) together to make our town beautiful.
2. The bank and the grocery store ______________ (**donate / donates**) money for a new park.
3. Parents and children ______________ (**plant / plants**) trees.
4. The mayor and police officers ______________ (**help / helps**), too.
5. A teacher or parent ______________ (**bring / brings**) shovels.
6. My teacher or my classmates ______________ (**water / waters**) the new plants.
7. The parents or the school ______________ (**take / takes**) photos.

B. **Complete each sentence with a compound subject to match the verb.**

8. _______________ and his _______________ volunteer on Community Day every year.

9. Victor's _______________ and their _______________ volunteer, too.

10. Some _______________ and _______________ pick up garbage at the park.

11. _______________ and her _______________ rake leaves.

12. A _______________ or two _______________ lead the volunteers at our school.

13. The _______________ or the _______________ is the best place to volunteer.

Write It

C. **Answer the questions about how you can help in your community. Use compound subjects correctly.**

14. What do you and your family do to help in your community? _______________

____

15. What do your friends and neighbors do to help? _______________

____

____

16. What problems in your community need to be solved? _______________

____

____

D. (17–20) **Write four sentences that tell more about what you, your family, or other people do to help in your community. Make sure you use at least two compound subjects.**

____

____

____

____

____

____

Name ______________________________

69 Can a Compound Subject Include a Pronoun?

Yes, and the Pronoun Comes Last.

A **compound subject** can include nouns and pronouns joined by **and** or **or**.

1. **My brother and I** share a bedroom. Our mother says our room is too messy.
2. **My father and she** tell us to clean up.
3. **My sister and they** call us slobs.
4. **My brother and I** put our dirty clothes in the hamper.
5. **He or I** empty our garbage.

How do you know where to place the pronoun?

- Nouns always come before pronouns.
- The pronoun **I** always comes last.

Try It

A. Complete each sentence. Write the correct compound subject.

1. ______________________________ decide to keep our room clean.
   I and my brother/ My brother and I

2. My friend Miguel gives us some advice. ______________________________ also share a room.
   His brother and he/He and his bother

3. ______________________________ put their clothes away every night.
   He and Pedro/Pedro and he

4. ______________________________ brings the dirty dishes to the kitchen.
   His brother or he/He or his brother

B. (5–8) Complete each sentence about a project. Use compound subjects that include at least one pronoun and the word and.

My parents decided to fix up our backyard. My uncle ______________ did most of the work. My uncle had a truck and lots of tools. My father ______________ replaced the concrete walk with bricks. My sister ______________ helped put down the bricks. She ______________ also planted flowers.

Write It

C. Answer the questions about a project you helped do with a family member or friend. Use compound subjects.

9. Describe the project you helped do. ________________ and I ________________
____.

10. Why did you do this project? ________________________________ because
____.

11. Will you and this person work together on another project? Why or why not? __________
____

D. (12–15) Write four sentences about a project you helped do with a family member or friend. Use compound subjects.

____
____
____

Edit It

E. (16–20) Edit the journal entry. Fix the five mistakes with pronouns.

May 26

Mom and Dad helped me fix up my room. I and they decided it was too childish. My old curtains and quilt have clowns on them! I and Mom picked out striped shades and a quilt. I and Dad chose a new lamp. They and my sister helped me put up movie posters. I and my family think my room looks great!

Proofreader's Marks

Transpose words:

I and Mom painted my room.

Change text:

He or me will take a photo. (S / I)

See all Proofreader's Marks on page xi.

Name ______________________________

70 What's a Simple Sentence?

A Sentence with One Subject and One Predicate

You can express a complete thought with a simple sentence. In statements, the subject usually comes before the predicate.

Subject	Predicate
Certain food **advertisements** (noun)	**target** (verb) children.
The **teacher** (noun)	**conducted** (verb) a taste test in class.
The **students** (noun)	**tasted** (verb) three snacks.

Mixing short simple sentences with longer sentences can improve your writing. Short sentences speed reading. They also help readers comprehend your writing.

Try It

A. Identify each phrase as either a subject or a predicate. Then write a complete sentence by adding the missing part.

1. our class ______________________________
2. tasted snacks ______________________________
3. the snacks ______________________________
4. voted on our favorite snacks ______________________________

B. Turn each group of words into a complete sentence by adding a subject or a verb. Underline the noun in the subject once and the verb in the predicate twice.

5. studied ads for each snack ______________________________
6. flashy images our attention ______________________________
7. our class the taste test again ______________________________

Write It

C. Answer the questions about an ad you like. Use simple sentences.

8. Which ads do you like? I like ______________________________.

9. What is memorable about this ad? ______________________________ is memorable because ______________________________.

10. What does this ad claim about the product? ______________________________

____

11. Do you think this claim is true or false? Why? ______________________________

____

D. (12–15) Write four simple sentences about an ad you have seen recently.

____

____

____

____

____

____

Edit It

E. (16–20) Edit the ad. Fix the five mistakes with subjects and predicates.

Hearty Oatmeal Cookies

Children need healthy snacks. love Hearty Oatmeal Cookies. Hearty Oatmeal Cookies the healthiest cookies around. They an all-natural taste just like homemade cookies. have no sugar. Everyone Hearty Oatmeal Cookies. You will love them, too!

Proofreader's Marks

Add text: are
Some ads ^ entertaining.

See all Proofreader's Marks on page xi.

Name ______________________________

71 How Are Phrases and Clauses Different?

A Clause Has a Subject and a Predicate.

- A phrase is a group of related words. A sentence must have a **subject** and a **verb**. It may have several phrases.

  On a TV show, / a **family** / of five / **struggles** / with daily problems.

On a TV show,	a family	of five	struggles	with daily problems.
adverb phrase	noun phrase	adjective phrase	verb	adverb phrase

  The phrases **On a TV show** and **with daily problems** both describe the verb **struggles**, so they function as adverb phrases. The phrase **of five** describes the noun **family**, so it is an adjective phrase. The phrase **a family** functions as the subject, so it is a noun phrase.

- A **clause** contains a **subject** and a **verb**. It can stand alone as a sentence.

  The last **episode** **was** funny.

Try It

A. Write one phrase from each sentence and tell how it functions in the sentence.

1. My favorite show airs on Friday evenings. ______________________________
2. The main characters seem like ordinary children. ______________________________
3. The parents help the children with problems. ______________________________
4. The problems on the show get solved so easily! ______________________________
5. My sister and I also like shows with superheroes. ______________________________
6. Sadly, our favorite program only aired for two seasons. ______________________________
7. On Saturday mornings, we watch reruns of old superhero TV shows. ______________________________

   ____

B. **Include each phrase in a sentence.**

8. a TV game show ______

9. the game show host ______

10. the main contestant ______

______

11. from our town ______

12. with his mom and dad ______

13. in a beautiful new car ______

Write It

C. **Answer the questions about television shows you watch. Be sure to use phrases and clauses correctly.**

14. What television shows do you and your friends watch? My friends and I ______

______.

15. When do your favorite TV shows air? ______

______

16. Who are your favorite characters in this show? ______

______

D. **(17–20) Write four more sentences about the television show you like. Be sure to use phrases and clauses correctly.**

______

______

______

______

______

______

Name ____________________

72 What's a Compound Sentence?

Two Clauses Joined by *And*, *But*, or *Or*

The words **and**, **but**, and **or** are conjunctions. They join the two clauses in a **compound sentence**. A comma (**,**) comes before the conjunction.

- Use **and** to join similar ideas.

  Americans love celebrities.
  Celebrities influence us in many ways.
  → **Americans love celebrities, and celebrities influence us in many ways.**

- Use **but** to join different ideas.

  Some celebrities support great causes.
  They don't always seem like experts.
  → **Some celebrities support great causes, but they don't always seem like experts.**

- Use **or** to show a choice.

  You can dress like your favorite star.
  You can develop your own style.
  → **You can dress like your favorite star, or you can develop your own style.**

Use compound sentences to add sentence variety and show how ideas are related.

Try It

A. Combine each pair of sentences. Use and, but, or or to make a compound sentence.

Proofreader's Marks

Delete:
You can wear anything you want.

Add a comma and text: , and
I watch movies on TV I also watch the news.

Do not capitalize:
Television Shows can be interesting.

See all Proofreader's Marks on page xi.

1. Young people want to be like their favorite celebrities. Some celebrities are good role models.
2. Some middle school students want to dress like hip-hop artists. Others want to dress like TV or movie stars.
3. Many celebrities care about the causes they support. Some seem more interested in getting a lot of media attention.
4. You can support a cause because you truly care about it. You can support a cause because it is trendy.
5. Celebrities can be our heroes. They can show us the dangers of money and fame.

B. Choose the correct conjunction to combine the two related sentences.

6. Celebrities get a lot of attention, ________________ they often use it wisely.
   and / or

7. Some celebrities are good role models, ________________ others set a bad example.
   or / but

8. My favorite rock star supports environmental causes, ________________ she appears in an ad about global warming.
   and / but

9. Some celebrities say they support a cause, ________________ their actions don't reflect their words.
   or / but

10. You can accept a celebrity's opinion, ________________ you can do your own research on the issue.
   and / or

Write It

C. Answer the questions about celebrities. Use compound sentences in your responses.

11. Which TV shows and magazines discuss the lives of celebrities? ________________ *and*
____.

12. Is the information in these sources true? ________________________________
How can you tell? ________________________________

13. How does this media attention affect people's opinions about celebrities? ________________
____

14. Is it fair for the media to report on celebrities' private lives? Why or why not? ________________
____

D. (15–20) Write six compound sentences about celebrities in the media.

____

____

____

____

____

Name ______________________________

73 What's a Run-on Sentence?

A Sentence That Goes On and On

- To fix a run-on sentence, break it into shorter sentences.

  Run-on: There are many television shows to choose from **and** I like entertainment shows **but** sometimes I also watch the news.

  Better: There are many television shows to choose from. I like entertainment shows, but sometimes I also watch the news.

- You can also break a run-on sentence into two clauses and separate them with a semicolon.

  Run-on: I like to watch news programs about real issues **and** I am not interested in news about celebrities.

  Better: I like to watch news programs about real issues; I am not interested in news about celebrities.

Try It

A. Edit the sentences that are run-ons.

1. Paula likes to watch celebrity news and I see why it interests her but I prefer to watch the national and international news.
2. I want to know about events that affect my life, and I think news about celebrities does not impact me closely.
3. I get so tired of hearing about celebrities and I don't really need to know every last detail about their clothes and relationships.
4. One time Paula visited me and she wanted to watch her celebrity news show and then I wanted to watch a real news show and she watched it with me and liked it!
5. We need to stop focusing so much on movie stars and musicians and instead, we should learn about the events and issues that affect us and people throughout the world.

Proofreader's Marks

Add a period:
People are interested in celebrities⊙

Add a comma:
This news is shocking, but is it true?

Capitalize:
we watch the news every night.

Delete:
He likes this show, and ~~and~~ I see why.

Add a semicolon:
I tire of celebrities; their lives seem silly.

See all Proofreader's Marks on page xi.

B. Revise each run-on sentence. Make two or more shorter sentences, or use a semicolon to connect two clauses.

6. My mother likes to watch TV news and she thinks it is important to keep up with politics and know about our government. ____________________

____

7. My grandfather says that TV news never tells the full story we should read the newspaper instead. ____________________

____

____

8. My older sister thinks we should also listen to public radio news programs and she likes shows in which listeners call in with questions and comments. ____________________

____

____

Write It

C. Answer the questions about TV and the news. Use two or more sentences or use two clauses connected by a semicolon.

9. What types of TV shows do you watch? I watch ____________________

____________________.

10. How do you learn about the news? ____________________

____

11. How do other people in your family learn about the news? ____________________

____

D. (12–15) Write at least four sentences that express your opinions about TV news. Make sure you do not use run-on sentences.

____

____

____

____

Name ______________________________

74 What's a Complex Sentence?

A Sentence with Two Kinds of Clauses

- A clause has a **subject** and a **verb**. An **independent clause** can stand alone as a sentence.

  I **saw** a basketball game.
  independent clause

- A **dependent clause** also has a subject and a verb. But it cannot stand alone.

  when my **family** **went** to the city
  dependent clause

- You can "hook" a dependent clause to an independent clause to form a **complex sentence**. The dependent clause can function as a noun, adjective, or adverb.

  I **saw** a basketball game when my **family** **went** to the city.
  independent clause — dependent clause

Try It

A. Create complex sentences about a trip to the city. Draw a line to connect each independent clause with a dependent clause.

1. My family goes to the city	when it is held again next year.
2. Last time, we saw crowds of people	whenever we get the chance.
3. The crowds were there	that he will play pro sports.
4. We decided to walk with this one group	when the team buses arrived.
5. Everyone cheered	who were really excited.
6. My brother hopes to play in the tournament	because a college basketball tournament was going on.
7. He honestly believes	that was moving toward the Athletic Center.

B. **Turn each independent clause into a complex sentence. Add a dependent clause that begins with the word in parentheses. Write the complex sentence.**

8. I want to join my middle school basketball team **(because)**

____

9. I love to play **(whenever)**

____

10. I won my first game **(when)**

____

11. I want a coach **(who)**

____

Write It

C. **Answer the questions about media coverage of sports. Use complex sentences.**

12. Do you follow professional or college sports? Why or why not? I ______________________ *because* ______________________________________.

13. Why do you think so many people like to watch sports events on TV? ______________________

____

14. When do most sports fans first become interested in sports? ______________________

____

15. What might happen if people could not watch sports events on TV? ______________________

____

D. **(16–20) Write five complex sentences that tell more about your attitude toward sports.**

____

____

____

____

____

____

Name ______________________________

75 Can a Clause Act Like an Adverb?

Yes, and It Often Tells When or Why.

- A **complex sentence** has one independent clause and one dependent clause.

  Newspapers include photographs (independent clause) **because they help readers understand events.** (dependent clause)

- When the **dependent clause** acts like an adverb, it begins with a **subordinating conjunction**. The conjunction shows how the two clauses are related. If the dependent clause comes first, it is followed by a comma.

Tells When:	**After I came home from school**, I flipped through the sports section of the newspaper.
Tells Why:	**Since I took tests all day**, I now wanted to read for enjoyment.
Tells What May Happen:	I will read any article **if it has an interesting photo**.

- More **conjunctions** include: before, when, whenever, while, until, because, unless, although.

Try It

A. **Turn each independent clause into a complex sentence. Add a dependent clause that acts as an adverb. Begin the clause with a subordinating conjunction.**

1. I read an article about last night's basketball game ______________________________
______________________________.
2. ______________________________, the photograph showed the emotions of the players.
3. I let my friend borrow the newspaper ______________________________.
4. ______________________________, we talked about the game.
5. We didn't realize how exciting it was ______________________________.

B. **Complete each complex sentence with a subordinating conjunction that tells when, why, or what may happen.**

6. Kristin looked through the newspaper ________________ she needed to find a current-events article for social studies. **(why)**

7. She planned to look through a news magazine ________________ she could not find anything in the paper. **(what may happen)**

8. ________________ she skimmed the headlines for ten minutes, she found an interesting article. **(when)**

9. Kristin thought the article was perfect for her presentation, ________________ it was about recent events in Africa. **(why)**

Write It

C. **Answer the questions about newspapers and magazines. Use a subordinating conjunction that tells when, why, or what may happen.**

10. When you look at a newspaper or magazine, do you pay more attention to the articles or the photographs? Why? I ____
because ____.

11. Describe a photograph in an article you have read. How did the photo help you understand the article? ____
____

12. If you were a newspaper or magazine photographer, what kinds of subjects would you want to photograph? Why? ____
____

D. **(13–15) Write three complex sentences about a photo in a newspaper or magazine. Use clauses that act as adverbs.**

____
____
____
____

Name ______________________________

76 Can a Clause Act Like an Adjective?

Yes, and It Often Begins with *Who*, *That*, or *Which*.

- A **complex sentence** has one independent clause and one dependent clause.

  My school has a newspaper **that comes out twice a year.**

  independent clause — dependent clause

- Some **dependent clauses** act like adjectives and tell more about a noun. They begin with a **relative pronoun**.
  1. Use **who** to tell about a person.
  2. Use **that** for things or people.
  3. Use **which** for things.

- Place an **adjective clause** right after the noun it describes.

  Other middle schools have newspapers **that come out monthly**.

  Our newspaper publishes old news, **which is boring to read**.

  I know lots of students **who agree with me**.

Try It

A. Complete each sentence by adding the relative pronoun who or that.

1. Students don't want to read news ______________ is three months old.
2. I know several people ______________ would help raise money for the paper.
3. I discussed my ideas with Ms. Jordan, ______________ is our principal.
4. Our school deserves a newspaper ______________ we can be proud of.

B. Turn each independent clause into a complex sentence. Add an adjective clause that begins with a relative pronoun.

5. My English teacher, ______________________________, likes the idea of publishing monthly.
6. She also wants to start a Web site, ______________________________.
7. We could read articles ______________________________.

Write It

C. Answer the questions about your school. Use relative pronouns that introduce adjective clauses.

8. Imagine that you are a reporter covering an event or issue at your school. What would you write about? I would write an article about ______________________________
______________________________.

9. What would you explain in your article? I would explain the idea ______________________________
______________________________.

10. What kinds of readers would be most interested in your article? ______________________________
____

D. (11–14) Write four complex sentences about a newspaper article you might write. Use adjective clauses.

____
____
____
____

Edit It

E. (15–20) Edit the article. Fix the six mistakes with relative pronouns.

The Clifton Panthers won their fourth straight basketball game last Thursday against the Easton Tigers, which had been undefeated. The Panthers took an early lead who they never lost. The girl which is the team's forward led with 20 points who were all scored during the first half. The girl which is the best defense player also did well. The 40–18 win was Clifton's first ever against a team who is one of the best in the league.

Proofreader's Marks

Change text:

Fans ~~which~~ who saw the game were amazed by their team's early lead.

See all Proofreader's Marks on page xi.

What's a Compound-Complex Sentence?

It's Complicated.

A **compound-complex sentence** has two or more independent clauses and one or more dependent clauses.

When Brad chose Carlos, he hoped he'd be goalie, but Carlos wants to play forward.
<u>dependent clause</u> <u>independent clause</u> <u>independent clause</u>

Carlos likes playing goalie, but he wants to try a position that he hasn't played before.
independent clause independent clause dependent clause

The sentence below has two independent clauses and one dependent clause. The **dependent clause** is in the middle of one of the independent clauses.

Brad, **who coaches the team**, understands, and he'll let Carlos play forward.

Try It

A. Add a subordinating conjunction (**often, because, before, if, since, when, while,** etc.) or a relative pronoun (**who, that, which**) to complete the dependent clause and form a compound-complex sentence.

1. _____ you are fit, you feel good, and you can enjoy sports.

2. I swim or I shoot baskets each day _____ I feel healthy.

3. _____ I have a good breakfast, I walk to school or I ride my bike.

4. My dad, _____ loves sports, played pro baseball, but he almost chose basketball instead.

5. Dad always wins _____ we shoot baskets together, but I still have fun.

B. **Combine the sentences to form a compound-complex sentence. Write the new sentence.**

6. When Dad was young, a woman saw him playing basketball. She told her college about him. ____

____.

7. Dad visited the college, and he met the school's coach. The coach offered Dad a scholarship. ____

____.

8. Dad went to the college. He played a game of pickup baseball. The coach saw him.

____.

9. In the end, they offered Dad a baseball scholarship. They needed an outfielder. Dad played baseball. ____

____.

Write It

C. **Add an independent clause with and, but, or or to change each complex sentence into a compound-complex sentence.**

10. Because Dad is so good, I'm learning from him, ____________________.

11. If you like exercise, basketball is a great game ____________________.

12. I shoot baskets ____________________ before I go to school.

13. Dad likes to play sports, ____________________ when we have time together.

14. I sing along ____________________ while Dad plays his guitar.

D. **(15–18) Tell about something you like to do with a favorite relative. Use at least four compound-complex sentences.**

____

____

____

____

____

____

Name ______________________________

78 Use Compound Sentences

Remember: **A compound sentence includes two independent clauses joined by and, but, or or.**

- Use **and** to join like ideas. Use **but** to join different ideas. Use **or** to show a choice.

  My brother and I want to get a dog, **and** we think we can get our parents to agree. My mom and dad love dogs, **but** they are worried about all the work involved. We have to walk the dog every day, **or** we won't be able to get one.

- Don't overuse **and**.

  My brother and I went to an animal shelter ~~and~~. It was really sad ~~and~~. There were so many dogs, and we wanted to adopt them all.

Try It

A. Edit the sentences. Form compound sentences when appropriate by using and, but, or or. Don't overuse and.

1. We also found a pet adoption Web site and it shows photographs of available pets but it describes their personalities.

2. The Web site has listings from different animal shelters and rescue groups and the pets come from all over the country and you can visit a shelter in person. You can have a pet sent to your area.

B. Combine each pair of sentences. Use and, but, or or to make a compound sentence. Don't overuse and.

3. Dogs make great pets. They are also a lot of work. ______________________

____

4. My parents want us to do most of the dog walks. They won't agree to get a dog. ________

____

Write It

C. Answer the questions about pets. Use compound sentences.

5. How do you feel about dogs and cats? In my opinion, dogs are ______ ______ cats are ______.

6. Do you have a pet? If so, what kind? If not, would you like to have one? ______

7. If a friend or neighbor wanted to get a pet, what advice would you offer? ______

D. (8–10) **Write three compound sentences that tell more about your attitude toward animals. Don't overuse and.**

______

______

______

Grammar at Work

E. (11–15) **Fix the three mistakes with compound sentences. Then fix the two mistakes with pronouns.**

My brother and I worked out a deal with my parents and we signed a family pet care contract! Chamith and I promised to walk the dog every day after school. Him will walk the dog four days a week, I will walk the dog three days a week. My parents will walk the dog in the morning and at night. Chamith also promised to feed the dog. He will do breakfast and I will do dinner. It won't be hard to keep our promises. Now us just have to find the right dog and get everyone to agree!

Proofreader's Marks

Add a period:
We want to get a dog⊙

Add a comma:
We asked our parents,
but they were worried.

Delete:
They think a dog is too much work ~~and~~ for us.

Capitalize:
we promised to take care of the dog.

Add text:
We will walk and feed the dog.

See all Proofreader's Marks on page xi.

Name ___________________________

79 Use Complex Sentences

Remember: Using a variety of sentences improves your writing.

Expand a simple sentence to a **complex sentence**.

- Add an **adjective clause** to tell more about a noun.
  Use a **relative pronoun** (that, which, who).

  I read a magazine article.

  I read a magazine article **that discussed global warming**.

- Add an **adverb clause** to tell more about an action.
  Use a **subordinating conjunction** (after, although, if, because).

  You should read this article **if you care about our planet**.

Try It

A. **Create complex sentences by adding an adjective or adverb clause to each sentence. Write the new sentence. Then write adjective or adverb to explain the clause's function.**

1. Young people worry about global warming. ___________________________

____

2. We need to take actions. ___________________________

____

B. (3–6) **Read the interview with a middle school student. Choose the correct words to form adjective and adverb clauses.**

Q. What are some things ____________ (**who / that**) middle school students can do to protect the environment?

A. They can use lunch boxes, ____________ (**which/who**) don't create as much garbage as paper and plastic bags. ____________ (**Because/If**) students live in a cold climate, they can ask their families to lower the heat. They can also switch to compact fluorescent lightbulbs ____________ (**because/if**) they save energy.

Write It

C. **Answer the questions about the environment. Use complex sentences that include adjective and adverb clauses.**

7. What is your biggest concern about the environment? Why? My biggest concern ________ ________ because ________.

8. What can young people do to help solve this problem? ________ ________

9. If you were an adult, what other actions could you take? ________ ________

D. **(10–13) Write four more sentences about what people can do to protect the environment. Use complex sentences.**

____

____

____

____

____

Grammar at Work

E. **(14–20) Fix the five mistakes with complex sentences. Fix the two mistakes with prepositional phrases.**

The Environmental Club at my school is a club who works on many projects. Last month we sold compact fluorescent light bulbs, which save lots of energy. If they cost more than regular bulbs, they last longer. Some people aren't crazy about them they can buzz. Yet students wanted to try these bulbs although we provided information about they. Next week we will hold a recycling fair that will encourage students to recycle more bottles and cans. Our club is important if these issues affect all of we!

Proofreader's Marks

Add text:

I joined the club ^when^ I was in seventh grade.

Change text:

I like the other students ~~which~~ ^who^ are in the club.

See all Proofreader's Marks on page xi.

Name ______________________________

80 Use Compound-Complex Sentences

Remember: You can improve your writing by using compound-complex sentences to show relationships among ideas and to add sentence variety.

- Combine **two independent clauses** with **one or more dependent clauses** to form a compound-complex sentence.

  Hiking is great. It is one way to keep fit. You need a good trail map.

  Hiking, which is one way to keep fit, is great, but you need a good trail map.

- A dependent clause may begin with a **subordinating conjunction** (when, if, because, although, etc.) or with a **relative pronoun** (that, which, who).

  You can get lost, **if** you go the wrong way, or you might fall off a cliff.

  Once, I hiked with a map **that** was out of date, and I got lost.

Try It

A. Expand each sentence by adding an adjective clause to form a compound-complex sentence.

1. My friend Jonah hiked through a forest ______________________, but he was really careful.
2. If you can, hike with someone ______________________, and carry plenty of water.
3. Bears, ______________________, roam in many forests, so you need to watch out for them.
4. Rabbits and squirrels ______________________ are cute, but you should not feed or pet them.

B. **Expand each sentence by adding an adverb clause to form a compound-complex sentence.**

5. Wear long sleeves or put on sunblock ____________________.

6. I put on insect repellent, or I hike in the middle of the day ____________________.

7. ____________________, I hiked in Central Park, but I loved it!

8. Now I hike in deserts ____________________, and I see glorious sunsets.

Write It

C. **Where could you enjoy the out-of-doors? Add independent or dependent sentences to form compound-complex sentences below.**

9. What country would you like to explore? If I could go to ____________________

____________________.

10. Where can you see nature at home? I can enjoy nature at home ____________________

____________________.

11. What animals would you like to see in the wild? I love wildlife, so ____________________

____________________.

D. **(12–14) Write three more compound-complex sentences about how you can enjoy nature or outside exercise.**

____

____

____

____

____

____

____

____

____

____

____

81 Why Do Verbs Have So Many Forms?

Because They Change to Show When an Action Happens

The tense of a verb shows when an action happens.

Earlier	Now	Later
Past ←	●	●	● → **Future**
	Past Tense visit**ed**	**Present Tense** visit visits	**Future Tense** **will** visit

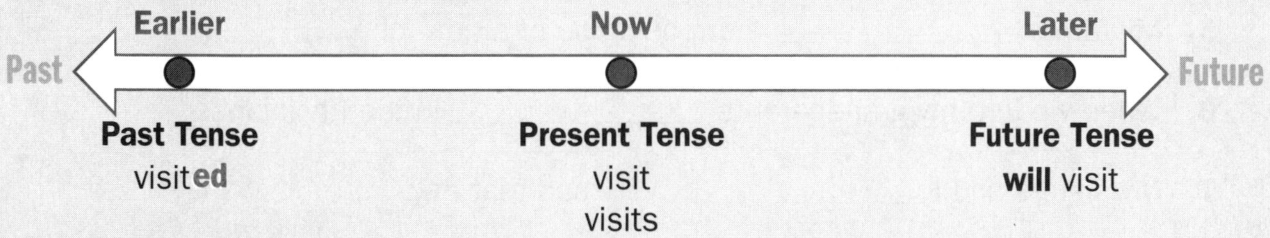

- **Present tense** verbs tell about actions that happen now or on a regular basis.

 I **visit** my grandparents. I always **go** to their house.

- **Past tense** verbs tell about an action that already happened. Add **-ed** to show the past, or use the correct form of an irregular verb.

 I **visit**ed my grandparents a year ago. I **went** to their house last July.

Present Tense	am, is	are	have, has	go, goes	see, sees
Past Tense	was	were	had	went	saw

- **Future tense** verbs tell about actions that haven't happened yet.

 I **will visit** my grandparents soon. I **will go** to their house next week.

Try It

A. Rewrite each sentence. Change each underlined verb to the past tense.

1. My family <u>lives</u> here. We <u>like</u> this neighborhood. _____

2. I <u>see</u> my grandmother every day. She <u>helps</u> me with my homework. _____

3. I <u>am</u> happy to live near her. We <u>have</u> a lot of fun together. _____

B. **Complete each sentence with a verb from the box. Use the correct tense of the verb: past, present, or future. You can use words more than once.**

are	call	come	live	miss	move	stay	visit

4. Last year, my family ______________ to New York.

5. My father ______________ here because of a new job.

6. When we left, my grandparents ______________ in the Philippines.

7. My sisters and I ______________ very sad that day.

8. Now, we ______________ very far from our grandparents.

9–10. A year ago, we ______________ next door to them. I still ______________ them.

11–12. They ______________ us every weekend. Next summer, we ______________ them.

Write It

C. **Answer the questions about moving to a new place. Use past, present, and future tense verbs.**

13. Who in your family moved to a new community? ______________________________

____

14. How do you stay in touch with family members? ______________________________

____

15. What family members did you visit in the past? ______________________________

____

16. What family members will you visit in the future? ______________________________

____

D. **(17–20) Write four sentences about family members who live far away. Use past, present, and future tense verbs.**

____

____

____

____

Name ______________________________

82 What If an Action Happened but You're Not Sure When?

Use the Present Perfect Tense to Tell About It.

- If you know when an action happened in the past, use a **past tense** verb.
  Last month, my mom **traveled** twice for her job.
- If you're not sure when a past action happened, use a verb in the **present perfect tense**.
  Mom **has traveled** for her job many times.
- To form the present perfect, use the helping verb **have** or **has** plus the **past participle** of the main verb. For regular verbs, the past participle ends in **-ed**.

Verb	Past Tense	Past Participle
like	liked	liked
shop	shopped	shopped
try	tried	tried

Try It

A. Complete each sentence. Use the past tense or the present perfect tense.

1. Three months ago, Uncle Jeffrey ______________ away.
moved / has moved

2. Just before he left, he ______________ a job in another city.
accepted / has accepted

3. We ______________ to visit him every week.
tried / have tried

4. I ______________ all our visits so far.
enjoyed / have enjoyed

5. Last weekend, my cousin ______________ to join us.
decided / has decided

6. He ______________ Uncle Jeffrey many times before, too.
visited / has visited

B. **Write the past tense or present perfect tense of the verb in parentheses.**

7. During the past month, my parents ________________ their work schedules. **(change)**

8. Yesterday, my father ________________ until nine o'clock. **(work)**

9. He ________________ late many times now. **(stay)**

10. Last week, my mother's boss ________________ her to work on Saturday. **(ask)**

11. A few times, my mother ________________ to work on Saturdays. **(agree)**

12. Over time, I ________________ to my parents' new schedules. **(adjust)**

13. Last night, I ________________ the house to help out. **(clean)**

14. Then, I ________________ my homework. **(finish)**

15. For the past few weeks, we ________________ to make the best of the situation. **(try)**

Write It

C. **Answer the questions about yourself and a recent change in your family. Use past tense and present perfect tense verbs in your sentences.**

16. In the last year, what change has occurred in your family? In the last year, ________________

____.

17. What effect has that change had on you? ________________________________

____

D. **(18–20) Write three sentences about how you help your family during busy times. Use past tense and present perfect tense verbs in your sentences.**

____

____

____

____

Name ______________________________

83 What If a Past Action Is Still Going On?

Then Use the Present Perfect Tense.

- Use the **present perfect tense** to show that an action began in the past and may still be happening.

  My dad **has owned** his own store for a long time. (He still owns it.)

  I **have helped** him in his store. (I am still helping him.)

Present Perfect Tense

has creat**ed** **have** enjoy**ed**

- A verb in the present perfect tense uses the helping verb **have** or **has** plus the **past participle** of the main verb. For regular verbs, the past participle ends in **-ed**.

Try It

A. Write a verb to complete each sentence. Use the present perfect form of the verb in parentheses.

1. My dad ________________ hard in his store. **(work)**

2. He ________________ me to help him. **(ask)**

3. I ________________ shelves for him. **(stock)**

4. I ________________ some money for my hard work. **(earn)**

B. Write the present perfect tense of learn, ask, start, or watch to complete each sentence.

5. I ________________ Dad use the cash register.

6. I ________________ to take care of customers.

7. My younger sister ________________ to help in the store, too.

8. She ________________ me to show her what to do.

Write It

C. Answer the questions about work you have done. Use the present perfect tense in some of your sentences.

9. Have you ever worked for somebody? I have ______________________________

____.

10. What has your mom or dad asked you to help with? ______________________

____

11. What chore have you started and not finished yet? ______________________

____

D. (12–15) Write four sentences about something your family or your friends have worked on together. Use the present perfect tense.

____

____

____

____

Edit It

E. (16–20) Edit the flyer. Fix the five mistakes with present perfect tense verbs.

Willie's One Stop has serve your neighborhood for years. We has provide "service with a smile." Our family has works hard to meet your needs. Our customers have ask for a new line of groceries. We has add them to our shelves. We have expanded our hours. Please shop with us.

Proofreader's Marks

Change text:

has opened
Dad's store ~~have open~~ on Sundays.

See all Proofreader's Marks on page xi.

Name ______________________________

84 Do All Past Participles End in *-ed*?

No, Irregular Verbs Have Special Forms.

- Past participles of irregular verbs have a completely new spelling.

	Verb	Past Tense	Past Participle
Forms of *Be*	am, is	was	been
	are	were	been
	give	gave	given
	go	went	gone
	see	saw	seen

- Use **has** or **have** plus the past participle to form the **present perfect tense.**

  My grandmother **has been** in the hospital.

  We **have gone** to see her every day.

Try It

A. Complete each sentence. Write the present perfect form of the verb in parentheses.

1. Grandma ______________ home from the hospital. **(go)**
2. I ______________ her every day. **(see)**
3. I ______________ her some help around the house. **(give)**
4. She ______________ really happy to see me. **(be)**

B. (5–8) **Write the present perfect form of a verb from the chart to complete each sentence.**

Grandma ______________ up and around a lot. She ______________ out for walks again. My friends ______________ Grandma out with her dogs. The dogs ______________ Grandma a lot of love and affection.

Write It

C. Answer the questions about someone who has been sick or hurt. Use the present perfect form of an irregular verb in some of your sentences.

9. Who in your family has been sick or hurt? ______________________________

____

10. What help have you given to that person? ______________________________

____

11. Where have you gone with that person? ______________________________

____

D. (12–15) Whom in your family have you visited recently? Write four sentences about your visit. Use the present perfect form of an irregular verb in each sentence.

____

____

____

____

Edit It

E. (16–20) Edit the letter. Fix the five mistakes. Use the present perfect tense of the verbs.

Dear Aunt Tanya,

Ben and I have been eager to share news about our baby cousin. We have went to visit him three times. Kevin been such a good baby. We has see him every day. I has give him his bottle twice! Ben is be even more helpful than I have been!

Your loving niece,

Janet

Proofreader's Marks

Add text:	She ^has given him a bottle.
Change text:	We ~~has~~ ^have seen the baby.
See all Proofreader's Marks on page xi.	

Name ______________________________

85 When Do You Use the Present Perfect Tense?

When an Action Happened, but You Are Not Sure When, or When a Past Action May Still Be Happening

- If you know when an action happened in the past, use a **past tense** verb.

  Yesterday, some students **volunteered** at school.

- If you're not sure when a past action happened, use a **present perfect tense** verb.

  Students **have volunteered** at school in the past.

- If an action began in the past and may still be happening, use a **present perfect tense** verb.

  Students **have volunteered** at school every day this year.

  (They are probably still volunteering.)

Try It

A. Write the correct form of the verb to complete each sentence.

1. On Tuesday, I ______________ out at school.
   helped / have helped
2. I ______________ for the past year.
   volunteered/have volunteered
3. Last week, my teacher ______________ me to move some desks.
   asked/has asked
4. She ______________ my help before, too.
   needed/has needed
5. Once, she ______________ me to hang some pictures.
   wanted/has wanted
6. Sometimes I ______________ books to her car.
   carried/have carried
7. I ______________ helping my teacher.
   enjoyed/have enjoyed
8. I ______________ a lot from her, too.
   learned/have learned

B. **Rewrite each sentence. Use the present perfect tense of the verb.**

9. The school librarian needs volunteers in the library.

____

10. My friends help the librarian every Wednesday.

____

11. Alex stacks books back on the shelves.

____

12. Paolo checks out books to students.

____

13. I study in the library on Wednesdays.

____

14. On some Wednesdays, my friends ask me to help out.

____

Write It

C. **Answer each question. Use a verb in the present perfect tense in your answer.**

15. How has the school librarian helped you? _______________

____

16. How have your teachers helped you? _______________

____

17. How have you volunteered at your school? _______________

____

D. **(18–20) What have students done to help out at your school? Write three sentences. Use the present perfect tense in your sentences.**

____

____

____

____

Name ______________________________

86 How Do You Show Which Past Action Happened First?

Use the Past Perfect Tense.

- Use the **past tense** of a verb to tell about an action that was completed in the past.
  Last week, I **missed** the game.
- If you want to show that one past action happened before another, use the **past perfect tense** for the action that happened first.
  I **had planned** to go before my parents **asked** me to help.

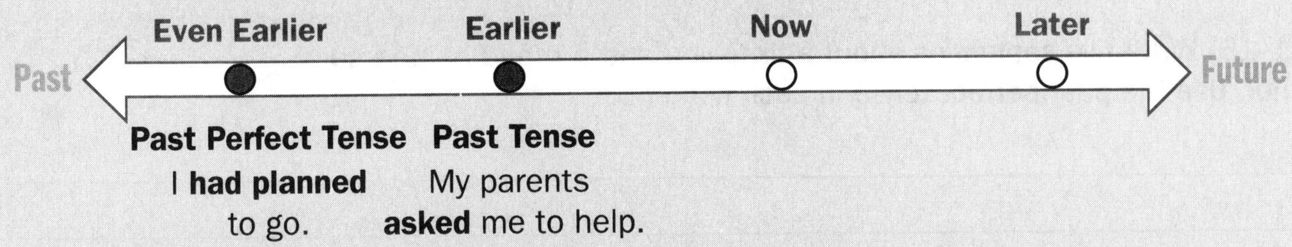

- To form the **past perfect tense**, use **had** plus the **past participle** of the main verb.
  I **helped** although I **had wanted** to see the game.

Try It

A. Write the past perfect tense of the verb in parentheses.

1. I ______________ to go to the game before I agreed to help my parents. **(plan)**
2. When Lauren called me, I already ______________ the job. **(start)**
3. I ______________ the job before Lauren arrived at my house. **(finish)**
4. We decided to stay at my house because the game______________. **(end)**

B. Complete each sentence by using the past perfect tense.

5. I was happy that Lauren ______________ me.
6. Lauren said she ______________ to spend time with me.
7. We ______________ some popcorn before we watched the movie.

Write It

C. Complete each sentence about how you helped at home. Use the past perfect tense.

8. Before I did my homework, I ____.

9. My friend wanted me to go to the movies, but I ______________________________.

10. Before I left for school, I ____.

D. (11–15) Write five sentences about a time you and a friend helped each other. Use the past perfect tense in each sentence.

____

____

____

____

____

Edit It

E. (16–20) Edit the journal entry. Fix the five mistakes.

January 23

I had be really nervous about my oral report before Mom helped me. Before she listened to me, I had practice in front of the mirror. I work for a long time before she listened. After she give me suggestions, I practiced again. Because Mom help me, I was ready to give my report. I did a good job.

Proofreader's Marks

Change text:

I had ~~hope~~ hoped to practice.

See all Proofreader's Marks on page xi.

Name ______________________

87 Can a Verb Act Like an Adjective?

Yes, When It Is a Participle.

- Verbs have **four principal parts**. For example:

Present	Present Participle	Past	Past Participle
cheer	cheering	cheered	cheered
worry	worrying	worried	worried

- Many **verbs** are made up of a **helping verb** and a **participle**.
  Present Participle: The fans **are** **cheering** for their team.
  Past Participle: They **have** **cheered** for the whole game.

- A **participle** can act as an adjective to describe a noun or pronoun.

  Cheering, people jump up and down.

  The **worried** fans hope their team wins.

- Insert a comma (,) after a participle that begins a sentence.

Try It

A. Combine sentences. Move the underlined participle to tell about a noun or a pronoun in the other sentence. Write the new sentence.

1. The basketball players come out onto the court. They are <u>running</u>.
   ____

2. The players pass the ball to each other. They are <u>practicing</u>.
   ____

3. The home crowd claps. The crowd is <u>encouraging</u>.
   ____

4. The game begins. The game is <u>exciting</u>.
   ____

B. **Complete each sentence. Use the present participle or the past participle of the verb in parentheses as an adjective.**

5. The ________________ fans root for their team. **(clap)**
6. ________________, one player runs up the court. **(dribble)**
7. ________________, the player scores three points. **(shoot)**
8. The ________________ fans clap and cheer. **(delight)**
9. ________________, the fans wait for the final buzzer. **(excite)**
10. The ________________ players on both teams shake hands. **(tire)**
11. The home team wins the ________________ game. **(thrill)**

Write It

C. **Complete each sentence about the fans or players during an exciting game. Use present or past participles as adjectives.**

12. Before the game, ____
____.
13. During the game, ____
____.
14. After the game, ____
____.
15. The best part for me is ____
____.

D. **(16–20) Write five sentences about a sports team. Use participles as adjectives.**

____

____

____

____

____

Name ______________________________

88 What Are Participial Phrases?

Phrases That Start with a Participle

- A **participle** is a verb form, but it can act like an adjective to describe a noun or a pronoun. It can stand alone or come at the start of a **phrase**. A participle often ends in **-ing**.

  Maria watches the **amazing** circus.

  Watching the circus, she joins the people **cheering for the performers**.

- You can create a **participial phrase** to combine two sentences. If the phrase begins a sentence, use a comma (**,**) after the phrase.

  Maria claps her hands. Maria applauds the performers.

  Clapping her hands, Maria applauds the performers.

- Place a participial phrase close to the noun or pronoun that it describes.

  Not OK: Maria eats some peanuts **feeling hungry**.

  OK: **Feeling hungry**, Maria eats some peanuts.

Try It

A. Use a participial phrase to combine sentences. Write the new sentence. Don't forget the comma after a participial phrase at the start of a sentence.

1. Maria watches the acrobats. Maria claps as they fly through the air.

____

2. She hopes to be an acrobat one day. She pays close attention.

____

3. The acrobats swing on the flying trapeze. The acrobats are fantastic.

____

4. Maria holds her breath. Maria does not take her eyes off them.

____

5. Maria gasps at the acrobats' tricks. Maria wants to see them again.

____

B. **Write the participle of a word from the box to complete each sentence.**

prance	grab	wish	parade	balance	ride

6. Maria watches the elephants ______________ around the ring.

7. ______________ onto each other's tails, the elephants form a circle.

8. ______________ on one elephant, a performer waves to the crowd.

9. Next, Maria sees the horses ______________ into the ring.

10. ______________ carefully, a performer walks across the tightrope.

11. ______________ she could join the circus, Maria watches each performer.

Write It

C. **Find each misplaced participle. Which noun does it describe? Correct each misplaced modifier. Rewrite the sentence.**

12. A woman dives from the platform into a small pool wearing a flaming suit.

____

13. A man crosses a pond full of alligators walking on stilts.

____

14. An acrobat descends from the roof of the circus tent dangling by only one foot.

____

15. Wheels spinning, a clown is carried across the tightrope on a bicycle.

____

D. **(16–20) Write five sentences about an act you would like to see at the circus. Use a participial phrase in each sentence.**

____

____

____

____

____

Name ______________________________

89 How Can You Improve Your Writing?

Combine Sentences.

- You can use a **participial phrase** to combine sentences.

  Jacob watches the parade. Jacob likes the sounds and colors.

  Watching the parade, Jacob likes the sounds and colors.
  participial phrase

- You can also use an appositive to combine two sentences. An **appositive** is a noun or noun phrase that identifies or explains the noun or pronoun that comes before it. Appositives are usually set off with commas.

  Mrs. Berg takes Jacob to the parade. Mrs. Berg is Jacob's aunt.

  Mrs. Berg, **Jacob's aunt**, takes Jacob to the parade.

Try It

A. Use participial phrases to combine each pair of sentences. Write each new sentence.

1. The drummers beat on their drums. The drummers march by.

   ____

2. Jacob listens to the band. The band plays lively music.

   ____

3. He watches the trumpeters. The trumpeters blow on their horns.

   ____

4. Veterans march in their uniforms. Veterans follow the band.

   ____

5. Jacob sees the veterans. The veterans wave to the crowd.

   ____

B. **Use appositives to combine the sentences. Write each new sentence.**

6. Anna marches by with the drum majorettes. Anna is Jacob's sister.

____

7. Anna tosses her baton high into the air. A baton is a hollow metal stick.

____

8. Jacob plays the trombone. The trombone is a brass instrument.

____

9. Mr. Peters invites Jacob to try out for the band. Mr. Peters is the band teacher.

____

10. Jacob will march in the parade next year. Jacob is a good musician.

____

Write It

C. **Answer the questions about a parade you saw. Use a participial phrase or appositive in your answers.**

11. Who was in the parade? ______________________________

____

12. What kind of music was played in the parade? ______________________________

____

13. What was your favorite part of the parade? ______________________________

____

D. **(14–15) Write two sentences about watching a parade. Use a participial phrase in one sentence and an appositive in the other.**

____

____

____

____

Name ______________________________

90 Use Verbs in the Present Perfect Tense

Remember: Use **have** or **has** plus the past participle of a verb to form the present perfect tense.

- The past participle of a **regular verb** ends in -ed.
  My sister **has acted** in many plays. **(act + -ed)**
  My parents **have loved** her in all of them. **(love [– e] + -ed)**
- The past participle of an **irregular verb** usually has a new spelling.

Verb	Past Participle
be	been
come	come
get	got or gotten

Verb	Past Participle
hold	held
show	shown
take	taken

Try It

A. Complete each sentence. Use the present perfect tense of the verb in parentheses.

1. My sister Beth ______________ more nervous recently. **(seem)**
2. I ______________ what is bothering her. **(wonder)**
3. Beth ______________ a new role in her school play. **(get)**
4. It ______________ hard for her to learn the lines. **(be)**
5. My parents ______________ home early to help her. **(come)**
6. The lines ______________ up a lot of their time. **(take)**

B. Add a verb in the present perfect form to complete each sentence.

7. Mom ______________ very helpful to Beth.
8. She ______________ Beth how to practice her lines.
9. I ______________ Beth learn some lines, too.

Write It

C. **Answer the questions about something you have learned. Use the present perfect tense.**

10. What special thing have you learned in the past year? ______________________________

____

11. Who has helped you? ____

____

12. What advice have friends given you? Has it helped? ____________________

____

D. **(13–15) Write three sentences about how you have helped your friends or family learn something new. Use the present perfect tense.**

____

____

____

____

Grammar at Work

E. **(16–20) Fix the <u>four</u> present perfect tense verbs. Fix <u>one</u> compound sentence.**

March 12

Beth have learn her lines. She has work really hard all week. She have show me what hard work can do. I has be a big help to Beth. We have been a great team she has done all the hard work.

Proofreader's Marks

Add text:

Beth ^has been busy.

Change text:

I ~~has~~ have been busy, too.

See all Proofreader's Marks on page xi.

Name ____________________

91 Use Present Perfect and Past Perfect Verbs

Remember: Use **has** or **have** plus a past participle for the present perfect. Use **had** plus a past participle for the past perfect.

- When you tell about the past, you may need to relate actions in time. First use the **past tense** to tell what happened.
  Yesterday, Jamal and Juan **talked** about baseball.
- Then use the **past perfect tense** to tell what happened before the discussion.
  Jamal and Juan **had discussed** baseball the week before, too.
- Sometimes a past action may still be going on. That's when you use the **present perfect tense**.
  Jamal and Juan **have enjoyed** sports together for a long time.

Try It

A. Complete each sentence. Use the correct form of the verb.

1. This year Juan played lacrosse, but he ____________ baseball until last year.
has played / had played

2. Yesterday, Juan ____________ to a lacrosse game.
went / has gone

3. Jamal ____________ baseball for years, and he still does.
has played / had played

4. He ____________ a pitcher since he started.
was / has been

B. Write the correct tense of the verb in parentheses. Use the past, past perfect, or present perfect tenses.

5. Before Juan moved here, he ____________ far away. **(live)**

6-7. Juan ____________ here when he ____________ ten. **(come, be)**

8. Juan ____________ best friends with Jamal ever since. **(be)**

C. **Complete each sentence about you and a friend. Use the past, present perfect, and past perfect forms of verbs.**

9. Yesterday, I ______________________________ with my friend, but before that we ______________________________.

10. Together, my friend and I always ______________________________ ______________________________.

11. For the past few years, I always ____________________, but my friend always ______________________________.

Write It

D. **(12–15) Write four sentences about how you met one of your friends. Use the past, present perfect, and past perfect forms of verbs.**

____

____

____

____

Grammar at Work

E. **(16–20) Fix the <u>four</u> mistakes with verb tense. Fix <u>one</u> adjective clause.**

Dear Sam,

Yesterday, my lacrosse team play in the championship game. My team have play well all season, and we still are playing well. Yesterday, before we scored our first point, the other team has score two. Before the game ended, we go ahead by four points. The fans attended the game were great.

Your friend,
Juan

Proofreader's Marks

Change text:
We ~~be~~ lucky. (have been)

Add text:
Before I did homework, I ^ gone to the game. (had)

See all Proofreader's Marks on page xi.

Name ______________________________

92 Combine Sentences

Remember: You can improve your writing by combining sentences.

- You can use a **participial phrase** to combine sentences.

  We enjoy family time. We spend one evening together each week.

  Enjoying family time, we spend one evening together each week.
  participial phrase

- You can also use an **appositive** to combine sentences. Appositives are usually set off with commas.

  Mary is my younger sister. Mary likes to bowl.

  Mary, **my younger sister**, likes to bowl.
  appositive

Try It

A. Use a participial phrase to combine each pair of sentences. Write the new sentence.

1. Mary wants to bowl. Mary chooses our activity this week.

____

2. We watch Mary's bowling ball. Mary's bowling ball is speeding down the lane.

____

3. Mary knocks down all the pins. Mary gets a strike.

____

B. Use an appositive to combine each pair of sentences. Write the new sentence.

4. Joanne is my older sister. Joanne likes to cook.

____

5. She makes fettuccine Alfredo. Fettuccine Alfredo is noodles in a cheese sauce.

____

6. Joanne finds the recipe in grandmother's cookbook. The recipe is a family favorite.

____

Write It

C. **Answer the questions about something your family does together. Use participial phrases or appositives in your answers.**

7. What is your favorite family activity? ______________________________

____

8. Where does your family usually spend time together? ______________________________

____

9. What new activity would you like to try with your family? ______________________________

____

D. **(10–12) Write three sentences about things you would like to do with your family. Use a participial phrase or an appositive in each sentence.**

____

____

____

____

Grammar at Work

E. **(13–15) Combine <u>two</u> pairs of sentences. Use a participial phrase and an appositive. Fix <u>one</u> misplaced modifier.**

Dear Grandma,

The whole family gets together every Friday night. I love board games. I chose to have a board-game marathon last night. Mary and Joanne were the winners. Mary and Joanne are board-game champs. I will choose a night at the mall next Friday night loving to shop!

Love,

Sara

Proofreader's Marks

Add text:

We ^played board games.

Change text:

Family night ~~were~~ ^was fun!

Delete:

Mary and Joanne ~~were~~ were winners.

See all Proofreader's Marks on page xi.